Beardie Basics
and Beyond

Should you,
while wandering in the wild sheep land,
happen on moor or in market
upon a very perfect gentle knight,
clothed in dark grey habit,
splashed here and there with rays of moon;

free by right divine
of the guild of gentlemen,
strenuous as a prince,
lithe as a rowan,
graceful as a girl,
with high king carriage,
motions and manners of a fairy queen;
should he have a noble breadth of brow,
on air of still strength
born of right confidence, all unassuming;

last and most unfailing test of all,
should you look into two snow-clad eyes,
calm, wistful, inscrutable,
their soft depths clothed on with eternal sadness—
yearning, as is said,
for the soul that is not theirs—

know then,
that you look upon
one of the line of the most illustrious
sheepdogs of the North.

Alfred Ollivant

Ch. Rich-Lins Royal Shag, ROM. Richard and Linda Nootbar, Richlin.

DEDICATED TO

the memory of
Barbara Hagen Rieseberg
for her selfless devotion to
helping the novice

and to

Mrs. Olive Willison
for her tireless work to revive
the Bearded Collie as a show breed

Beardie Basics
and Beyond

The Complete Guide to Bearded Collies

Barbara Hagen Rieseberg

and

Betty J. McKinney

Third Edition revised by

Jo Parker

Alpine
PUBLICATIONS

Alpine Publications, P.O. Box 7027, Loveland, CO 80537

BEARDIE BASICS AND BEYOND

ISBN: 0-931866-78-2

Library of Congress Cataloging-in-Publication Data

Rieseberg, Barbara Hagen.
    Beardie Basics and Beyond / Barbara Hagen Rieseberg and Betty J. McKinney. —
3rd ed. / revised by Jo Parker.
        p.   cm.
    Includes bibliographical references (p.   ) and index.
    ISBN 0-931866-78-2
    1. Bearded collie.   I. McKinney, Betty Jo.   II. Parker, Jo.   1923-
    III. Title.
    SF429.B32R54   1997
    636.737'4—dc21   96-48735
                                                                           CIP

Also by the authors: *Sheltie Talk,* Alpine Publications, 1976, 1985.

Alpine books are available to clubs, organizations, and breeders for premiums
and fund-raising at special discounts. For information write to the attention of
the Special Markets Director, Alpine Publications, at the above address.

Edited by: Dianne Nelson
Design and layout: Shadow Canyon Graphics
Cover design: B.J. McKinney

Cover photo: Am. Can. Ch. Britannia Ticket to Ride, HC, ROMX, owned by
Michele Ritter. Photo copyright Chet Jezierski.
Back cover photo: Ch. Parcana Piece of the Action, owned by Judy Panzini and
Joanne Williamson, Photo courtesy of Jo Parker; copyright Chet Jezierski.

1 2 3 4 5 6 7 8 9
Printed in the United States of America

Contents

Foreword to the Third Edition   xi
Foreword by Jennie Osborne, Osmart   xii
Acknowledgements   xiv
About the Authors   xv

1 **The Beardie Charisma**   1
   Temperament and Personality 2 • A New Start for An Ancient
   Breed 4

2 **Ideals and Interpretation**   7
   Official AKC Bearded Collie Standard 8 • British Standard 14

3 **Moving Out**   17
   Side Gait 18 • Rear or "Going" Gait 22 • Front or "Coming"
   Gait 25

4 **Love at First Sight**   29
   Some Obvious Questions 30 • Where Do You Find Your Dog 32 •
   Beardie Rescue 33 • Making the Purchase 33 • Importing 36

5 **The Comforts of Home**   37
   Early Training 38 • Housing 39 • Keeping Your Beardie Safe 43 •
   Finding A Lost Beardie 44 • The Jet-Set Beardie 45

6 **The Beardie Beautiful**   47
   Tools and Equipment 47 • Evaluating the Coat 48 • Table
   Manners 49 • The Grooming Process 50 • Routine Care 54

7 **Shaping Up**   61
   The Healthy Beardie 61 • Feeding 62 • Conditioning Through
   Exercise 65 • Caring for the Older Beardie 66

8 In Sickness and In Health 69
Immunizations 69 • Parasites 70 • When Your Beardie Is Not
Feeling Well 73 • First Aid 77

9 Beardie Be Good 83
The Psychology of Training 83 • Training Guidelines 84 •
Training Tips Specific to Beardies 87 • What Every Beardie
Should Know 87 • Show Training 90 • Canine Good
Citizens 92 • Obedience Training 92 • Other Activities
for Beardies 92

10 Building A Better Beardie 97
The Building Blocks 97 • Genetics and Health 101 •
Controlling Genetic Defects 109

11 Color Schemes 111
Genetic Profiles 112 • White Markings 113 •
Tan Markings 114 • Graying 114 • Predicting Adult Color 115
• Eye Color 115 • Pigmentation 117 • Acceptable Color
Breedings 117

12 Laying the Foundation 119
Finding Your Foundation Stock 120 • Develop A Plan 123 •
Understanding Pedigrees 123 • Practical Applications 126

13 Planned Parenthood 127
The Brood Bitch 128 • Selecting a Mate 132 • The Stud
Dog 134 • Breeding Difficulties 136 • Culturing and
Treating Infection 140

14 The New Generation 141
Whelping Box 143 • Whelping Supplies 145 • Signs of
Approaching Labor 146 • Whelping 147 • Postwhelping
Care of the Bitch 151

15 All Beardies Great and Small 153
Examining the Puppies 154 • Early Environment 156 •
Weak Puppies 157 • Puppy Diseases 160 • Evaluation of
Your Puppies 161 • Dewclaws 163 • The Toddler 164 •
Evaluating the Older Puppy 166

16 Bye Bye, Beardie 171
Advertising 172 • Preparing Your Puppies for Sale 174 •
Making the Sale 174 • Follow-Up 180

17 Showing Off 181
How Dog Shows Are Organized 182 • Match Competition
187 • Entering A Show 187 • Shows in England 188 •
Showing Your Beardie 189

18 The Happy Herder 197
Working Standard 198 • Herding Instinct 198 • Temperament
in a Herding Dog 199 • Choosing A Herding Dog 200 •
Introducing the Beardie to Stock 102 • Training Pointers 202 •
Herding Organizations 206

**19 Kennels in England, Canada, and the
United States** 211
English Kennels 211 • Canadian Kennels 228 • American
Kennels 235

20 Judge for Yourself 251
Part One: Outline by Cynthia Mahigian Morehead 251 •
Part Two: Side Gait by Jo Parker 254

21 Bearded Collie Club of America 257
BCCA Specialty Winners 257 • Top Producers 263 •
Performance Awards 264 • Register of Merit Instinct 266

Other Sources of Information 267
Index 269

Melita's Poppy's A Poppin' ROM, with owner Jean Richland, Melita Bearded Collies. Mike Lidster photograph.

BEST OF
BREED

CONTRA COSTA

KENNEL CLUB
JUNE 1985
MIKE LIDSTER
PHOTOGRAPHER

FOREWORD TO THE THIRD EDITION

Much has happened since we first published *Beardie Basics* in 1979. I fondly remember the joy we shared when it was released at the 1978 Specialty match, held on the grounds of the elegant Stanley Hotel in Estes Park, Colorado. Entries were few in those days, and Beardies were so new to the show scene that everyone was excited about the breed and how "naturally" they were shown.

Well, many things have changed since then. Beardies are growing in popularity and numbers, they have proven their mark in the Group and Best in Show rings, in herding, in agility, in obedience, and many other realms. No longer a rare, unrecognized breed, neither are they, unfortunately, quite as natural. Barbara Rieseberg, who died suddenly after surgery in 1980, would not be so pleased about the latter. But she would be pleased about the achievements her beloved breed has made during the past eighteen years, and she would be quite proud to see what close friend and co-breeder Jo Parker and others have accomplished with their Beardies, many of which stem from Silverleaf stock.

Since I was never personally involved in the breed, it seems so right that Jo Parker has agreed to revise *Beardie Basics* and update it for a new generation of Beardie lovers. Jo's love and knowledge of the breed comes through boldly; her ideals and standards for the breed paralleled Barbara's, and her expertise as a licensed AKC judge lends credibility. Thank you, Jo, for your hard work and dedication!

Betty J. McKinney
November 1996

FOREWORD TO THE FIRST EDITION

When I was asked to do the foreword for *Beardie Basics*, my first thought was, "Yes, it's easy." But when I picked up my pen, suddenly I realized this was not going to be a simple task.

It's fifteen years since our first Beardie entered my life. Alas, she left us in December, but it's entirely due to Bluebelle that I am in a position to write today.

Beardies first caught my eye because of their shaggy appearance. They looked, and are, rather mischievous, friendly family dogs that really steal your heart.

When I first entered the show ring there didn't seem to be two Beardies that looked alike. Some, in fact, were filthy, ungroomed animals that looked as if they had just come in from a hard day's work in muddy fields. There was a wide range of sizes; coats varied from short to floor length and from straight to tight curls. In fact, at that time you could virtually fit the Standard to any shaggy dog.

I am often asked how Beardies have changed over the years. Size is still a problem in the breed, and coats still vary in length and texture, but now at least the Bearded Collies do look like a breed. They are shown well groomed and clean. But how I deplore the habit of parting the hair down the spine, and then draping it like curtains over the dog's sides! Coats are straighter, but many are soft and far too long. Eyes seem to be getting lighter, and nasal pigmentation is often lacking. Now, some dogs are very obviously being trimmed.

The Beardie is comparatively new to your country. Now is the time for you to decide if you want a glamorous show-stopper, or if you prefer an elegant, yet workmanlike dog that could, with training, still do the job for which he was destined. Fashion is fickle. Here in England, to my joy, the judges are again ignoring the "pretty long-coated dog with the hackney action" and reverting to his elegant, yet workmanlike, ground-covering brother whose coat, though thick and abundant, does not obscure his outline.

Like me, you must have been attracted to the Beardie for his handy size, adaptability, and of course his appearance. His future is in your hands. Search your conscience, examine the photos of the early winners (i.e. Benjie, Bravo, Beauty Queen, Bronze Penny, Blue Bonnie, etc.), then compare them with today's winners. Remember — it was these original Beardies that attracted you to the breed in the first place.

In conclusion, I wish the Beardie well in the country of his adoption. I hope this book will prove useful to experienced and novice breeders alike.

Jenny H. Osborne SRN
President, Bearded Collie Club
Osmart Kennels
Bacup, England
1978

ACKNOWLEDGEMENTS

We wish to thank all of the breeders and owners who supplied photographs for this book. Special thanks are due to Barbara Iremonger, Jennie Osborne, Jackie Tidsmarsh, and the many other English breeders who supplied priceless historic photos and assisted us with our research. Thanks to judge Margaret Osborne for her endless help in locating breeders in the United Kingdom.

We are grateful for the help of the staff of the Valley Veterinary Clinic, Longmont, Colorado, and the Colorado State University Veterinary Medicine Clinic, Fort Collins, Colorado; as well as to Dr. Phyllis Holst, D.V.M., for assistance on the medical and breeding chapters.

And finally, special thanks to all the breeders and exhibitors who contributed photographs and kennel histories, to the Bearded Collie Club of America for helping us with statistics, and to Beardie lovers everywhere for making this book possible.

About the Authors

A longstanding friendship between the authors began in the late 1960s, and together they traveled to Great Britain in 1977 to research the first edition of *Beardie Basics* and to purchase breeding stock.

The authors' first book, *Sheltie Talk*, published in 1967, was conceived because they wanted to give the Sheltie fancier a badly needed source of basic information specific to the breed— information which the authors had difficulty obtaining during their early years as breeders. The book has since become the most widely recommended work on the Shetland Sheepdog.

Barbara Hagen began breeding Shelties in 1961, at the age of fourteen. Over the next sixteen years she bred or owned a dozen champions in Shelties and various other working breeds. In 1970, Barbara married Freedo Rieseberg, who previously had been involved in breeding German Shepherd dogs, and the two continued breeding and showing under her kennel name, Silverleaf. They obtained their first Bearded Collies from England in 1973, with the help of international judge Margaret Osborne, and went on to produce numerous champion and ROM Beardies. In April of 1980, Barbara Rieseberg died—a great loss not only to Freedo, but to the Beardie world as well. Silverleaf Kennel has since become inactive.

B.J. McKinney began breeding and showing Shelties in 1966, under the name Kinni Kennels. Her interest in publications dates back to her twelfth year of age when, with camera and pen, she put together her first "book," a story about a litter of Sheltie puppies. She has been involved in publishing since 1974, and has bred several champion Shetland sheepdogs.

Jo Parker has been a breeder/exhibitor of Bearded Collies since 1974, and is also a licensed AKC judge. Her Parcana kennel has produced many champions, including Best in Show and Group winners. Prior to her involvement with Bearded Collies, she bred Shetland Sheepdogs for nearly thirty years. She is a former President of BCCA, was breed columnist for the *AKC Gazette* for many years, and has written numerous articles. She holds a B.A. in journalism from the University of Alabama.

1 *The Beardie Charisma*

The Bearded Collie is a "super dog" to those who love him. While not perfect for everyone, the breed is unique in its capabilities, endearing qualities, and timeless beauty. He is truly a gift from the past—with a heritage all but lost in many of today's breeds. The "Beardie" comes unchanged in beauty and spirit over the centuries. Today's breeder is faced with the awesome responsibility of preserving the virtues of the breed—virtues that are beyond price and that, once lost, can never be recovered.

The quotation in the front of this book depicts one aspect of the Beardie. A less romantic but more practical statement was made by Major James G. Logan of Scotland, a longtime Beardie fan:

> A Beardie is a dog of almost over-powering friendliness, extremely active, boisterous, an expert in escapology, a dog with a loud bark who is not afraid to use it. It is not a dog for the house proud or car proud or the fanatical gardener or for parents of nervous children or for those who are forced to leave it in the house all day, but for anyone who is prepared to train it and control it, to exercise it and to look after its coat, to put up with mud, sand or worse that it will bring into the house, and can keep it occupied, there is no breed which will provide more faithful companionship or greater entertainment.

There is no doubt that the more a Beardie is made a member of the family, worked with, talked to, and loved, the more personality he will develop.

*Britannia Ride to Blue Heaven as she appeared on the front page of the Citizen in Prince George, Canada.
Courtesy Velda Fitchett, D'Arbonne.*

The Beardie charisma is a phenomenon not easily described. It has to do with the temperament and personality of each dog, but it is more than this. It is an interrelationship between person and dog that transcends mere ownership. It encompasses devotion, companionship—and perhaps most of all—a mutual respect. It instills in the person lucky enough to feel this bond a sense of responsibility to a particular animal.

TEMPERAMENT AND PERSONALITY

You have to live with a Beardie to appreciate his worth and character. Each individual is different from all others, yet all possess some traits that are uniquely Beardie—characteristics shared by others within the breed but that set Beardies apart from other breeds of dogs. Beardies are usually happy. They forgive easily and never hold grudges, yet they never miss a lesson along the way. Their enthusiasm for life and all that it offers can be contagious. They often make you laugh, not because they are intentionally clowning, but because they are just having fun, and they laugh with you. Beardies bubble over with love for everyone. They assume that everyone welcomes them with equal abandon, and a visitor may be surprised by a bear hug and kiss from the family Beardie.

Temperament is inherited. It dictates if a Beardie will be timid or aggressive, boisterous or quiet, responsive or stubborn. These basics cannot be changed drastically, and they will be passed on to offspring. Luckily, most Beardies are self-assured, steady, and sensible. To pick an individual that is anything less is to jeopardize your chance for a happy relationship with your dog. There is a wide range of acceptable temperaments, but neither a dog that is very timid nor one that is offensively aggressive should be considered "typical." Some Beardies are reserved with strangers and some are openly affectionate with everyone, but all must respond to their owners to be correct working dogs.

Temperament can be modified by the dog's environment. Proper socialization and training are beneficial, while abuse or neglect can create character flaws. Personality, on the other hand, is acquired by association with man. It is the full expression of individual characteristics developed within the limits of the dog's inherited temperament. Character, an important element in the Beardie charisma, is a combination of the dog's temperament and personality. A dog with sound character is one that behaves predictably and intelligently under any circumstances and that has enough personality to be an interesting companion.

When selecting a Beardie, choose one whose temperament appeals to you, as long as it falls within reasonable limits. One person might prefer a rambunctious animal, while another might select a sweet, quiet individual. The most important requisite at any age is responsiveness to the owner. This determines trainability, the ability to communicate, and the will to please.

Instinctive Behavior and Needs

In addition to temperament, any given individual inherits instinctive responses. In Beardies, the dominant instinct is to herd. This makes them extremely suitable as family dogs but also causes them to have certain requirements. Be aware that Beardies can be rather independent, and you as the owner must exert enough dominance to maintain control. Herding dogs have an inborn will to please yet a compulsion to complete a job with single-minded fanaticism. Beardies have been selected for centuries on the basis of intelligence balanced by responsiveness to people.

Beardies are also protective of their charges, which can include children, puppies, and other animals in place of a flock of sheep, and they may try to bunch their charges together. A Beardie is happiest if all members of his family are together, and if they are in separate rooms, he often will go back and forth between them. A mother dog will worry her puppies until she has them grouped together. The Beardie is not a guard dog, but he makes an outstanding nursemaid. It is believed that the original Nana in James Barrie's *Peter Pan* was a Bearded Collie. Do not expect him to attack an intruder; unless his people are actually threatened, such action would be contrary to a Beardie's nature.

Beardies are active and intelligent and are easily bored if neglected. Although they are well mannered and capable of amusing themselves, they crave a fair amount of personal contact and mental stimulation. A neglected Beardie may become unintentionally destructive. Beardies need owners who are consistent about training and who offer a firm but fair authority. Good parents usually make good Beardie owners.

House Dog or Kennel Dog?

Most Beardies make admirable house dogs. They like to keep their quarters clean and require little conscious housebreaking, and, of course, their personalities flourish best when they are part of the family. Although exuberant outdoors, they settle down and are well mannered after the initial greeting in the house.

Beardies do well under kennel conditions also, but they must be given adequate exercise and enough human contact for proper socialization. When you select a dog, be sure that he shows evidence of good socialization. A friendly, responsive Beardie will adjust well as a pet regardless of whether he has been raised in the house or in the kennel.

*Beardies are expert jumpers. Am. Can. Ch.
Bedlam's Go Get 'em Garth Can. Am. CD
in the air. Courtesy Alice Bixler.*

"eye" while working. History credits them with being herders but also records their service as drovers, working behind livestock being driven to market. Apparently Beardies excelled in both functions. This is remarkable, because most breeds specialize in only one of these tasks and must be taught the other chore against their instincts. Some modern herding books reference the Beardie as a drover, but this is not justified by the instinct tests that usually show the Beardie to be a herder. In fact, Beardies are one of the very few breeds capable of rivaling the Border Collie at its trials. Beardies have been able to command respect from Border Collie trainers who have seen them in action.

Documentation of the breed's history is incomplete, because Beardies belonged to the

A wildly exuberant, hesitant, or destructive dog is likely showing signs of neglect and will need individual attention before he behaves more favorably. He will probably adjust well with patience, but you will need to expend more effort than with a properly socialized puppy. It is far easier to get control of an extrovert than to give confidence to a timid dog.

A NEW START
FOR AN ANCIENT BREED

To appreciate the intricacies of the Beardie's nature, you must look to his heritage. Until very recent times, he has been strictly a working stock dog. Most Beardies exhibit herding characteristics similar to those of the Border Collie—they circle and bunch the flock, and some even display

*An acrobatic puppy shows off.
Courtesy Alice Bixler.*

hill shepherds rather than catching the noble-man's eye as a show breed. However, they are mentioned throughout several centuries and appear to be one of the oldest British breeds, tracing probably as far back as A.D. 1540 in recognizable form.

Records show that in about 1514, three Lowland Polish Sheepdogs—two bitches and a dog—were traded to a Scottish shepherd for a valuable ram and ewe. These individuals probably founded the breed that is known as the Bearded Collie. Some researchers believe that the breed was already established in Britain at the time of the Roman invasion. It is universally accepted that the Bearded Collie, like the Puli and most other shaggy sheepdog breeds, is descended from the Komondor of the Magyars in Central Europe

By the 1700s, Beardies were showing up regularly in British portraits and writings. Prior to 1900, the breed was often called the Highland Collie and was sometimes mentioned as the Hairy Moued [mouthed] Collie or the Mountain Collie. The word "collie" is derived from the Scottish term for any sheepdog, which is thought to be "coaley" [black] or the Welsh "coelio" [faithful].

By 1800, the breed was quite popular, and some individuals were even being bred for showing in southern Scotland. There were two distinct varieties. The Border or Lowland type was a large, slate-colored dog with long, harsh, straight hair. He often measured as tall as twenty-four or twenty-five inches at the shoulder. The brown-colored Highland variety was smaller and more agile. He had a shorter, curly coat. The two varieties were crossed to combine the best qualities of both in the modern Beardie. The curly coat has been bred out, and coat quality (either straight or slightly wavy) is now the same in all colors.

Although the Beardie was well established as a breed, no Standard or breed club existed until 1912. This led to the virtual extinction of the breed as a recognized entity. The breed was kept alive only by a few shepherds who raised Beardies to work sheep, and although

the lineage was kept pure, there were no records or registrations. The Beardies were saved only because of their working ability and their resistance to the cold, rainy Scottish climate

Beardies are believed to figure prominently in the background of the more recent Border Collie and Old English Sheepdog breeds, and possibly the Kerry Blue Terrier. Indeed, a specimen with Beardie coat and characteristics still crops up now and then in registered Border Collie litters. The occasional smooth Beardie is an indication that the Border Collie could have been bred down from the Beardie with careful selection and perhaps a few outcrosses. Since Border Collies have always been selected for working ability rather than for type, it is likely that both rough and smooth varieties will be tolerated for some time in that breed. In Beardies, however, where the type has always been more uniform and distinctive, breeders chose to eliminate and not register the occasional smooth specimen. As a result, the smooth coats have virtually been eliminated.

Revival of the Show Beardie

In 1944 in England, Mrs. G.O. Williston accidentally acquired a brown Beardie bitch puppy while searching for a working Shetland Sheepdog. It took her some time to realize that "Jeannie" was a Bearded Collie and not just a sheepdog cross, and by that time, Mrs. Williston had been thoroughly won over by the Beardie charm. From this bitch and from a few other Beardies of working lineage who became certified as purebred come all of the registered Beardies in the world today. Mrs. Williston engaged in a long and frustrating search for a suitable mate for Jeannie and eventually acquired a slate male whom she called Bailie of Bothkennar. The breed made a cautious comeback under her fostering. The Bearded Collie Club of Great Britain was formed in 1955, and in 1959 the breed gained championship status in England.

This is my kind of herding. Ch. Bedlam's Unreachable Star. Courtesy Alice Bixler.

Beardies quickly spread to other countries. The first litter whelped in the United States was bred by Mr. and Mrs. Lawrence Levy in 1967. The Bearded Collie Club of America (BCCA) was founded in 1969. The tireless efforts of a few early members resulted in the American Kennel Club (AKC) granting miscellaneous recognition to the breed in 1974 and entering the Bearded Collie in the AKC Stud Book with full working breed status in October 1976. Beardies began their show career in the United States on February 1, 1977, when the breed became eligible to compete in the Working Group. Their existence was made obvious to all when Ch. Brambledale Blue Bonnet CD won an all-breed Best in Show, a remarkable feat for any bitch, especially for one of a new, rare breed. Ch. Shiel's Mogador Silverleaf CD put the males in the record by taking a second Best in Show during the first year of recognition. Several other notable dogs won group placements, and a number of champions finished during 1977. The Bearded Collie established his reputation as a sound, stable working dog by show definition as well as by his proven herding ability. In January of 1983, the Working Group was divided, and the Beardie was put into the new Herding Group.

2 Ideals and Interpretation

An evaluation of any animal must involve comparing him to what he should be. In the show ring, the contender is judged against the other entrants. To the breeder, however, every individual must be compared to the ideal specimen of the breed. But what is ideal? Is this different for each person, or is there a common goal? Must the beginner be influenced by the opinion of only one established breeder? Where can you turn to find a *universal* concept of the perfect Beardie? The flawless Beardie does not exist, but the mental image of what he looks like is necessary for the breeder or fancier. It provides a goal toward which to strive with every selection and breeding.

Each recognized breed of dog has a written description of the "ideal" for that breed. This word picture is known as the Standard and is the final authority to which all breeders, judges, and students of the breed must turn. The Standard is often referred to as the blueprint for the breed; it allows for individual interpretation while drawing boundaries of acceptable variations

The original Standard was extremely vague and could actually have described a number of shaggy breeds. The AKC approved a revised Standard for the Bearded Collie in 1978. It was a great improvement over the original, but many members of the Bearded Collie Club of America feel that it still needs clarification, correction, and added details. Also, the AKC would like for all breed Standards to fit a uniform format. Any change in a Standard must be undertaken seriously, and the final product must be worthy of representing the breed for generations to come. Breeders must never presume to make the Standard fit the dogs; the dogs should always be bred to conform to a well-written Standard.

OFFICIAL AKC BEARDED COLLIE STANDARD

CHARACTERISTICS: The Bearded Collie is hardy and active, with an aura of strength and agility characteristic of a real working dog. Bred for centuries as a companion and servant of man, the Bearded Collie is a devoted and intelligent member of the family. He is stable and self-confident, showing no signs of shyness or aggression. This is a natural and unspoiled breed.

GENERAL APPEARANCE: The Bearded Collie is a medium-sized shaggy dog with a medium length coat that follows the natural lines of the body and allows plenty of daylight under the body. The body is long and lean, and, though strongly made, does not appear heavy. A bright, inquiring expression is a distinctive feature of the breed. The Bearded Collie should be shown in a natural stance.

HEAD: The head is in proportion to the size of the dog. The skull is broad and flat; the cheeks are well filled beneath the eyes; the muzzle is strong and full; the foreface is equal in length to the distance between the stop and occiput. The nose is large and squareish. A snipey muzzle is to be penalized. (See Color section for pigmentation.)'

Eyes: The eyes are large, expressive, soft and affectionate, but not round or protruding, and are set widely apart. The eyebrows are arched to the sides to frame the eyes and are long enough to blend smoothly into the coat on the sides of the head. (See Color section for eye color.)

Ears: The ears are medium sized, hanging, and covered with long hair. They are set level with the eyes. When the dog is alert, the ears have a slight lift at the base.

Teeth: The teeth are strong and white, meeting in a scissors bite. Full dentition is desirable.

NECK: The neck is in proportion to the length of the body, strong and slightly arched, blending smoothly into the shoulders.

FOREQUARTERS: The shoulders are well laid back at an angle of approximately forty-five degrees; a line drawn from the highest point of the shoulder blade to the forward point of articulation approximates a right angle with a line from the forward point of articulation to the point of elbow. The tops of the shoulder blades lie in against the withers, but they slope outwards from there sufficiently to accommodate the desired spring of ribs. The legs are straight and vertical with substantial, but not heavy, bone and are covered with shaggy hair all around. The pasterns are flexible without weakness.

BODY: The body is longer than it is high in an approximate ration of five to four, the length measured from point of chest to point of buttocks; the height measured at the highest point of the withers. The length of the back comes from the length of the ribcage

Eng. Ch. Pepperland Lyric John at Potterdale, Potterdale, a male of outstanding type.

Multi-group placing Ch. Lochengar Never Surrender exhibits femininity in a bitch.

and not that of the loin. The back is level. The ribs are well-sprung from the spine but are flat at the sides. The chest is deep, reaching at least to the elbows. The loins are strong. The level back line blends smoothly into the curve of the rump. A flat croup or a steep croup is to be severely penalized.

HINDQUARTERS: The hind legs are powerful and muscular at the thighs with well-bent stifles. The hocks are low. In normal stance the hocks are perpendicular to the ground and parallel to each other when viewed from the rear; the hind feet fall just behind a perpendicular line from the point of buttocks when viewed from the side. The legs are covered with shaggy hair all around.

Tail: The tail is set low and is long enough for the end of the bone to reach at least to the point of the hocks. It is normally carried low with an upward swirl at the tip while the dog is standing. When the dog is excited or in motion, the curve is accentuated and the tail may be raised but is never carried beyond a vertical line. The tail is covered with abundant hair.

FEET: The feet are oval in shape with the soles well padded. The toes are arched and close together, and well covered with hair including between the pads.

COAT: The coat is double with the undercoat soft, furry and close. The outer coat is flat, harsh, strong and shaggy, free from wooliness or curl, although a slight wave is permissible. The coat falls naturally to either side but must never be artificially parted. The length and density of the hair are sufficient to provide a protective coat and to enhance the shape of the dog, but not so profuse as to obscure the natural lines of the body. The dog should be shown as naturally as is consistent with good grooming, but the coat must not be trimmed in any way. On the head, the bridge of the nose is sparsely covered with hair which is slightly longer on the sides to cover the lips. From the cheeks, the lower lips and under the chin, the coat increases in length towards the chest, forming the typical beard. An excessively long, silky coat or one which has been trimmed in any way must be severely penalized.

COLOR: All Bearded Collies are born either black, blue, brown or fawn, with or without white markings. With maturity, the color may lighten, so that a born black may become any shade of gray from black to slate to silver, a born brown from chocolate to sandy. Blues and fawns also show shades from dark to light. Where white occurs, it only appears on the foreface as a blaze, on the skull, on the tip of the tail, on the chest, legs, and feet, and around the neck. The white hair does not grow on the body behind the shoulders nor on the face to surround the eyes. Tan markings occasionally appear and are acceptable on the eyebrows, inside the ears, on the cheeks, under the tail, and on the legs where white joins the main color.

Pigmentation: Pigmentation on the Bearded Collie follows the coat color. In a born black, the eye rims, nose, and lips are black, whereas in the born blue, the pigmentation is a blue-gray color. A born brown dog has brown pigmentation and born fawns a correspondingly lighter brown. The pigmentation is completely filled in and shows no sign of spots.

Eyes: Eye color will generally tone with the coat color. In a born blue or fawn, the distinctively lighter eyes are correct and must not be penalized.

SIZE: The ideal height at the withers is 21 to 22 inches for adult dogs and 20 to 21 inches for adult bitches. Height over and under the ideal is to be severely penalized. The express objective of this criterion is to insure that the Bearded Collie remains a medium-sized dog.

GAIT: Movement is free, supple and powerful. Balance combines good reach in forequarters with strong drive in hindquarters. The back remains firm and level. The feet are lifted only enough to clear the ground, giving the impression that the dog glides along making minimum contact. Movement is lithe and flexible to enable the dog to make the sharp turns and sudden stops required of the sheep dog. When viewed from the front or rear, the front and rear legs travel in the same plane from shoulder and hip joint to pads at all speeds. Legs remain straight, but feet move inward as speed increases until the edges of the feet converge on a center line at a fast trot.

SERIOUS FAULTS:
Snipey muzzle
Flat croup or steep croup
Excessively long, silky coat
Trimmed or sculptured coat
Height over or under the ideal

There are some prevalent discrepancies from the Standard to be seen in the show ring today. One of these is an increasing disregard for the insistence on naturalness. Dogs are seen with artificial parting down the back and obvious trimming, especially on the feet and legs, but also on necks, tails, belly lines, and faces. Much of this is done by professional handlers who think that it is necessary for Group and Best in Show competition. Other exhibitors, seeing a trimmed dog win, feel that they must do the same. If the dog is a good one and the owner tells the handler not to trim, the dog will still do his share of winning. It is permissible to do some judicious trimming of straggly areas that would be considered good grooming, but this should never be obvious or give a "sculpted" look.

Another area of divergence is the tendency toward shorter, broader dogs, rather than the long, lean look. These cobbier dogs are a move away from true working-dog type because they lack the endurance and agility necessary for a day's work. Their movement is somewhat more plodding rather than being free and supple. This tendency may be attributable to judges or breeders who have faulted Beardies for being too close in the rear. It stands to reason that a lean dog will have his hind legs closer together than a broad dog, but he can still have the correct straight line from hip to pad. Of course, if the dog is cow-hocked or crosses over, he should be penalized.

Several areas need to be addressed in any future changes in the Standard. One of these is the ear set. It would be better if the wording read, "The *orifice* of the ear is set level with the eyes." The current wording might encourage a houndlike ear. When a dog with correct ear set lifts his ears at the base, the lift should bring the ear about level with the top of the skull. This ability to lift the ear slightly is important, because it increases hearing capability and probably aids in ventilating the ear, thus avoiding problems such as ear infection. Hound ears lack the ability to lift.

The correct eye shape has been omitted in the Standard. A large, oval eye is preferred. Length of upper arm also is omitted. This should be equal in length to the shoulder blade. In the Standard, croups are described only in a negative manner. The correct slope for a Beardie should be about twenty-five degrees, which is slightly flatter than the thirty-degree slope common to most other working breeds. The Beardie developed this trait to be able to leap straight upward to facilitate his sheep herding on the rough Scottish countryside. The flatter croup and corre-

Lovely head type. Eng. Ch. Bravo of Bothkennar, Osmart.

Parcana Possibility, Silverleaf, shows correct coat texture.

spondingly squared-off topline are distinctive breed characteristics.

Recent studies indicate that a well-laid-back shoulder may actually measure less than the accepted forty-five degree angle. Dogs with ideal layback that were previously assumed to have a forty-five degree shoulder angulation probably measure closer to thirty-nine degrees. This discrepancy is due strictly to methods of measurement and is not intended to advocate straighter shoulder angulation.

Some minor comments concerning the color section are in order. First is the color of the pigmentation of fawns. While fawn could be considered just a lighter shade of brown, it actually has a distinctly mauve tone. This is the surest way to distinguish between a true fawn and a light brown. Two other areas are more a matter

of interpretation than a need for change. The phrase, "The white does not grow on the face to surround the eyes," should never, by any stretch of the imagination, be interpreted to fault a blaze that arches over the eyes as the hair lengthens. The unacceptable white is seen as a predominantly white head or a blaze so wide that it encompasses the eyes at the skin line.

The reference that pigmentation should have no spots means that no flesh-colored spots should appear on the nose leather, the visible part of the lips, or the eye rims. It does not refer to a pink spot on the bridge of the muzzle---a normal occurrence in any breed that has white markings on the face.

A most desirable change in the Standard would be to eliminate the list of Serious Faults and to substitute the statement, "The foregoing

Bites: left, correct scissors bite; right, overshot bite — incorrect for an adult, but may correct if seen in a puppy.

Bottom left: correct ear set.
Bottom right: ears set too high.

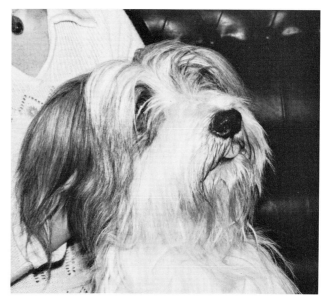

PARTS OF THE BEARDIE

1. Foreface or muzzle. Well filled below the eyes. Broad and blunt.
2. Stop. Nose to stop should be equal to or slightly shorter in length than stop to occiput. Stop should be well defined.
3. Occiput.
4. Line indicating center of gravity.
5. Withers. The point to which height is measured.
6. Back. Moderately long, strong, and level.
7. Loin. Close coupled and muscular. Loin is the area between last rib and hipbone.
8. Croup. Should have slight downward slope.
9. Tail. Must reach at least to the hock. Low carriage is preferred.
10. Thigh. Well muscled and long.
11. Hock. Low set and flexible.
12. Stifle. Should be long and well bent.
13. Flank. Slightly tucked up.
14. Elbow. Depth of chest should reach at least to this point.
15. Pastern. Should be strong and moderately sloped.
16. Upper arm. Angle of upper arm is measured where a line from point of shoulder to point of elbow intersects the perpendicular.
17. Point of shoulder.
18. Throatlatch.
19. Underjaw. Should be of sufficient length to provide for correct bite and allow lips to meet evenly.
20. Nose. Should be large and square.
21. Length of body measured from point of shoulder to point of hip. Standard calls for five-to-four ratio of length to height. Much of this length is due to proper angulation and length of rib cage.

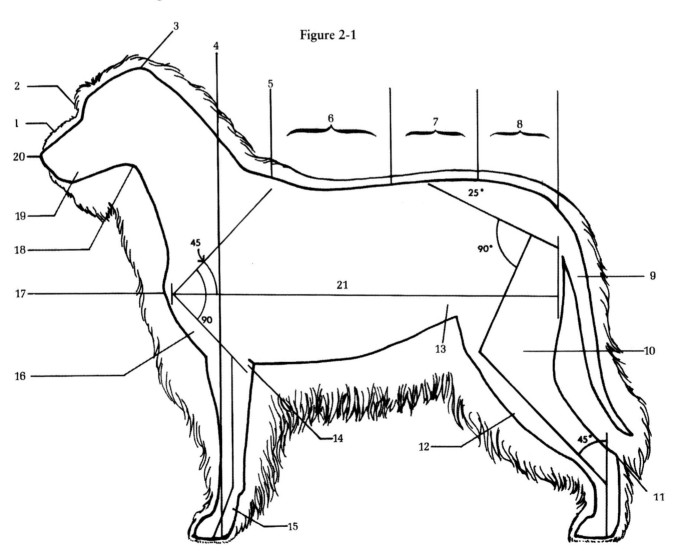

Figure 2-1

STRUCTURE OF THE BEARDIE

1. Skull. Should be broad and flat.
2. Neck. Moderately long and arched.
3. Rib cage. Long, sloping well back, with moderate spring flattened at the bottom.
4. Thoracic vertebrae.
5. Lumbar vertebrae.
6. Croup (sacrum).
7. Pelvis (ilium).
8. Pelvis (ischium).
9. Upper thigh (femur). "Rear angulation" refers to the angle at which the upper thigh meets the pelvis.f The ideal is ninety degrees.
10. Stifle joint (patella).
11. Stifle (tibia and fibula). Should be equal to or preferably longer than the thigh bone.
12. Hock joint.
13. Metatarsus.
14. Elbow (olecranon).
15. Feet (phalanges).
16. Pastern (metacarpus).
17. Pastern joint.
18. Forearm (radius and ulna).
19. Upper arm (humerus). Should be equal in length to the shoulder blade. Actual length of bone is measured rather than to point of elbow.
20. Breastbone (prosternum). Projects slightly in front of point of shoulder, but should not be prominent.
21. Shoulder blade (scapula). "Front angulation" refers to the angle at which the scapula and humerus meet. Ideal angle is ninety degrees. Shoulder blade should be set at a forty-five-degree angle.
22. Cheekbones. Should be flat and merge smoothly with the skull without dips or ridges.

Figure 2-2

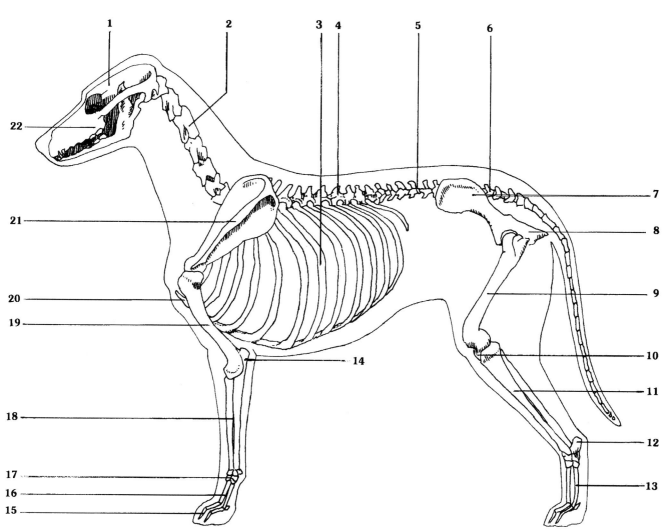

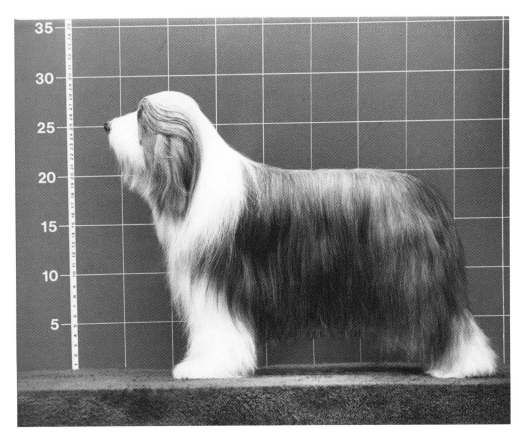

Am. Can. Ch. Bendale Special Lady UD HC in ffront of a grid board to show body proportion. Courtesy MicheleRitter.

is a description of the ideal Bearded Collie, any deviation to be penalized according to the extent of the deviation."

On the whole, this Standard is a tribute to those who compiled it. It is to be hoped that any changes will be as carefully thought out. It is interesting to compare the BCCA Standard with that of the Bearded Collie Club in England.

BRITISH STANDARD

GENERAL APPEARANCE: Lean, active dog, longer than it is high in an approximate ratio of five to four, measured from point of chest to point of buttock. Bitches may be slightly longer. Though strongly made, should show plenty of daylight under body and should not look too heavy. Bright, enquiring expression is a distinctive feature.

CHARACTERISTICS: Alert, lively, self-confident and active.

TEMPERAMENT: Steady, intelligent working dog, with no signs of nervousness or aggression

HEAD AND SKULL: Head in proportion to size. Skull broad, flat and square, distance between stop and occiput being equal to width between orifices of ears. Muzzle strong and equal in length to distance between stop and occiput. Whole effect being that of a dog with strength of muzzle and plenty of brain room. Moderate stop. Nose large and square, generally black but normally following coat colour in blues and browns. Nose and lips of solid colour without spots or patches. Pigmentation of lips and eye rims follows nose colour.

EYES: Toning with coat colour, set widely apart and large, soft and affectionate, not protruding. Eyebrows arched up and forward but not so long as to obscure eyes.

EARS: Of medium size and drooping. When alert, ears lift at base, level with, but not above top of skull, increasing apparent breadth of skull.

MOUTH: Teeth large and white. Jaws strong with a perfect, regular and complete scissors bite preferred, i.e., upper teeth closely overlapping lower teeth and set square to the jaws. Level bite tolerated but undesirable.

NECK: Moderate length, muscular and slightly arched.

FOREQUARTERS: Shoulders sloping well back. Legs straight and vertical with good bone, covered with shaggy hair all round. Pasterns flexible without weakness.

BODY: Length of back comes from length of rib cage and not that of the loin. Back level and ribs well sprung but not barrelled. Loin strong and chest deep, giving plenty of heart and lung room.

HINDQUARTERS: Well muscled with good second thighs, well- bent stifles and low hocks. Lower leg falls at right angle to ground and, in normal stance, is just behind a line vertically below point of buttocks.

FEET: Oval in shape with soles well padded. Toes arched and close together, well covered with hair, including between pads.

TAIL: Set low, without kink or twist, and long enough for end of bone to reach at least point of hock. Carried low with an upward swirl at tip whilst standing or walking, may be extended at speed. Never carried over back. Covered with abundant hair.

GAIT/MOVEMENT: Supple, smooth and long reaching, covering ground with minimum effort

COAT: Double with soft, furry and close undercoat. Outer coat flat, harsh, strong and shaggy, free from wooliness and curl, though slight wave permissible. Length and density of hair sufficient to provide a protective coat and to enhance shape of dog, but not enough to obscure natural lines of body. Coat must not be trimmed in any way. Bridge of nose sparsely covered with hair slightly longer on side to cover lips. From cheeks, lower lips and under chin, coat increases in length towards chest, forming typical beard.

COLOUR: Slate grey, reddish fawn, black, blue, all shades of grey, brown and sandy with or without white markings. When white occurs it appears on foreface, as a blaze on skull, on tip of tail, on chest,

legs and feet and, if round the collar, roots of white hair should not extend behind shoulder. White should not appear above hocks on outside of hind legs. Slight tan markings are acceptable on eyebrows, inside ears, on cheeks, under root of tail and on legs where white joins the main colour.

SIZE: Ideal height: Dogs 53 to 56 centimeters (21 to 22 inches); bitches 51 to 53 centimeters (20 to 21 inches). Overall quality and proportions should be considered before size but excessive variations from the ideal height should be discouraged.

FAULTS: Any departure from the foregoing points should be considered a fault and the seriousness with which the fault should be regarded should be in exact proportion to its degree.

NOTE: Male animals should have two apparently normal testicles fully descended into the scrotum.

A comparison of the two Standards shows far more similarities than differences. The English Standard more precisely defines the amount of white allowed on the hind legs, the size of the skull, and the ear placement. The American Standard gives more detail on the rib shape and a far better description of gait. The English ask for eyebrows to arch upward and forward, while the Americans say to the sides, although this is probably as much a matter of grooming as genetics. The English have a much better section on Faults. It covers all bases and puts all faults in proportion. The American Standard gives the erroneous impression that faults not listed are not really serious. It would be absurd to think that a trimmed coat, which is non-hereditary, could be more serious than a structural fault, which is not only genetic but could be incapacitating. It is to be hoped that any future change in the American Standard would adopt the English version. Many other breed Standards use this wording.

Ch. Parcana Jake McTavish in top form!

Ch. Parcana Lord Corwin CD HC BIS.
© Debrah Helen Muska, Animal Images.

Left: Am. Can. Ch. Britannia Ticket To Ride HC ROMX;
Right: Ch. Britannia Sweet Lady CD.

Am. Can. Ch. Bendale Special Lady UD HC.

Am.Can. Ch. Britannia Just Jeffrey HC and his daughter, Am. Can. Ch. Britannia Sweet Libeardie.

Ch. Bedlam's Nemesis in New York's Central Park.

Bridgrove Black Rory.

*Above:
Am. Can. Ch.
Britannia Ticket
to Ride HC
ROMX winning
BOB at
Westminster
Kennel Club,
1993. Owner
handled by
Michele Ritter.
He went on to a
Group Second.*

*Right:
Ch. Daybreak
Rising Sun
UD, CD.
Breeeder/owner
Barbara Prescott.*

Ch. Aretisan Bronze Paladin HS.

Flyball is an exciting sport enjoyed by Alice Bixler's Beardie.

Ch. Highlander Double Enchanted HC, owned by Don and Elodji Means and Beth Tilson.

Britannia Master Thinker UD, HI, Can. CD, sporting his herding ribbons. Owned by Sandy Weiss.

Ch. Highlander Spellbound HC, ROM, CGC retrieving in the water.

Beth Tilson with three lovely veterans (left to right): Ch. Highlander Lorna Doone CD, HC, ROM, ROM I at age seven years; Ch. Parchment Farm's Mr. Kite CD HC ROM, at ten years; and Parchment Farm's Annie Laurie HC at eleven years.

Five-week-old brown, fawn, and black puppies.

A rainbow of colors in one litter. Left to right: brown, blue, black, fawn, brown, and tricolor.

A black Beardie: Am. Can. Ch. Crisch Midnight Magic, HC ROM. Graham Photo.

A fawn puppy:
Parcana Sir Raggs of Genesee.

A lighter fawn adult: Ch. Britannia Fawn Lady.
Photo by Jezierski.

A rare black and tan Beardie, Ch. Higllandglen
Gruff McDuff. This color was written out of the
British Standard in the 1960s.

Four colors of Beardies:
Left to right, a black, a fawn, a brown, and a gray.

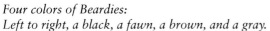

A slate: Ch. Madigan's Born for Adventure.

A brown Am. Ch. Willowmead Red Ruariridh.

Fawns: Ch. Stonehaven's My Lady Amber, left, and her dam, Ch. Stonehaven's Picture Perfect.

3 *Moving Out*

A Beardie's effectiveness as a working dog is primarily determined by his physical ability. He must be swift, tireless, and capable of sudden starts, stops, and turns. He also has developed the unique ability to leap straight upward from any position, a feat that is useful in coping with the rough terrain and the half-wild sheep found in the Beardie's native habitat.

While some aspects of structure influence efficiency of movement more than others, a dog's conformation can be evaluated quickly and relatively accurately by watching how he moves. Show-ring evaluation of movement is made from three angles—as the dog approaches the judge, as he gaits away from the judge, and from the side as he circles the ring. Equal emphasis should be placed on each segment of gait. A dog that moves correctly is said to be "sound." (This term can also refer to proper health and temperament but usually is applied to gait.)

When evaluating soundness, a judge looks for straightness and strength of legs, ligamentation of joints, and musculature. These traits determine how well a dog will move within the limitations of his skeletal structure. Evaluation is also made on strength of topline and smoothness of motion, on where the feet hit the ground, and on the balance of the trot as determined by skeletal proportions and angles. If everything is correct, the Beardie will exhibit a long, easy, effortless stride that he can continue to use mile after mile. Conditioning the muscles will enable a dog to exhibit his greatest potential (*see* Chapter 7).

The natural working-dog gait is the trot. Because this is also the gait at which structure can most easily be evaluated, it is the only gait used in the show ring. The trot is achieved when the diagonal legs move in unison. It is a two-beat gait, with periods of suspension between each beat in which all four legs are off the ground at once. Length of stride is determined by the dog's "angulation." Front angulation is measured at the point of the shoulder; ideally, ninety degrees between the shoulder blade and the upper arm, which should be of equal length for maximum efficiency. Rear angulation is measured at the junction of the hip and thighbone—also a ninety-degree measurement in the ideal specimen. The thigh should be relatively long to allow for strong drive. In order for the trot to remain balanced, front and rear angulation must be the same. Therefore, if the ideal is not available, it is preferable to have a dog with a balanced front and rear angulation even though the angle is not perfect, rather than an individual that is well angulated at one end but poorly so at the other. The unbalanced dog cannot trot properly and must compensate in some aspect of his movement. Any gait deviation creates a weak point that, under prolonged stress or old age, is subject to breakdown.

SIDE GAIT

The speed and endurance of a dog is determined by his side gait. To many breeders, this is the most important aspect of gait, because it has the greatest effect on the dog's efficiency. Unfortunately, it is also the most difficult for a beginner to recognize. It is imperative that any serious Beardie enthusiast learn to analyze side gait.

The correct trot viewed from the side is effortless and powerful. The feet should be lifted only enough to clear the ground with a minimum of wasted vertical motion. This gives a Beardie the appearance of almost floating across the terrain. A bounce or roll to the topline is evidence of improper action. The topline should remain firm and level at all times

The hindquarters provide the forward propulsion known as "drive." The front should move in line with and at the same efficiency as the rear in order to accept the drive and provide the primary balance and directional control. The front action is referred to as "reach."

The right hind leg and the left front leg move together, and the left hind leg and right foreleg move in unison. One set of diagonals hits the ground, completes the stride, and lifts for a period of suspension; then the second set of diagonals strikes the ground and propels the dog forward before another moment of suspension. Then the process repeats. As one set of diagonals is projecting the dog forward, the other is clearing the ground and stretching forward to start the next stride. The hind foot will usually strike the ground at the point where the front foot on the same side just left. Legs on the same side come together under the body in a "V", then extend fully to the front and rear as the legs on the other side come together. To rec-

Figure 3-1
The correct trot. At full extension, all four feet are off the ground.

ognize a correct trot, watch for the diagonals moving in unison and for good length of stride.

Breaking down the trot even further, let's examine the front alone. The shoulder layback, the length and angle of the upper arm, and the leg and pastern all contribute to proper reach. The feet must be strong and resilient to absorb the shock. The front leg reaches as far forward as possible (in a good mover it should extend as far forward as the tip of the nose or slightly farther) and strikes the ground in unison with the hind diagonal. It then carries the dog forward until the front foot is underneath the body as far as possible, lifts just enough to clear the ground, and again reaches forward to accept the next stride. The hind foot follows a similar pattern. It reaches underneath the body and pushes the dog forward. Once it passes the vertical, it begins the portion of the stride known as follow-through, which provides much of the forward push. The foot should remain on the ground until both stifle and hock joints are at full extension, then lift only enough to clear the ground as it again moves forward.

Croup, thigh, stifle, hock, and foot, plus muscling, all contribute to proper rear action. The Beardie has a slightly flatter croup than most working breeds. This allows for an extended follow-through in drive, and, combined with the strong muscles and lighter frame, permits the freedom for flat-footed leaps. When all of this is put together, you see a graceful, startlingly agile dog in action. The longer and better balanced a trot, the longer and more effortlessly a dog can function

Faults of Side Gait

Unbalanced Stride. The least severe side fault is one in which the dog is balanced but poorly angulated and must take more steps to keep up. With this fault, timing and cadence are still correct. More severe side faults are usually due to incorrect skeletal proportions. The cause of these faults can vary from unbalanced angulation to disproportionate length of individual bones

A dog that has good rear angulation but inadequate shoulder layback is an all-too-common sight in many breeds, including Beardies. Although a dog with this fault has good drive, the front cannot keep up. The dog loses cadence in his trot and throws his front feet in an

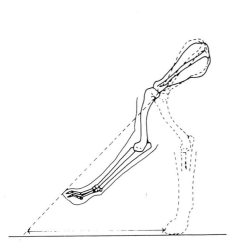

Figure 3-2
*Maximum reach is limited
by shoulder angulation.*

Figure 3-3
Front feet lifted too high due to straight shoulders.

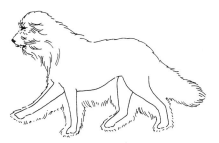

Figure 3-4
Downhill runner.

Figure 3-5
Kicking up.

Figure 3-6
Pounding or dwelling.

attempt to keep them away from his hind feet. Usually the front feet are lifted too high in a jerky motion. In a severe case, the hind feet strike the front legs and the dogs looks as if he is trying to kick his chin. The shoulder is fairly rigid and lacks flexibility. Some individuals take short, picky steps and lift the rear feet very high in order to expend the extra drive. In any case, the back does not remain level, but instead bounces when the animal is in motion.

Likewise, a dog that is better in shoulder than in stifle angulation has problems. Probably he will appear to be running downhill when on the level, because as he moves, his rear remains higher than his withers. A dog that is straight in rear angulation usually has a kick-up, or at least inadequate follow-through. His hind foot never reaches the print left by the front foot. Because the stride is shorter, power of the drive is reduced severely. Again, timing is thrown off and efficiency is below par.

When synchronization of gait is disturbed, a dog may exhibit "pounding" or "dwelling." The front foot reaches full extension, hesitates in midair, then crashes down after the hind leg has begun the next stride. This is extremely hard on the entire front assembly. It may be difficult to detect at first; watch for the diagonals moving together as an indication of correct gait.

Another indication is to look for the two inverted "V"s made when the legs are at full extension. The front and rear "V" should be equal in width, should not overlap, and should be simultaneous. A narrower front "V" denotes lack of reach, a narrower rear "V" a lack of

drive. If they overlap, the dog is too short in body and probably crabs. If the "V"s are not simultaneous, the timing of the trot is off.

Hocks Set Too High. This is an imperfection that often (but not always) accompanies straight stifles. When both faults appear, the dog usually is high in the rear. The hind legs lack flexibility and the stride is shortened. Kick-up sometimes occurs and is quite noticeable in a dog with high hocks.

Sickle Hocks. This is a condition in which the metatarsus curves slightly inward from hock to foot. Follow-through becomes virtually impossible, and a stiff, stilted rear action results. Kick-up always occurs with sickle hocks. This condition is more common in Beardies than in many working breeds and should be faulted severely.

Short Upper Arm or Stifle. The upper arm should be equal in length to the shoulder blade. Regardless of angulation, a short upper arm throws off gait. (Upper-arm length is measured by the actual length of the bone, not to the point of elbow.) A hackney or prancing gait, with the front feet lifted high, is often indicative of a short upper arm. Less common is the proportionally shorter stifle. This results in a choppy rear action, which again lacks in follow-through.

Incorrect Pastern. The pastern is designed to absorb shock from the forequarters. It needs

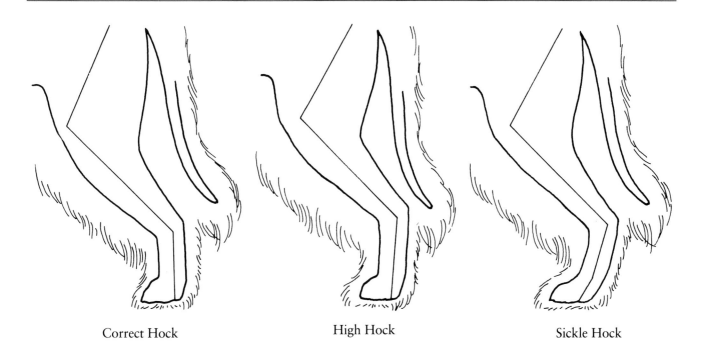

Correct Hock   High Hock   Sickle Hock

Figure 3-7
Correct and faulty hocks.

to be moderate in length and slope to perform its function efficiently. Too much slope results in loose, extremely weak wrists, a problem often accompanied by a crooked front. The other extreme is a too-steep pastern, which usually is short and often occurs in conjunction with a straight shoulder. Either condition is restrictive, and jarring strains the entire front assembly. The pastern is primarily a shock absorber, and under stress, a front assembly with poor pasterns will become sore and break down.

Pacing. Pacing is an action similar to trotting but one in which the legs on the same side (instead of the diagonals) move in unison. Sometimes a dog will pace quite rapidly. Unless the handler is aware of the difference in gait, a dog might pace in the show ring. Because structural analysis cannot be made from a pace, an individual that fails to trot readily will not be considered in a conformation class. The dog will often pace if the handler moves too slowly or if the dog is tired. A quick jerk will usually put the animal into a trot.

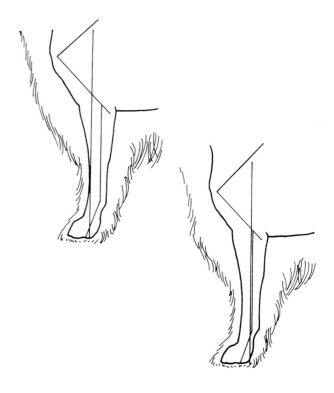

Figure 3-8
Length of upper arm.
Right: Short upper arm, causing foreleg to be set too far forward.

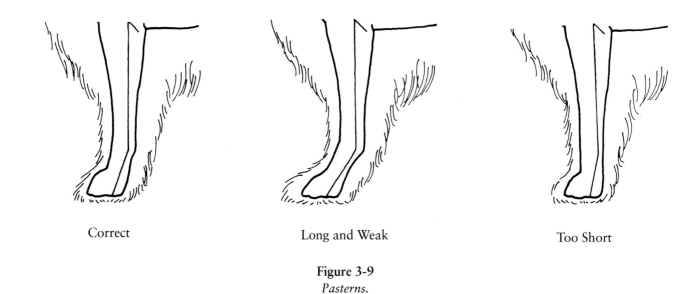

| Correct | Long and Weak | Too Short |

Figure 3-9
Pasterns.

Crabbing. Crabbing is the lack of alignment of the body in motion. The dog moves somewhat sideways, with the rear tracking to the left or right of the front. This last consideration of side gait is more easily seen coming or going. In some instances, crabbing is a way for the dog to avoid striking his front legs with his hind feet—the result of too short a body or of having more angulation in the rear than in the front. Crabbing may also be simply a bad habit.

Crabbing.

REAR OR "GOING" GAIT

The primary function of the dog's rear legs is to produce the drive that propels the body forward. However, the Standard also calls for the stance to be square and the gait true going away. It is certainly more pleasing to the eye this way and also avoids encouraging weaknesses that may break down under stress. A dog with a less-than-perfect stance but that moves well is superior to an individual that stands correctly but cannot move properly. Stance can always be trained or "stacked," but movement is proof of structure.

To determine how well a dog is tracking in rear, draw an imaginary line down the center of each hind leg (as viewed from the rear), from hip to hock to foot. When the dog is standing, these lines should be straight, vertical, and parallel to each other. A deviation at the hock or foot, either in or out, indicates a weakness. When the animal is moving, these lines should remain straight but come together in a "V" shape as speed increases. The inside edges of the feet converge on a center line; thus the term "singletrack" describing correct gait in a Beardie. Beardies sometimes appear a bit narrow because of their long stifles and leaner builds. Also, the long coat can be deceptive. Brush hocks thoroughly, or better yet, wet them down, before evaluating rear action.

Far left: Correct rear stance.

Figure 3-10
Left: Singletrack viewed from the rear.

Figure 3-11
Below: Pawprints made when a Beardie singletracks. Dark and light prints represent opposing diagonals.

Rear Faults

Hocking Out. Hocking out is probably the most serious of the rear faults because it puts terrific stress on the ligaments and is likely to restrict the drive of the hindquarters. The condition is permissible in young puppies because it is likely to be caused by loose ligamentation that will tighten as the dog grows. Very slight hocking out is like any other fault—the severity is judged by its degree rather than by its nature.

Cow Hocks, Toeing Out, and Close Rears. The term "cow hocks" is used when the hocks turn inward and the feet turn outward. If the legs are straight at the hocks but the feet turn outward, the dog is said to "toe out." True cow hocks exhibit both problems.

Among the first faults that a novice learns to recognize are light eyes, wavy coats, gay tails, and cow hocks. Because cow hocks are eventually determined to be the most serious of these faults, the novice will think of them as

Figure 3-12
Hocking out.

Figure 3-13
Cow hocks.

Figure 3-14
Toeing out.

Figure 3-15
Close parallel rear.

Figure 3-16
Crossing over.

Figure 3-17
Wide parallel rear.

paramount among structural faults. But the truth is that there are many worse and harder-to-detect faults than cow hocks. Cow hocks do not affect the rest of the dog unless they are so extreme as to constitute an actual deformity. A dog may appear cow hocked standing but still move true. This is a lesser fault than moving cow hocked.

To a lesser degree than cow hocks, toeing out and close rears are undesirable. In the latter two cases, the efficiency of gait is not badly restricted. Toeing out sometimes affects stance only, whereas a close parallel rear is also obvious in motion. A close parallel rear is one that, in motion, is parallel from hock to foot with an angle at the hock. This condition is often accompanied by a narrow pelvis.

Crossing Over. Crossing over is a a fault in which the feet overstep the center line and cross to the opposite side. The legs actually cross when gaiting, and the entire rear of the dog usually bounces from side to side as the center of gravity is shifted with each step. The fault becomes more obvious with speed.

The Wide Parallel Rear. A Beardie with this fault often (though not necessarily) stands perfectly; in fact, he is often touted as not being able to stand incorrectly. He is built like a table with unyielding vertical legs that remain the same distance apart at the feet in a swift trot as when standing. The wide parallel gait is more obvious at a slow gait, because the fast trot forces the legs toward a singletrack for balance. Wide rears are seldom seen in Beardies, and when this fault does occur, it is usually accompanied by a short or straight stifle. Occasionally, a wide mover, particularly one that is wide both front and rear, develops a characteristic "roll" from throwing his weight from side to side. This dog varies from the individual that hocks out in that the hocks of a wide mover remain in line and appear strong. Wide rear rarely affects side gait.

Hitching. Hitching occurs when one hind leg is lifted higher than the other as it is brought forward. This can be observed from the side as well and causes an imbalance in the gait. This possibly results from a difference in the amount of muscle in the legs and is rarely structural.

FRONT OR "COMING" GAIT

Beardies should also singletrack in front at a brisk trot. When the dog stands, his legs should be in straight parallel lines from elbows to pasterns to feet.

Correct front action is partially dependent on correct rib spring. Proper ribs are rounded at the top half to allow plenty of room for the heart and lungs but are flattened on the bottom half to allow for unrestricted swing of the front leg backward along the side of the dog. If the sides are too rounded (barrel-ribbed) or too flat (slab-sided), the plane in which the elbow moves is distorted and some of the efficiency in gait is destroyed. Barrel ribs often lack depth, and their roundness causes the elbows to swing out to avoid interference. A slab-sided individual lacks substance and appears frail and narrow. Although a normal condition in a young dog, slab-sidedness usually causes a faulty front action because the front is not adequately supported. Be wary of the young dog that is extremely well-developed in ribs and chest for his age because he may very well continue to develop and end up being too broad and heavy in front.

Front Faults

Crooked Front Legs. Crooked front legs are somewhat comparable to cow hocks in the rear. The legs bow outward at the top, inward at the pasterns, then out again at the foot. A dog with a crooked front may move well, but he often possesses other front faults that complicate the issue. Carried to the extreme, this front is known as "fiddle front." Beardies with narrow, crooked fronts should not be bred.

Out at Elbows. This fault is similar to hocking out. The elbows project out from the body rather than moving straight back and forth when the dog trots. This action can also be caused by excessive weight but is often a result of barrel ribs. Elbowing out is often found in conjunction with crooked legs, toeing in, a short upper arm, or loose ligamentation.

Wide Front. This fault means that the dog does not move in a singletrack. The dog usually stands nicely, but his legs remain vertical and parallel when in motion. This condition is similar to a wide parallel rear and can be caused by barrel ribs.

Figure 3-18
Singletrack viewed from the front.

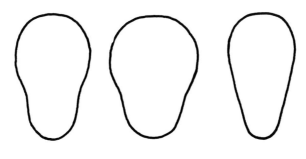

Figure 3-19
Ribspring.
Correct, barrel, and slab-sided.

Figure 3-20
Crooked front.

Figure 3-21
Out at elbows.

Figure 3-22
Wide front.

Figure 3-23
Narrow front.

Figure 3-24
Paddling.

Figure 3-25
Winging.

Figure 3-26
Crossing over.

Narrow or "Tied-In" Front. This refers to a dog that is narrow-chested and too close or pinched at the elbows. The legs may or may not be straight, but they lack adequate support from the rib cage and chest. As a result, the front exhibits an eggbeater motion or is thrown randomly from side to side. This type of front in a young dog may improve as the chest broadens with maturity provided the legs are straight. However, the feet often point outward. An individual that exhibits this fault should be considered a very questionable risk, even as a youngster.

Paddling. Paddling occurs when the dog throws his leg in an outward circle from the elbow as he moves. A dog that paddles usually tracks wide.

Ch. Sunkap Sir Knight HT at seven months of age showing proper front and rear extension and correct balance of stride.

Winging. Winging is often erroneously called "paddling." While both faults involve throwing the feet outward, winging originates at the pastern rather than at the elbow. Winging is seen more frequently than true paddling.

Crossing Over. Crossing over is the same fault as crossing in the rear. The feet pass beyond the center line, and the center of gravity shifts, causing a choppy, bouncing appearance. Crossing in front is usually due to a narrow chest.

Poor fronts have long been a problem in all breeds and are particularly noticeable in a sound working breed such as the Beardie. Once lost from a line, correct front structure is difficult to regain, but once obtained, it can be bred consistently with little effort. Breeding for good fronts should be a high priority in the breed.

Anything that interferes with the desired smooth-floating trot is faulty. The problems described above are examples, but they do not cover every possibility for faults. The complex interrelationship between parts of the body can easily be disturbed, so it is imperative to breed only individuals that are correct in structure.

"Bonnie and friend," *courtesy of Melita Bearded Collies.* Photo by Bill McKnown.

4 *Love at First Sight*

Almost everyone loves to shop—especially when the object of their search is a cuddly, lovable puppy. Before you get all wrapped up in the excitement of buying, make some practical deliberations. Your new Beardie will probably be a member of your household for a decade or more, and his selection deserves careful consideration.

As a potential dog owner, you may not have given any real thought to what type of dog will fit your needs. You may be attracted to a particular breed, such as the Beardie, because a friend has one or because you have seen pictures of the breed. However, you may not have stopped to assess the suitability of the breed to your family or situation. Before you embark on a dog-shopping spree, take time to research a number of breeds. Learn about their temperaments, care and space requirements, size, and hereditary strengths and weaknesses. Excellent sources for this information include books, veterinarians, the local kennel club breeder-referral or rescue service, and, of course, breeders themselves.

Will the breed that you admire fit in with your home? Consider your lifestyle, the age of your children, and your own temperament, as well as your space limitations. What will your dog be—a family pet, the foundation for a kennel, a working dog, an obedience dog for competition or a 4-H project, a show dog, or a combination of these? Where will you keep him? Do you have the time and money to provide him with proper care and attention?

Do not start looking for a Beardie until you are sure that this is the breed for you and that you are willing and able to make him a true member of your family. He will need your companionship and a reasonable amount of training. He will also need regular grooming. A Beardie is not a dog that you can leave alone in the backyard for weeks and then suddenly decide to bring in the house for a while. If this is your idea of the way to have a pet, you better look for another breed because you would not be happy with a Beardie.

SOME OBVIOUS QUESTIONS

Once you have decided on a Beardie, three additional questions are of major importance and should be considered before you shop. They are: what sex, what age, and what quality of dog do you need?

He, She, or It?

There are many old wives' tales about which makes a better pet—a male or female? Basically, it is a matter of personal preference, because either sex makes a marvelous pet. Beardies show more differences between individual puppies than between sexes. Rather than consider only one sex, it is better to look for the temperament that would best fit your lifestyle. This could be found in either a male or female puppy. A responsible breeder will be able to help you determine which puppy will best fill your needs. Once a pet is neutered, there is even less difference in the sexes.

Most reputable breeders require the neutering of a pet-quality Beardie when he is old enough. Neutering benefits both you *and* the breed by preventing unwanted litters and the perpetuation of mediocre-quality Beardies. It also eliminates the bothersome heat periods in a female or the tendency for a male to wander and fight. A neutered Beardie will be a more affectionate pet and a better worker, less prone to being distracted, and he will be easier to manage. There are health benefits as well, primarily reduced risk of mammary-gland or testicular cancer.

Neutering is safe, easy, and relatively inexpensive. Sluggishness, unwanted weight gain, temperament change, or other side effects rarely

Who can resist the adorable face of a Beardie puppy? Bedlam's Photogenic. Courtesy Alice Bixler.

occur provided the neutering is performed when the dog is old enough to have an adequate supply of sex hormones (approximately eight months of age). *Nothing* is gained by allowing your male to sire puppies or your bitch to whelp a litter before having him or her neutered. In fact, either could have negative effects.

Of course, if you want to breed or show, a neutered dog is not for you. Neutered animals or ones with a nonbreeding registry cannot be shown in conformation classes at any licensed show, but they can be shown in obedience or herding events.

The foundation for a breeding kennel should be the best bitch that you can find (*see* Chapter 11). It is usually not advisable to start

Seven-week-old Beardie puppies bred by Pat McDonald.

with a male, because the best males in the country are readily available for your use. Never start a breeding kennel with a male/female pair. Even if you are lucky enough to find suitable mates, they may not produce well together, and if perchance they do, you will still have to go outside to continue your program after the first couple of litters.

Males are impressive and are apt to become top show winners; therefore, some exhibitors prefer to start with a male. Even if you do not plan to breed, a top winning male can be promoted at stud if you can take the time and provide the facilities to handle visiting bitches.

Toddler, Teenager, or Adult?

Generally, you will think of getting a puppy at weaning age—seven to nine weeks—but there are many good reasons to buy an older Beardie. If you have very young children, a twelve-week-old puppy may better contend with their rough handling. If you work away from home during

the day so that feeding and housebreaking are difficult, consider a three- to four-month-old puppy that is already trained and able to go longer without attention. If you are buying a show or breeding prospect, the more mature the dog, the surer the choice and, generally speaking, the higher the price. The proven, older brood bitch, the retired show dog that needs a new home, or the mature male that is ready to show may be just right for your situation. Don't shy away from such opportunities for fear the older dog will not adapt. It may take the older Beardie a little longer to accept you as his master, but he usually will adjust and make an ideal pet. Most breeders who place an older dog will do so on a trial basis.

Pet, Breeding, or Show?

Most breeders classify their Beardies in one of three basic categories—pet, breeding, or show prospects. One of the breeder's first questions is bound to be, "Do you want a show dog or a family dog?"

A Beardie sold as a pet is meant to be just that—a wonderful companion. He will look like a Beardie and will have the typical temperament and personality that may have prompted you to choose a Bearded Collie in the first place, but he will not have all the fine points of conformation necessary to qualify him for the show ring or breeding kennel. The pet Beardie is ideal for herding livestock and for competing in obedience work, tracking, or other practical work, and you won't need to be as concerned about his sustaining slight injuries or damaging his coat as you would if you used a show dog for this type of activity. (Yes, a show dog *can* do these things, too.)

The most important consideration in a pet is temperament. Even at weaning age, the young Beardie exhibits much of his adult personality. By watching a litter at play for a while, you can probably pick out the quietest, the boldest, the most aggressive, and the pup showing the strongest herding instinct. It is best not to select an extremely frightened or aggressive puppy

Breeding and show Beardies are very similar, if not identical, in quality. The young puppy is usually referred to as a "show prospect" because it is difficult to determine with total accuracy just how an eight-week or twelve-week puppy will mature. Exceptional Beardies that are six months of age or older may be classified as "show quality" and will be sold for higher prices than the young "prospects." At six months, the structure is evident, gait and coat are beginning to mature, and type is obvious. Because puppies may be shown at six months of age, the dog may even have begun to prove his mettle in the show ring. A show dog must be an excellent specimen of the breed, possessing all the qualities of temperament, personality, showmanship, and correct conformation that could make him a winner.

"Breeding quality" also denotes show quality or a Beardie that is only slightly less than perfect. The major difference is often the lack of poise or showmanship of the breeding-quality Beardie, especially in females. A dog purchased for breeding should have good temperament and good health and should exhibit no major faults. A show dog lamed by an injury or one that has lost an ear or a tooth or has been scarred in a fight may also be sold for breeding quality. (*See* Chapters 11 and 14 for more information on breeding and show-dog selection.)

WHERE DO YOU FIND YOUR DOG?

Finding the right Beardie may not be easy and it may take time, but he is well worth waiting for. If you can locate one or more breeders within driving distance, this is the place to start. You may also find Beardies exhibited at a local dog show (watch the ad column of your local newspaper for dates and places). You can probably locate breeders through your local kennel club referral service or by writing the American Kennel Club for the address of the parent club (the Bearded Collie Club of America). The BCCA can then send you a list of breeders. You may also find advertisements in national dog magazines (*see* "Other Sources").

A good way to develop an eye for a Beardie and to meet the breeders is to attend a dog show. Observe the judging carefully and ask a knowledgeable spectator to help you understand the reasons for the placements. After the breed has been judged, go quickly to the grooming area to discuss buying a puppy with a breeder/exhibitor whose Beardies attracted you. Most exhibitors are busy with preparations prior to ring-time but will be happy to talk with you immediately after the breed classes.

Before you actually make a purchase, try to visit the breeder at home. One clue to a good kennel is consistency of quality and type throughout the kennel, especially if evident through several generations. Another clue is the cleanliness and the kind of socialization and care provided. If overall type is varied or poor, temperaments are questionable, or kennel conditions unclean, look elsewhere.

What if you can't visit the breeder in person—can you still purchase a good Beardie? Yes, if you are careful. Rely on referrals from knowl-

*A playful older puppy owned by
Larry and Michelle Abramson.*

Hopefully, you will not find a Bearded Collie in a pet shop—a source that is definitely not recommended. Always buy from a breeder. Most breeders are reputable people who will help you select the right dog for your needs and become your friend and advisor while you are getting started in the breed. Some breed clubs maintain a rescue service—a placement service for older Beardies—that is worth looking into.

BEARDIE RESCUE

This is a very important function of the Bearded Collie Club of America, operating nationwide. Beardies that have been abandoned, abused, or left in shelters are taken in by volunteers and rehabilitated. Costs of veterinary care are paid from the Rescue Fund. Good homes are then found for these dogs. The director of this program is Paul Glatzer, (516) 724-0871. There are regional representatives throughout the country.

MAKING THE PURCHASE

Every AKC-registered dog should be sold with a signed litter or individual registration slip, a pedigree, and a sales contract that includes a guarantee. If the litter registration papers have not come back to the breeder from the AKC, the contract should contain a statement guaranteeing that they will be signed over to the purchaser as soon as they arrive. The seller may hold the registration certificate until certain contractual conditions such as neutering and payment completion are fulfilled.

The AKC has made available a limited registration that prevents any offspring of that animal from ever being registered. The sales contract should contain this provision. A dog with this registration cannot be shown in breed competition in a licensed or member dog show. He is eligible, however, to be entered in any other licensed or member event, such as obedience or herding.

edgeable handlers or judges or from breeders with an established reputation. Sometimes a professional handler will see and purchase a dog for you if you cannot travel in person. If you choose to write to breeders without a referral, take time to get to know them through letters or calls before you make a purchase

When you are buying a dog from another area of the United States, you often can have him shipped "on approval." Under these circumstances, you purchase the Beardie with an agreement that he may be returned for a full refund within a specified time period (usually a few days) if you find that the dog does not suit your requirements or feel that he was misrepresented. You pay all shipping expenses and assume responsibility for the dog while he is in your possession during the approval period.

SAMPLE SALES CONTRACT FOR PET PUPPIES

On (date) ——————————— XYZ KENNELS agrees to sell the following Beardie Collie

to: (name) ——————————————————————————————————

of: (address) ——————————————————————————————————

———————————————————— telephone: ——————————————

for the sum of $ ——————————

Color: ——————————————   Sire: ——————————————————

Sex: ——————————————   Dam: ——————————————————

Whelped: ——————————————   Reg. #: ——————————————————

REGISTRATION PAPERS:

1. Limited registration (non-breeding) papers will be given with the puppy (or will be transferred to the buyer immediately upon receipt from AKC if they are being processed) provided the animal has beenpaid for in full.

    OR

2. If the animal has not been fully paid for at the time it is transferred, limited registration papers will be held by the seller until payment has been made in full.

    OR

3. In the case of a pet bitch, the animal must be neutered before the registration papers are transferred. On receipt of a veterinarian's certificate that the bitch has been neutered, the limited registration papers will be transferred with no additional charge.

It is understood at the time of sale this dog is not considered to be of show or breeding quality, but it is representative of its breed and is structurally and temperamentally suited as a compaion or obedience or herding dog. Beginning training classes are highly recommended for any family dog to insure a happy relationship.

This dog is guaranteed for 48 hours against any health or temperament irregularities, and it is recommended the buyer have the puppy examined by a reputable veterinarian during this period. (Note: any puppy going to a new home may be a bit unsure of himself until he becomes familiar with his surroundings.) A full refund will be given for any pup found not satisfactory during the first 48 hours and returned in good condition. The buyer will be responsible for only shipping charges. No other guarantee is given or implied except in the case of an *hereditary* defect that develops (before the age of three years) to the extent that it renders the dog unsuitable as a pet. In this instance, a replacement will be given when one becomes available. Buyer will be responsible for only shipping charges.

Neutering of males is strongly recommended. Neutering of females is mandatory.

Special provisions: Signed: ——————————————————

                                   Signed: ——————————————————

                                   Address:——————————————————

                                   ——————————————————————

                                   Telephone:——————————————————

Guarantees

Ask for and expect a written sales contract/guarantee. A pet generally will be guaranteed to be in good health for a specified period from date of purchase. He also may be guaranteed for good temperament and/or against any debilitating hereditary defects up to the age of two or three years. (This generally includes crippling dysplasia and blindness.)

A breeding-quality Beardie should carry a guarantee that the dog will be capable of reproducing, and either a show or breeding animal should be guaranteed against hereditary defects occurring before three years of age. Monorchidism, or cryptorchidism (failure of one or both testicles to descend into the scrotum), is a disqualification in any breed, and this should certainly be included in the guarantee on a show or breeding male.

Contracts for show Beardies may carry any number of terms. Some breeders guarantee that the dog will finish his championship. Others guarantee that the dog will be show quality by their definition at a certain specified age. The more protection you are given, the higher the price you can expect to pay.

Almost every registered Beardie should be sold with some type of contract to protect the buyer and seller. It is important that you understand and agree to these terms.

Payment Terms

There are many ways to buy a dog. The best and most usual is an outright cash purchase. A few large breeders will accept major credit cards or take time payments, in which case you will be asked to sign a contract and agree that the registration papers will be held by the seller until the last payment has been made.

"Breeder's terms" refer to the sale of a male with stud privileges (use of the dog for breeding retained by the seller) or the sale of a bitch with puppies or even litters to be given back to the seller. Sometimes exceptional show

Choosing the right puppy can be a difficult decision.

animals are sold this way to ensure that they and their offspring are properly bred and exhibited. Partial value of the puppies or litters is deducted from the sale price, and the bitch is usually co-owned until the payment in puppies has been fulfilled. If the terms are agreeable to both parties and the two individuals can work together reasonably, such arrangements can be advantageous to both. Terms must be spelled out in writing and clearly understood by both parties.

Permanent co-ownerships offer another method of obtaining a good Beardie. Co-ownerships may be offered by breeders who want to hold on to a Beardie for breeding but do not have the space or time to keep another dog. Some breeders will sell co-ownership only to a novice so that they can place the dog but essentially retain control and assure that the dog is shown, promoted, and bred properly. If the beginner is willing to cooperate with the experienced breeder, this may be an excellent way to obtain top-quality stock. Usually the person purchasing the co-ownership is expected to keep the dog. The two owners may split stud fees or litters, and the contract should specify in writing how this is done and who is to be responsible for maintenance, show, and advertising expenses.

Occasionally, it may be possible to lease a Beardie for a start in breeding without the permanency or expense of buying. Bitches are leased for a five- or six-month period, and the lease must be registered with the AKC. The lessee is generally responsible for the shipping charge, the stud fee, and all other expenses when leasing a bitch for a litter, or for the promotion costs and showing fees when leasing a stud dog. The lessee is held liable for the dog while the animal is in his care. About the only way to obtain a good Beardie on lease is to become acquainted with breeders and ask to be considered if they become interested in leasing a particular Beardie.

IMPORTING

Many of the Beardies in the United States at this time are either imported or are the offspring of imported dogs. The breed is relatively new to this country, and many breeders initially travelled to England in search of top-quality Beardies from the country of the breed's origin. Recently, some dogs have been imported from other countries as well as from England.

Importing, however, is expensive, risky, and not advisable for the novice breeder. A good puppy can be purchased in England for around $1,000, but the air fare, the duty, the crate, and the health certificate can greatly increase this amount. If you wish to import a dog, the best way is to make a trip to England and pick the dog after a tour of the major kennels. If you cannot do this, you may find an international judge who will select a good puppy for you.

Brave individuals may want to try writing to breeders in Great Britain and selecting their puppy by correspondence. Select a breeder who is well known or who has been recommended by another importer. A few English breeders want to send some of their best dogs out of the country, while others are concerned about not knowing what kind of home or promotion the dog will receive and are therefore reluctant to export their best.

The seller usually can arrange for transfer of papers and shipping. The airlines require that dogs be shipped in extremely large, heavy, usually wooden crates--hence the high freight rates. Upon entrance to the United States at either Los Angeles, Chicago, or New York City, the dog will be delayed for several hours for a health check. He then must clear customs at your nearest international airport.

Once the dog is here, he cannot be returned, so don't expect him to be shipped on approval. (Dogs going into England are kept in quarantine for six months.) Any guarantee for replacement will be strictly according to the charity of the breeder/seller. Because it is very difficult to purchase an adult, you will probably be importing a young puppy and therefore taking a greater risk in obtaining the quality you want.

The exporter must supply you with a three-generation export pedigree and British registration form for your dog. You must write to the American Kennel Club for an imported dog registration form. The AKC will instruct you how to apply for registration in this country.

5 The Comforts of Home

The first day at home with a new puppy is always enchanting. He will want to explore every corner, every door, every other animal, and, of course, every member of the family. His reactions may range from hilarious clowning to fright to a well-pulled-off bluff. You will hardly be able to take your eyes or hands off the lovely new creature. You will want to play with him, handle him, cuddle him, get acquainted, and, at the same time, reassure him.

But puppies, like babies, need time for sleep, and they do best if their mealtimes are quiet and undisturbed. You may want to keep your new Beardie closer to the family for the first few weeks while he's getting acquainted, but remember to allow him privacy and rest. His sleeping box, prepared before you bring him home, should be in a warm, draft-free corner away from the mainstream of family activities. A few rawhide chips or rawhide "bones," a Nylabone, a rubber ball, and a braid made of old nylon stockings will help entertain him and keep his teeth occupied on something other than dad's new slippers. A rug, old towel, or blanket provides comfortable bedding. If the box is large, you can prepare a bed at one end and spread papers for his toilet at the other end.

For the first few days in his new home, the best procedure is to let your Beardie become acquainted at his own pace. Don't push him to accept new sights, sounds, and experiences. He'll discover them in his own time and be much more confident than if he is rushed. As your puppy begins to feel at home, you can introduce him to all of the various aspects of his new life—car rides, hikes, other children, livestock, etc. Some Beardies will be hesitant and will need encouragement from you, while others will bounce right into anything and will need to be taught to heed your cautions.

Wybnellas River Pilot, "Baron," owned by Mr. and Mrs. F. Jaques.

The first month in a new home, especially for a two- to three-month-old puppy, is a very impressionable period in which the dog-owner bond is being formed. Take advantage of this period to form a relationship of mutual trust and respect with your Beardie.

EARLY TRAINING

Begin almost immediately to teach your Beardie what is expected of him. Even very young puppies are fully capable of learning, but their attention span is short. It is important to keep each lesson brief and to give lots of praise. A play period at the end is an excellent reward. If you are fortunate enough to have a Puppy Kindergarten class in your area, by all means enroll in it.

Discourage unruly behavior in the house by keeping your Beardie on a leash or confined to a small area at first. Discourage chewing on the wrong things, but because all puppies investigate their environment partly by chewing, provide him with rawhide or hard rubber toys. Praise him when he chews them. Never give him objects that he can easily tear into small pieces and swallow, except for rawhide.

Beardie puppies need to learn that you are the "boss." You will be off to a good start with your new relationship if you establish dominance, *without being harsh.* One way to establish dominance is to hold your puppy on his back while you talk sweetly to him. He probably will struggle, but keep him there until he lies still, then release him with lots of praise.

A very important lesson is the meaning of the word "NO," and some physical correction may be needed until this is learned. Tone of voice usually is sufficient correction. If not, you may discipline the puppy with a quick jerk on the collar, by picking him up by the scruff of the neck and shaking him, or by pushing his head to the ground and holding it there for a minute. Another good corrective measure is a swat with a rolled-up newspaper, but only if it is handy. *Corrections must be given within three seconds or not at all.* Always accompany the punishment with the command "No." Do *not* swat him with your hand.

Praise is the most important part of training. Always praise your Beardie lavishly when he performs as expected and as soon as he stops the behavior that you are correcting. If your Beardie is not responding well to your attempts at training, it may be that you are not giving him enough praise.

Ch. Bedlam's Nemesis enjoying her own bed. Courtesy Alice Bixler.

Come

You will probably also want to include the word "Come" in your puppy's early training. Call him to you often while he is with you in the house, rewarding him with praise and a goodie when he comes. If there are two people in the household, you can make a game by calling him back and forth between you. Don't be surprised, however, if your Beardie catches on so quickly that he runs back and forth without being called!

Housebreaking

Housebreaking can begin almost immediately, but don't expect your puppy to be perfectly dependable until he's at least three months old. In the beginning, it's up to you to anticipate when he has to relieve himself so that you can prevent accidents from happening.

The easiest method of housebreaking is to confine your puppy to a small area—a box, crate, or pen—at night. First thing in the morning, take him immediately to the area where you want him to relieve himself, and wait until

he does so. (It is best to avoid the intermediate step of paper breaking and take the puppy outside from the beginning.) Praise him immediately, then take him to the house for a romp. During the day when the puppy is inside, take him out to the same area whenever he is restless, when he wakes from a nap, shortly after a meal, or about every hour. The more vigilant you are in preventing accidents, the quicker he will learn. You will be surprised at how short a time it takes for him to become housebroken.

HOUSING

Beardies need space for exercise and play in order to keep their energy level manageable. If you must keep a Bearded Collie confined, allow time in your schedule for walks and romps in the open for at least an hour each day. If they are provided with this minimum requirement, Beardies adjust remarkably well to nearly any home

Although most Beardies are house dogs, some owners prepare a space in the yard or garage for their adult Beardies. A draft-proof doghouse or a raised, enclosed box in the corner of a garage or porch will do nicely for one or two dogs. Just remember that they still need their daily human companionship.

Crates

A Bearded Collie is much too active to be routinely confined to a crate. However, crate training can be a definite asset to any dog. There may come a time when your Beardie must be left at the veterinarian's office, stay with a friend, or be shipped to another location. The crate-trained dog will take this in stride.

Select a crate large enough for your Beardie to stand comfortably without ducking and to lie stretched out without being cramped. Wire crates are excellent for kenneling a dog in the house, but wooden or fiberglass crates are preferable for shipping. A shipping crate that is too large may cause the dog to be tossed about and possibly injured.

Crate training is easy. Simply put your Beardie in the crate for a short period at feeding time. Leave him there until he cleans up the food, then release him. This leads to pleasant associations and minimizes bad habits like scratching and whining. Gradually increase the confinement time to several hours or overnight. Give your Beardie a chew toy to alleviate boredom, but don't baby him. If he cries or claws at the crate, correct him immediately by scolding or by slapping the crate with a rolled-up newspaper. Your Beardie's ego is much tougher than he would like you to believe at times. In fact, a Beardie that continually gets his way will never really be well adjusted.

How much should you crate a Beardie? Opinions are varied. English breeders dislike crates and believe that much harm is done by using them. While this may be true in isolated incidents, there is a definite need for the use of crates in the United States. They are a necessity at unbenched dog shows; they provide safety while traveling in a car; and they furnish a clean, readily available in-house kennel where a Beardie can eat and sleep or be confined while you are entertaining, when you are out of the house, or when you just don't want a dog underfoot. The maximum time for confining any dog to a crate is seven or eight hours. Obviously, the longer the period of confinement, the more conscientious you must be to provide exercise. If you have only one dog, do not assume that he will exercise himself, even in a large yard. Teach him to retrieve a ball or a Frisbee, or take him for long walks.

Kennels

If you intend to keep several Bearded Collies for breeding or show, you will undoubtedly want a kennel. There are as many kennel variations as there are breeders. Styles range from made-over poultry or livestock sheds to elaborately constructed custom buildings that architecturally harmonize with the home. Some are unheated, while others boast heating, air conditioning, and even septic systems.

Regardless of style or complexity, certain basics such as dryness, good ventilation, and sanitation must be met. You will also have to consider the zoning regulations imposed by your city, county, or state health department. Always check local regulations before you begin to build.

Either wood or cement-block building materials are acceptable. Wood is drier, but concrete is easier to disinfect and clean. With either material, place a layer of heavy plastic sheeting beneath the floor to keep out moisture.

The building should be well ventilated yet as draft free as possible. Louvered ventilator windows or fans near the roof at each end of the kennel will provide ventilation; in addition, you may want several screened windows above the dog boxes for air and light. Louvered mobile-home windows are excellent if you can obtain them. Another possibility, borrowed from poultry sheds, is to have windows at one end and a big exhaust fan at the other end.

The partitions between "stalls" should be sturdy, smooth, and about six feet high. A good size for stalls is four feet square, with a larger pen for a bitch and her puppies. Each stall

Fences should be six feet high if you plan to keep your Beardie confined. Ch. Meadows' New Kid on the Block doing what he does best. Courtesy Mary Billman.

should have an opening large enough to accommodate a grown Beardie. A swinging door or rubber flap will prevent drafts, and a guillotine-style door on the inside will keep the opening firmly closed when desirable. Commercial doors are available, or you can build your own by making a sliding wooden door and hanging a rubber automobile flap over the opening.

Runs should be at least 4 x 12 feet (4 x 24 feet would be better) with six-foot-high chain-link fencing. Concrete flooring, definitely the easiest to clean, is costly to install and will wear off the hair on your Beardie's feet and legs. Three-quarter-inch or the smaller "pea" gravel is preferred by many breeders

In either case, dig the area for the runs to a depth of at least sixteen inches. Lay a four- to six-inch layer of rock or very coarse gravel, and sprinkle it with Boraxo to help kill odors and worm larvae. Then lay the top surface with either fine gravel or concrete. The top half of the surface gravel will need replacing every couple of years for good sanitation.

Hard dirt runs or grass areas are difficult to keep clean, and because they encourage infestations of parasites, they are not recommended. You can get by with dirt or grass in a large exercise yard, but be aware that your grooming time will increase substantially if your Beardie is kept on these surfaces.

Sanitation

Cleanliness is essential in a kennel or any dog facility, and the more dogs you keep, the more important and time consuming this becomes.

Food and water dishes should be washed often. Hard-rubber or stainless-steel dishes resist damage and can be disinfected easily. Heavy ceramic bowls are also easy to clean and are nearly impossible to tip over, but be sure that they are made in the United States so that they do not contain lead. Soapy water with a little Clorox added is an old standby for any kennel owner. In addition to cleaning the dishes, use this solution to wash down the

Clean water, gravel, and chain-link fence provide safe kenneling for this Beardie puppy.
Ch. Willowmead Pollyanna.

building and runs several times a year. Commercial disinfectants are also available. Frequent spraying of runs with Clorox and water will help to control odors.

Pick up feces at least once daily. If flies, mosquitoes, or hookworms are a problem, remove the dogs and spray the premises with Malathion, following the instructions carefully. You must keep the dogs out of the area for twelve to twenty-four hours after spraying. Rock salt will aid in killing roundworm larvae. Sodium borate (commonly sold as Boraxo) applied at the rate of ten pounds per hundred square feet may be used to control hookworm larvae. Both substances can be harmful to the dog's feet and should be well raked into the gravel or applied to concrete

and left on an empty run for a day and then washed off with water.

Disease control in the kennel is facilitated by placing a one-foot-deep concrete barrier at the base of the fencing between each run. If the runs are gravel, at least six inches of the barrier should be beneath the surface. A six- or eight-foot solid board fence around the periphery of the kennel is used by many commercial kennels to block airborne germs and noise. If you plan to raise, breed, or ship a number of dogs, a quarantine or isolation run removed from the rest of the kennel is essential. This run may be smaller than the others and should definitely have a concrete floor as well as an enclosed top for the safety of visiting Beardies.

KEEPING YOUR BEARDIE SAFE

In addition to the fact that you probably paid a lot of money for your Beardie, he is a living, breathing, cherished part of your family, and you want to do everything you can to protect him. Yet many purebred dogs die needlessly each year because their owners did not think about safety.

It seems like mere common sense to check your yard, kennel, or other facilities for holes or broken wires, cracks near a gate, insecure latches, and other precarious situations before you bring your dog home. Many new dog owners are not aware that a Beardie (or any dog) in a strange place can become a very adept escape artist. And because Beardies are quite capable jumpers, you will want to decide if your fences

Wybnellas River Pilot at home in Reading, England. Courtesy F. Jagnes.

are high enough. Any height less than six feet is questionable until your Beardie learns that this is his new home, after which he will probably stay inside fences over which he could easily leap.

While you are checking the premises, look also for chewable items such as accessible electrical cords, exposed fiberglass insulation, or other harmful or poisonous substances. Even adult dogs are likely to chew or swallow foreign objects; it is up to you to keep harmful items out of reach. In general, anything that might harm a child should also be kept away from your Beardie. Puppies are apt to tip things over, cut themselves on glass or tin, or step on sharp objects.

The Beardie's inborn herding tendencies can get him into a lot of trouble around livestock, so keep your dog away from stock unless he is supervised closely or is fully trained to work.

Although it seems unnecessary to warn you not to leave your Beardie locked in a closed car in summer, hundreds of dogs die annually of heat stroke from this very cause. When outside temperatures approach 80 degrees, the inside of your automobile will register more than 100 degrees.

Poisonous Substances

Many common items are poisonous to dogs if ingested. Among these are chlorine bleach, antifreeze, cleaning fluid, gasoline, fungicides, insecticides, herbicides, rat poisons, tar, suntan lotion, wax, paint and paint removers, hair-setting lotions, hair-coloring lotions, matches, mothballs, shoe polish, children's crayons, some household detergents, disinfectants, aspirin, and other drugs.

It is best to keep all house plants away from your Beardie. Many of them are poisonous to dogs, including dieffenbachia, philodendron, poinsettia, and mistletoe. Gardeners should also be concerned that many bulbs, vines such as wisteria, bittersweet, and sweet peas, and bushes such as euonymus, rhododendron, laurel, and yew can be harmful to your dog. Castor beans, especially the seed, are extremely poisonous.

Tattooing

Dognapping has become so common that any dog in any community is a potential victim. Tattooing is inexpensive and painless and takes only a few minutes. It can be done by a veterinarian or at one of the many tattoo clinics held in conjunction with dog shows and matches. Microchips are also becoming a popular method of identification. The chip is implanted under the dog's skin by a veterinarian.

Your social-security number (or another number such as your dog's AKC registration number) is tattooed permanently on the inside of your Beardie's right thigh. Always keep this area clipped so that the tattoo is readily visible. (Tattooing on the lip or ear is not recommended.) Tattooing or microchips are the only acceptable, positive legal identification recognized by law-enforcement authorities.

This number, along with your name, address, and telephone number, may be registered with the National Dog Registry (NDR), a nationwide organization that aids in the identification of lost, stolen, or stray dogs. Any dogs that you own are tattooed with the same number, and a notice is sent to the NDR. The listing lasts for a lifetime. (If you use the AKC number, each dog must have a separate number and a separate NDR listing and fee.) If your dog is lost, there is a very good chance that he will be returned to you because state and local police, humane societies, and more than 1,500 research labs, medical schools, and other organizations that work with dogs have been asked to verify through the NDR any dog that is delivered to them bearing a tattoo

The NDR also provides a name tag that your dog should wear any time he travels. The tag warns, "Tattooed dog registered with NDR." Similar warning signs are available for your car, crates, and kennel. For information and registration forms contact the National Dog Registry.

The AKC now requires positive identification of each dog if you own more than one of the same breed and sex. This can be done by adding a separate code to your social-security number,

such as your initial plus a number. The first dog would show P-1, the next P-2, etc. Your number plus the code should be written on each dog's AKC registration certificate in your file.

FINDING A LOST BEARDIE

If your Beardie wanders or becomes lost, there are a number of steps you can take to help locate him. Number one—don't panic! A high percentage of lost dogs are eventually returned to their owners.

If your dog becomes frightened and simply runs away, try to 'keep him in sight *without* making him feel that he is being pursued. As soon as he calms down, he probably will respond to your call. If he doesn't, try running away from him and he often will follow. Or try sitting down on the ground with your back to him and calling him. If several people are available to help, you can often corner your fleeing dog against a fence or building.

If your Beardie disappears and you can't sight him, act quickly. First call the local humane society, the dog-control officer, and your local radio station, giving a complete description of your dog and the place where you last saw him. Leave your name and phone number, along with the name and number of a friend who can be reached in case you are out. If the dog is newly purchased, contact the old owner in case your Beardie tries to return to his former home. Run an ad in the paper, offering a reward for information leading to your dog's return.

In case your dog is injured, call any veterinarians in your general region, then begin a house-to-house inquiry covering the entire area where your dog was last seen. Ask these residents to call you if your dog is sighted, and to please not chase him themselves. This keeps your dog from becoming more frightened, and he probably will seek water and shelter instead of continuing his flight.

Another possibility is to have fliers printed with your dog's description and a picture if available. These can be posted around the area and handed out to school children or other groups. You also might contact mailmen or meter readers who work in the area. Go to the local humane society or pound daily, rather than just calling, and show a picture of your Beardie. Be patient; many dogs are found after one, two, or even more weeks away from home.

THE JET-SET BEARDIE

About as many dogs as people travel these days. If your Beardie is accustomed to going along on family outings, to visiting relatives, and to taking jaunts down to the ice-cream parlor from the time he is a puppy, he will eagerly anticipate an automobile ride. On the other hand, if the only place you ever take him is to the vet's for a vaccination or to a few shows now and then,

he'll probably be nervous and may even get carsick. It is far better to start him out slowly at a young age with a few rides to the store or around the block. If he still has a tendency to get carsick, a Drammamine™ tablet given about thirty minutes before departure may help.

If you are going on a long trip with your Beardie, or if he will be flying, make sure that he is wearing a collar with an ID tag, rabies tag, and tattoo notice. Don't feed him for twelve hours before traveling, and withhold water two hours before departure. (If he is flying, follow the airline rules about food and water.) Feed and water him only lightly during the trip. It is always a good idea to take plenty of his regular food and drinking water, because unfamiliar food and/or water easily cause digestive upsets. It helps to have a bag containing plenty of newspapers, paper towels, a

"Are we there yet?" Life in a motor home. Courtesy M. Billman.

washcloth, Drammamine, Kaopectate, and a laxative or suppository. This will prepare you for almost anything.

If you will be crossing state lines, take a health certificate and rabies vaccination tag or papers. You may never have to show them, but it may save you time and trouble. If you are going into Canadaor Mexico, they are required.

Shipping by Air

Thousands of dogs fly throughout the United States each year with relative ease and safety. New regulations make air-freight shipments even safer than before. Anyone involved in breeding or showing Beardies extensively will one day ship a dog by air.

Proper preparation helps to ensure your Beardie a safe trip. The basics are simple:

1. Make reservations with the appropriate air-freight office several days in advance. *Choose a nonstop, direct flight* if possible. If a transfer is necessary, allow plenty of time for it. Ask the freight agent about regulations regarding type of crate and air temperatures at point of takeoff and destination. If it is too hot or too cold, your dog may have to wait until a more moderate day.
2. Prepare the crate. *Be sure that the size is comfortable but not too large.* Spread a layer of newspapers on the floor, topped by a second layer of shredded paper. Apply a label that notes "Live Dog. Do Not Place Near Dry Ice. Do Not Open Crate Except in Emergency." Prepare a shipping label prominently displaying the name, address, phone number, city, and airport to which the dog is being shipped, as well as your name, address, and phone number.
3. *Obtain a health certificate.* Interstate-commerce regulations require that all dogs crossing state lines be checked by a veterinarian within ten days or so (depending on the state) and certified to be in good health. A current rabies vaccination is required. To

avoid overstressing your Beardie, take him in for the examination a day or two before shipment.

The freight office will request that you have your dog at the airport about two hours before takeoff to allow adequate time for safe and correct loading. Always place a collar (not a choke collar) with ID tag on your Beardie before shipment, and put only one dog in each crate. Exercise your dog just before leaving him at the airport.

At the airport, check the air bill carefully to make sure that all information and phone numbers are correct. You might watch the agent place the air bill on the crate to make certain that the correct air bill goes with the dog. Unless you declare a value and insure your dog, the airline will pay only a minimum figure in case of loss, so be sure to buy insurance.

Your dog will be placed in the crate and weighed. If you wish, double-check the latch, then leave the rest to the airline. You should remain available, either at the airport or near your phone at home, until takeoff in case some emergency would prevent shipment. As a final precaution, always request that the receiving person phone to let you know that your dog has arrived safely at his destination.

Flying With Your Beardie

Most of the same requirements will apply. You must make a reservation for your dog, have a health certificate and rabies vaccination, and a proper-size crate. You will take your dog to the passenger check-in rather than to the freight office. You will need to pay an excess baggage charge. If you are flying with a very small puppy, it may be possible to take him into the cabin with you, but ask the airline about this.

If possible, watch to see that your dog is loaded into the plane before you take your seat. If you can't do that, ask the flight attendant to check with the pilot to see if your dog is on the plane. This is your right, so be firm about it.

6 *The Beardie Beautiful*

It is important for breeders to impress upon prospective Beardie owners that coat care is a major factor to consider. As an owner you must be willing to spend the time and effort for proper grooming or be prepared to take your dog to a professional groomer regularly. A third option is to keep your dog in a kennel or utility clip. Thorough grooming is important, not only for appearance, but for the health and comfort of your Beardie.

The Bearded Collie is a "natural" breed, which means that no obvious trimming or sculpturing of the coat is allowed. Just what is consistent with good grooming can be quite a borderline decision. Obvious sculpturing, such as is done on the neck, tail, and belly line of setters, on the feet of Cocker Spaniels, and on the knitting-needle parts of Shih Tzus, certainly goes way beyond grooming and is to be abhorred, because it completely destroys the natural look. On the other hand, hair sometimes grows in such a way that it makes a dog look bad when he really isn't, and it could be argued that a bit of judicious trimming would be merely good grooming. A clean, healthy, well-brushed dog can grace the show ring or present his best appearance as a pet.

TOOLS AND EQUIPMENT

Requirements for grooming tools are minimal. The most important item is a good-quality bristle brush. Do not economize on this tool. If possible, get a Mason-Pearson bristle or bristle-and-nylon brush. These come in a variety of sizes and, though high in price, are a good investment because they last for years, will keep

Commonly used grooming tools.

maintain and produces the typical *shaggy* outline. The formula for cultivating a beautiful coat is simply to keep it clean, healthy, and brushed. Assuming the coat has adequate genetic potential, it will develop length and shine in direct proportion to how much effort you exert. An adult pet needs to be brushed thoroughly only once a week. Depending on the dog, his environment, and the efficiency of your technique, this will take from fifteen minutes to an hour

Puppies tend to develop coat in one of two distinct manners. The first type of coat is rather sparse, wiry, and not overly attractive in the puppy stages. This type, however, is usually worth waiting out, because the adult coat will come in very harsh, easy to groom, and with a tendency to fall perfectly into place and stay there. Many of the more glamorous puppies

An ungroomed Beardie — the original "shaggy dog." Courtesy Sterling.

the coat in beautiful condition, and will cut your grooming time. If you can't justify the cost, get the best brush that you can afford. In addition, get a pin brush with stainless-steel bristles, a slicker brush, a wide-toothed comb, and a medium-toothed comb. The slicker brush is good for removing loose undercoat during a shed, the pin brush works well for routine brushing of pets, and the bristle brush is for finishing. Only use the bristle brush for grooming a show dog.

Add to your list three general-care items—a nail clipper, a tooth scaler, and a long forceps for plucking hair from the ear canal. For bathing your Beardie, get a good brand of dog shampoo, a bottle of liquid bluing, perhaps some coat conditioner if you live in a dry climate, a bottle of shampoo formulated for use on white hair, and a few old towels. If you become an expert, you may want to add a few extras of your own, but remember that a natural look is an essential element of Beardie type. There are plenty of breeds available for the frustrated hairdresser; the Beardie is *not* one of them.

EVALUATING THE COAT

The correct coat for the Bearded Collie is moderate in length, harsh in texture, and easy to

actually have soft, wooly coats verging on Old English Sheepdog type. This is alright in a *puppy*, but the coat should change in character until there is less undercoat and a long, harsh, straight outer coat by the time the dog is three years old.

Surprisingly, the profuse puppy coats are more difficult to keep up than the adult coats, because they tangle more easily and require more frequent brushing. Likewise, an incorrect adult coat, tending toward that of either the Old English Sheepdog or the Afghan Hound, will be much more difficult to groom and will need constant attention to look neat. The Old English coat may be curly and carry too much undercoat for a Beardie. The Afghan-type coat is usually dead straight but silky and limp to the touch. Either coat, though sometimes glamorous, is absolutely incorrect for a Beardie.

The Beardie coat has one unusual feature. Like human hair, it will continue to grow unless it is cut or broken off.

TABLE MANNERS

You may groom on a standard grooming table, on a portable top placed on a crate, on a card table with nonslip footing added, or even on the floor (this is suitable only for routine brushing of a well-trained animal). Table training definitely takes the work out of grooming and has other applications as well. It can provide a simple, impressive means of showing off your dog. On the table, he looks animated and unrestrained, yet he is confined to keep him from becoming pushy or overbearing to people.

Start putting your puppy on the grooming table when he is young, and get him accustomed to lying down while being brushed. All puppies and new adult Beardies try to jump off, but attempt to prevent this until your dog reliably understands what is expected. If he does escape, grab him, add a sharp verbal "No," and lift him backward onto the table. Then give him a Stay or Wait command and plenty of praise. Your dog must be praised for obeying even if you are forcing him to obey; otherwise, he has no incentive to do as you ask. If you know that your dog is thinking about jumping off, correct him before he actually leaps. Be sure to praise him. He should *never* jump off of a grooming table (or out of a car) until given the command to do so. Most dogs love their table and never resent this training once they understand what is wanted.

If you want the convenience of having your dog jump onto the table, this is how to teach

Right: Lift the dog and gently lay him on his side.

Far Right: Hold the feet until the dog stops struggling and will lie quietly on his side.

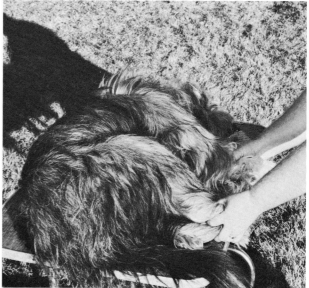

him. Do this exercise only with an adult dog that is already trained to lie on the table. Always lift puppies and pregnant bitches both on and off the table.

With your dog on lead, use the command "Up" and pat the table. He may put his front feet up the first time. If he does this, praise him lavishly and lift his hindquarters onto the table. If your dog isn't inclined to listen, talk in a happy, excited voice, repeating "Up" as you drag him onto the table by the collar. After you have pulled him up once, try again, leaving the lead slack and giving him a chance to do it himself. He'll probably be hesitant, so praise is most important. If he turns away, jerk him back. After a few times, he'll jump eagerly onto the table

The command "Up" is useful to get Beardies onto other objects besides tables, such as the platform used at shows for photographing group wins. It never hurts to think positively. You never know when you'll need it.

"Down Boy, Down"

Grooming is decidedly easier if your Beardie will lie on his side and allow you to brush him. In fact, it is the *only* way to thoroughly groom the underside of a Beardie single-handedly. With the dog on his side, you can probably groom him completely in the time it takes to whisk over the top while he is standing.

To teach him, stand him on the table and face his side. Encircle him with your arms approximately at hock level and clasp your hands together. In one motion, lean your body into his and pull his feet toward you. Try to lay him gently onto his side rather than throwing him like a rodeo calf. He will probably struggle and may become panicky for a few moments. Talk to him soothingly and keep him pinned with your body until he relaxes. Once he feels limp, rest a hand on his neck to steady him, then straighten up. Brush him lightly for a few minutes, then allow him to stand. Again, use a specific command to allow your dog to stand up. Repeat it a few times, and he will soon learn to

get up and lie down on command, or at least remain passive as you place him in position.

If your dog tries to get up, hold his head flat on the table and repeat the Stay command. He will not be able to get up unless he maneuvers his legs on the bottom side underneath himself, and he is unlikely to manage this unless he raises his head. Grasp his foreleg on the underside in one hand and his corresponding hind leg in your other hand. Pull until his legs are straight toward you and your dog is again flat on his side. You can then begin brushing. You may either stand (this is preferable at first because you may have to steady your dog) or pull up a chair and sit down while grooming. To help keep your dog relaxed, keep up a steady stream of chatter, relieving his boredom and making it a game.

THE GROOMING PROCESS

The single technique that must be learned for grooming Beardies is called line-brushing. This is a method of separating the coat into sections and brushing against the lay of the hair until the entire dog has been brushed. The hair must be brushed clear to the roots to separate the undercoat and remove dead hair. A dog that is line-brushed completely once a week should sport a healthy, well-groomed coat. (A damaged coat may need more frequent attention, preferably daily brushing with the addition of some coat oil in the spray during the conditioning period.)

With your dog lying on his side, spray the entire coat lightly with water. You will also spray every four or five inches along the line of brushing as you progress along the body. Start on your dog's muzzle and brush a few hairs at a time forward over his nose. Advance toward his neck, brushing a few more hairs with each stroke. It helps to hold the unbrushed hair with your free hand and slide this hand ahead of the brush as you progress.

If you come upon a mat or piece of tangled hair, separate it with your fingers and brush it apart. If necessary, insert the end tooth of your

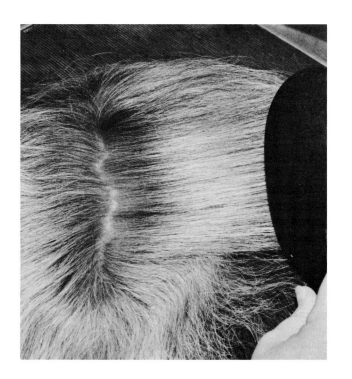

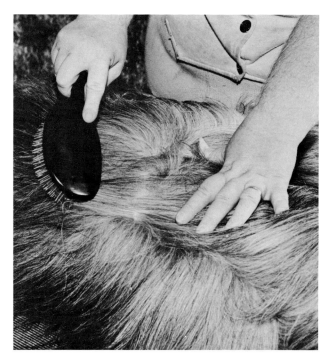

Top left: Separate the coat into sections.

Top right: Linebrushing.

Middle left: Pluck hair growing over the inside corner of the eye.

Middle right: Whisk the coat back into place.

Bottom: Comb the whiskers down and the beard forward.

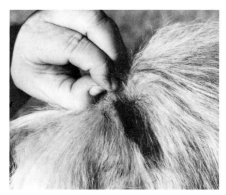

comb and split the tangle, then loosen it with your fingers and comb it out. If you take your time, even the worst mats will come out without your cutting or tearing a hole in the coat. Weekly brushing will prevent formation of any but the most insignificant tangles, and if your Beardie has correct coat texture, he will rarely mat.

Half of the grooming should take place between the nose and the withers. Areas of very dense hair growth under the ears and on the sides of the neck are often overlooked. Lift the ear up so that the underside is exposed. Line-brush under the line of attachment of the ear from muzzle to neck. Don't worry if you can't reach the whole beard. You are to groom only half of the dog from this side, and you will need to touch up areas later.

Separate and brush the hair on the inside of the ear, and check to see if any hair is growing inside the ear canal. If you find hair, pluck it out carefully following the technique described at the end of this chapter. Next, place the ear back in its normal position and brush the outside fringes. Start at the middle of the skull (remember, you're grooming half of the dog) and line-brush to blend with the completed area. Progress back along the neck. If you have a dog with profuse undercoat, you may want to rebrush this area at right angles to the original brush lines. You will see the difference in the finished look and in the lack of mats behind the ears. Before going any farther, brush the hair away from your dog's eyes and nose. He will lie much more patiently if he can watch what's happening. If you have trouble getting through the coat on a puppy, remember that he will become easier to groom as the coat matures.

Next, separate the coat vertically from the middle of the back downward along the edge of the brushed area. Spray one squirt of water along this line and continue brushing. Always move toward the rear of the dog. The coat is still being brushed toward the head, with the brush moving up and down the part and including slightly more hair in each stroke. The body area will be easy to maintain once it has been initially groomed. Repeat the pattern from top to bottom along the dog's side until you reach the loin area.

Now go back and do the front leg. Lift the leg and brush the chest hair and the area around the elbow. Spiral down and around the leg, spraying and line-brushing as you go. Brush the hair on the leg straight up toward the body. Separate this hair thoroughly, paying special attention to the elbow and toes. Brush clear to the tips of the toes, using the comb to separate the undercoat whenever necessary. Examine the toenails to determine if they need clipping. (*See* the end of this chapter for instructions.) Next, continue your line-brushing across the hip and down the hind leg. Be sure to separate all of the hair in the skirts (the long hair behind the thigh). When this is completed, turn your dog over and repeat the procedure for the other side. It is easier if you have your dog's legs toward you as you groom.

When this is finished, have your dog stand and line-brush down the center of his back. The mature coat should fall into a natural part. You may wish to brush the hair down each side to encourage this but do *not* part the back with a comb or other tool. Let your dog shake, then lightly whisk all hair back down into its natural lay.

Next, go to the front of your dog and start line-brushing, working downward on his chest from his throat. Brush the hair upward, but progress down the chest with the brush. When you are finished, whisk this hair back down also. Then work from the throat to the chin and separate every hair in the beard. You will probably have to comb the beard and face as a finishing touch. The sides of the muzzle are combed down, the top of the skull is combed straight back from the eyes, and the beard is combed forward. The only part left is the tail, which is simply line-brushed around and around from base to tip, with the feather brushed back into its natural plume. You may need someone to hold the dog if he objects to having his tail brushed. When you're finished, he will probably shake. The hair can then be whisked back into position.

Bathing

A Beardie should be bathed only when necessary and at least five days prior to a show so that the texture can return to the coat. The white parts will have to be rebathed the day before the show.

The most important step in bathing your Beardie is to give him a *thorough* line-brushing from head to toe, regardless of how dirty he is. If you bathe your dog unbrushed, the undercoat will pack tightly against his body and create a solid mat. Brushing him out afterwards will then be more difficult and will tear out considerably more undercoat. The anal glands can be emptied immediately before a bath so that any residue can be washed off. (Refer to the end of the chapter for details.)

Set out your towels, shampoos, bluing, and a container for mixing. A hand-held spray attachment is extremely helpful and can be purchased to fit almost any shower head. Stand your dog in the tub and wet him thoroughly. Start at the neck and work backward, leaving the head for last.

Work some shampoo into the hair around the neck, then lather along the back, down the legs, and finally around the skirts and tail. Let the soap set for two or three minutes, then rinse. Work through the coat with your fingers as you rinse to be sure that the soap is washing out completely. Wet the hair on the skull, ears, and muzzle, being careful to avoid the eyes and ear canal. Rub a small amount of shampoo between your palms and wipe it over the skull and ears. The beard and muzzle should then be thoroughly washed with a shampoo formulated for white hair. After the head is carefully rinsed, lather the feet, the tip of the tail, and the chest with the whitener shampoo. Rinse and repeat if necessary until these areas are clean.

If the coat is dry, a creme rinse or a diluted oil-base conditioner may be helpful. Do not apply creme rinse just before a show, because it softens the coat. As a final touch, rinse the white parts with a bluing solution. Use just enough bluing to color the water sky blue—roughly eight to ten drops to two quarts of water. The hair will dry a sparkling white.

Squeeze excess water from the coat and rub your dog's head with a dry towel. Blot water from the body coat and rub the legs briskly. Allow your dog to shake. When he is partially dry, line brush his coat throughly, and repeat when he is completely dry. The line-brushing will go very rapidly if you brushed your dog properly before bathing.

You can encourage the hair to part and fall to each side in a natural manner. While your Beardie is still wet after his bath, part the hair down the middle of his back, using a comb. When he is dry, brush the hair toward the tail, and then let him shake. The hair should fall to the sides without an exact part.

Chalking

Some exhibitors just brush and show their dogs. Others work a "chalk" powder into the slightly damp legs and whiskers for whitening and texture. Grooming chalk, cornstarch, calcium carbonate, or a mixture of these elements are used most frequently. After it dries, all chalk must be brushed out. No artificial substance should remain in the coat when the dog enters the show ring, and, in fact, is grounds for disqualification.

Grooming the Show Dog

Grooming the show Beardie takes more time and care. You must spray and brush your dog daily using only a bristle brush, because any other will tear the coat. The Beardie Standard states that the dog should be shown as naturally as is consistent with good grooming, but the coat must not be trimmed in any way. Unfortunately, trimming for the ring has become more and more common. The difference between "good grooming" and "trimming" is a fine line indeed, and to an extent, it is a personal decision. Good grooming, however, should leave a Beardie looking natural and *never* looking sculptured. If a handler is showing the dog, it is the responsibility of the owner to insist that the dog look natural

The hair on the feet can be so long that the dog is tripping over it. Often, the hair grows longer to one side so that the feet look crooked when they really are not. In these cases, the feet certainly are in need of proper grooming. To avoid a "trimmed" look, try the following. Stand your dog on the grooming table. Comb the hair outward around the leg and foot. Using forty-six-tooth thinning shears, hold them pointing downward, parallel to the leg. Cut in this position around the foot, trimming the hair back to about the same distance as the leg hair grows. Do not cut around the foot with the scissors parallel to the table.

Your Beardie may have an excess of undercoat in one or more places that can make him look unbalanced. A fine stripping knife can thin out some of the undercoat. Work from underneath so that the outer coat will not be affected. Use the stripping knife as if it were a comb, combing down against your thumb with a slight twist of your wrist. Take out just a little bit at a time and keep combing to judge your progress.

Brush out your dog completely, ready for the ring, before preparing the head. It's easier to do with your dog lying on the table.

Start with the hair on the backskull brushed back (Photo 1). Use a comb to create a triangle from one outside corner of the eye to the other (Photo 2). Comb the hair forward, hairspray the roots of the section, then backcomb close to the roots (Photo 3). If you have an exceptionally good head, this is all that you will need to do — just enough to keep the hair out of the eyes. If the head could use a little help, make several more sections parallel to the first, repeating the process. It may even be necessary to do a little backcombing on the sides just below and behind the eyes, depending on the individual head that you are grooming. Carefully smooth the hair back from the eyes with your hands (Photo 4) and *lightly* go over it with a brush. Put a little hairspray on your index finger and run this up the stop, then lightly go over it all with the hairspray. It should *not* feel stiff. Hold the head until the spray dries and *voilá*, a beautifully groomed head that stays that way (Photo 5). Do not go overboard and make

the head look overdone (Photo 6). Afterward, carefully remove the backcombing, spray with water to dilute the hairspray, and condition.

If You Are Not Showing Your Beardie

Trimming to make your dog easier to care for is perfectly alright. He will track in less mud or debris if his feet are trimmed closely. To keep hair out of his eyes, you can use a barrette or you can trim the hair over his eyes into slightly overhanging eyebrows. He can even be clipped all over, although he will lose some of "Beardie look." It is best if the hair is left about an inch long rather than being clipped to the skin. His face can be clipped into a terrrier style with whiskers and eyebrows, and the hair on his tail either left long or trimmed about two-thirds of its length with the end plume left. If you have a groomer doing the clipping, be sure to talk it over first and explain exactly what you want so that there are no unpleasant surprises

ROUTINE CARE

The following procedures should be performed at regular intervals. It is best to set up a schedule so that they are not neglected. A well-cared-for dog will live a longer, happier life and will have fewer problems over the years.

Ear Care

Any hair growing from the ear canal should be removed. If left, it can form an air blockage and contribute to ear infections. If you do not have a long forceps, pluck as much hair as you can reach with your fingers. This will help but will not remove hair that extends into the canal. This hair is not anchored, and plucking is not painful to your dog. If you have forceps, *carefully* reach as far as possible into the canal and clamp onto the hair. Do not reopen the forceps, but twist around and around until all of the hair

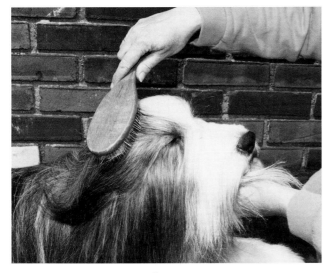

Photo 1

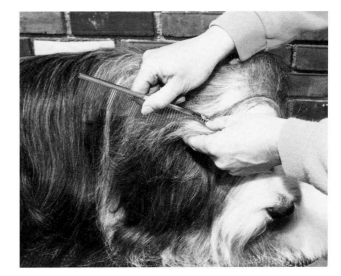

Photo 2

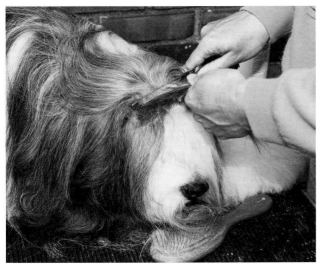

Photo 3

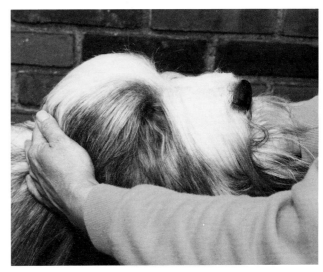

Photo 4

Photo 5

Photo 6

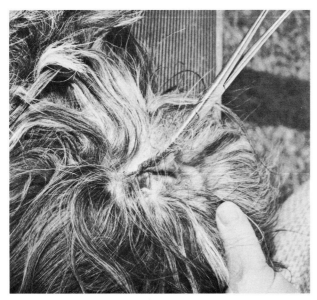

Pluck hair from the ear canal.

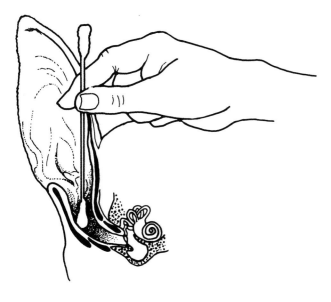

Figure 6-1
Carefully clean the visible portion of the ear canal with a cotton swab.

canal. If your dog scratches his ears continuously, shakes or tilts his head a great deal, or cries out when his ears are touched, he may have ear mites, an infection, or a foreign object imbedded in the ear. Have a vet check your dog if you suspect any of these problems.

Toenails

Toenails should be clipped at least every two weeks unless your dog is very active and wears down his nails on a hard surface. Long toenails cause the foot to spread or splay, making footing difficult. Long nails also force the weight of the body onto the heel of the pad instead of distributing it evenly, resulting in tender, broken-down feet and pasterns.

If your dog's dewclaws (fifth toe located on the inside of each front leg, almost at the pastern) have not been removed, be sure to clip them. They do not wear down like the nails on the feet do and can grow in a complete circle and back into the leg in time. Dewclaws are particularly dangerous on Beardies because the breed is active and prone to tearing the claws

Figure 6-2
Trim the nails almost to the quick.

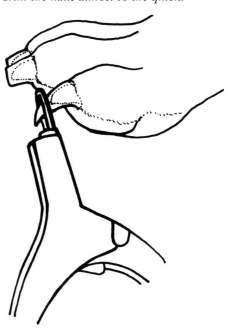

pulls loose. Repeat if necessary. If you are still uncertain about this procedure, have a vet or a good groomer show you how easy it actually is.

Occasionally, you will want to clean your Beardie's ears. Use rubbing alcohol on a cotton swab. Do not worry about alcohol getting into the canal—it will assist in wax removal and will evaporate harmlessly. Clean only the visible surfaces with your swab; never probe into the

off in the underbrush. Also, the coat on the legs hides the dewclaws from view so that they are easily forgotten and allowed to grow too long

Hold the foot as illustrated and cut the nail almost to, but not into, the blood line (the pink center of the nail). If you cannot see the quick, remove only the hooked portion of the nail and you will not cut too deeply. After the nail is trimmed, the blood line will recede somewhat as your dog brings his foot in contact with the ground; conversely, in a nail that has not been trimmed for some time, the quick will grow longer so that it reaches close to the tip of the nail. Because such a nail cannot be cut back as far as it should be with the first trimming, you will have to cut only a tiny bit, then repeat the process every few days until the nail has been trimmed back to the proper length. If you cut too deeply, the nail will bleed but the injury is not serious. A little styptic powder or Kwik Stop will control the bleeding. Your Beardie may remember and be a little touchy about his feet at the next grooming session, however. The properly trimmed nail should just clear the floor when the dog is standing on a hard surface

There are several kinds of nail clippers, and all of them work well. Most breeders prefer the type illustrated here. When your nail clippers become so dull that the nail is pinched or crushed instead of cut, it is time to buy a new pair. Always hold the clipper with the handle *below* the nail, tilting slightly backward. Cutting with the clipper to one side or on top tends to crush the nail rather than make a clean cut.

Foot Care

Because of the requirement for leaving hair between the toes, be sure to check thoroughly for grass seed and stickers, which can become imbedded in the foot. The hair actually protects against the majority of foreign bodies, but those that persevere are harder to detect and may be more easily overlooked than on a trimmed foot. If neglected, they can cause a serious infection.

"Cheat-grass" seed or foxtails are the worst offenders. In areas where these weeds predominate, it may be necessary to comb your Beardie's feet daily or, if he is not being shown, some trimming between the pads may be warranted.

Sore pads are fairly common in any active breed. They can be caused by excessive dryness or cracking, by a bruise, or from too much running on hard or uneven surfaces. Salt used to thaw ice in winter or kill worms in gravel runs may also cause sore feet. There are several commercial preparations such as Tuf-Foot or Pad-Kote that you may apply, or just try a little petroleum jelly or hand lotion to heal the cracks. Splinters or other foreign objects in the pad can usually be removed with a tweezer. Swab the area with rubbing alcohol, remove the splinter, then apply first-aid cream.

Teeth

Like humans, dogs need the tartar removed from their teeth in order to avoid gum disease. Puppies generally clean their teeth by chewing, but most adult dogs need assistance, especially as they grow older. Dogs that have had their teeth scaled regularly are less likely to lose their teeth with age. Rawhide chews, Nylabones, dry kibble, and other products made especially for this purpose are helpful, but if you check your Beardie's teeth at each of your weekly checkups, you will probably find some buildup of discoloring tartar

Your vet can remove this tartar for a significant fee that usually includes anesthesia, but if you are economy-minded, buy a tooth scaler and train your puppy to allow you to do the job yourself. If done regularly, cleaning takes only a few minutes. A good-quality, sharp scaler, obtainable from your dentist, your vet, or a dog-supply catalog, is essential

Begin with the upper incisors. Hold the lip away from the teeth with one hand and, with the other hand, use the scaler to scrape from just under the edge of the gum downward. Use short, firm strokes, cleaning only a small area of

Tartar must be scaled from teeth regularly.

Occasionally, these glands become clogged, accumulating a foul-smelling mass. Irritation of the glands results.

Clogging may be caused by injury to the region, by bacterial infection, or by migration of segments of tapeworm into the ducts of the glands. Obesity and lack of muscular tone may be contributing factors in old dogs. Chronically soft feces will also cause retention of the fluid. Closely confined dogs appear to have more difficulty than active dogs.

The most common early sign of anal irritation is when the dog licks or bites at the perineum. As the condition progresses, the dog may drag his anus across the floor or rub it against any rough surface. This action almost always indicates that the anal glands need to be emptied rather than that the dog has worms (as the old wives' tale would have us believe). If the glands

the tooth with each stroke. Be careful not to jab the tongue or lower jaw as you pull downward, but use enough pressure to chip the tartar loose.

After you have cleaned all of the upper teeth on both inside and outside surfaces, including the molars in the back of the mouth, repeat with the bottom teeth, scraping from the gum upward. Rinse the scaler in an oral antiseptic several times during the process. Complete the job by polishing the teeth with powdered pumice or toothpaste on a soft cloth. Several brands of toothpaste flavored to appeal to dogs are available from pet suppliers.

If your Beardie has bad breath even though his teeth are clean, try swabbing his teeth and gums with baking soda or Happy Breath. Strong, persistent breath odor may indicate that your dog has abscesses or that he has poor digestion or other health problems. Call this to the attention of your veterinarian at your Beardie's next checkup.

Anal Glands

These two small glands located below and on either side of the anus secrete a lubricant that enables the dog to expel his feces more easily.

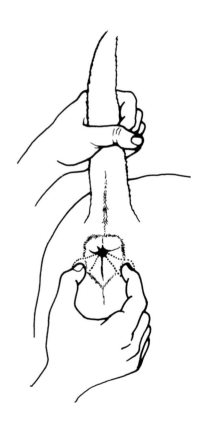

Figure 6-3 Press firmly to express the anal glands. Position of the glands is indicated by the dotted line.

become severely clogged, infection will set in and sacs may abscess. The only way to correct the abscess is to have the glands surgically removed.

Removing the accumulated fluid regularly will prevent impaction and will make your Beardie more confortable. Seize the tail with your left hand and encircle the anus from the bottom with your right hand. Press the anus firmly between your thumb and forefinger, expelling the vile-smelling mass. It may squirt some distance, so either do this outside or in an easily cleaned area, or cover the anus with a tissue or a piece of cotton. Repeating this procedure once a month is ample to keep the glands cleaned out, and, as stated earlier, the best time to check is just before a bath. Be sure to empty both glands.

Eye Care

Prolonged watering or irritation of the eyes is cause for concern, although it will probably occur for a few weeks as the puppy coat grows out and reaches a length where it gets into the eyes. You can help to avoid this by plucking the hair in the inner corner of the eyes. This problem corrects itself as the coat lengthens.

For mild irritation, a rinse made from one-fourth teaspoon salt in one-half cup water may be used, or you can buy a bottle of artificial tears for contact-lens wearers and use that as an eyewash. Severe irritation, mattering eyes, mild inflammation that does not clear up in a few days, or dilated pupils, haziness over the eye, or a foreign object in the eye signal a quick trip to your veterinarian. Don't put it off. And don't use old medication for a new eye problem. Drops or ointments for use in the eye are very specific to a particular condition and may cause serious injury if used to treat a different condition. Use medications only under the direction of your veterinarian. Avoid giving hepatitis vaccine to a dog with any eye irritation. It can create a severe reaction and possible blindness.

Beardie a la naturale!

Am Can. Ch. Classical Mystique, CD likes to sailboard. Courtesy Bridgette Nowak.

7 Shaping Up

THE HEALTHY BEARDIE

Optimum condition is essential in a show, working, or breeding Beardie, and it is important for the pet dog as well. Top condition is not achieved haphazardly but is the result of a skillfully planned and followed program. Conditioning is an ongoing project. The needs and condition of your Beardie will change from time to time during his life-span due to age, environment, stress, and other factors, so you will find it necessary to make adjustments in his diet and routine to compensate for these changes. Each Beardie is a little different. There are guidelines to help, but you will want to experiment a bit with your individual dog.

If you are to maintain your Beardie in glowing health and condition, you must first learn to recognize the signs of good health as well as the symptoms of illness or poor condition. Whether your dog lives in the house with you or in the kennel, be constantly alert to his condition and check him at least twice weekly. At first this will take conscious effort, but as you become familiar with your Beardie, the routine will become second nature.

Good health is dependent upon many factors—heredity, environment, diet, exercise, and grooming, to name a few. A healthy Beardie is bright and active with a happy, enthusiastic personality. His movements are effortless and smooth with no signs of stiffness or limping, and he does not tire easily. His coat appears glossy and unbroken, and beneath it you will find the skin smooth, pliable, and free from dandruff, scabs, red spots, or parasites.

61

A Bearded Collie in good condition carries just enough weight so that you can feel his ribs but cannot press a finger between them. Individual show Beardies may look better with just a bit more flesh, but they should never be fat. The muscles should be firm and supple, not soft and flabby. The flesh should fit the body firmly; loose, bouncing rolls of flesh are an indication of poor muscle tone

You can tell a great deal about your Beardie's health by observing the key areas—eyes, ears, and mouth. A Beardie's eyes may be the window to his soul, and they are also the first to clue you that he is not well. In a healthy Beardie, the eyes are clear, bright, expressive, and alert. The inside of the eyelids, as well as the third eyelid (the membrane at the inner corner between the upper and lower lids) are pink in color. (The third eyelid may have a dark pigment instead of a pink color.) Redness or swelling in these areas indicates a problem, and so do dull, cloudy eyes. The eyes should not water or contain mucus.

Lift your Beardie's ear leather and you will find the inside of the ear canal to be pale pink in color. It will be clearly visible if you have kept it free of hair (*see* Chapter 6). Bright pink or red ear membranes are abnormal. The ear should have only a small amount of brown wax. Large amounts of brown, orange, or foul-smelling wax are not normal.

The gums are also a vital key to good health. Become familiar with the normal color of your Beardie's gums and mouth. Normal gums are either pink or black, and they feel firm and fit tightly around the base of the teeth. Red, pale pink, yellowish, or white gums are abnormal. A red line along the gums, which appear to have shrunk away from the teeth, may indicate gum disease

During grooming, run your hands over your Beardie's body. You should find no lumps, swellings, or sores. Become familiar with your dog's respiration patterns both while at rest and after running. (Observe his usual sleeping, eating, bowel-movement, and urinating patterns.) Paying attention to these little details while he is well will enable you to notice quickly any

abnormal behavior or appearance. You will detect an illness before it becomes serious and will be able to make minor adjustments in your dog's environment or conditioning program that will keep him in top shape at all times.

FEEDING

Your Beardie's diet is the greatest factor in achieving optimum condition and health. Therefore, you will want to choose a high-quality, properly balanced commercial ration. The best commercial dog-food manufacturers have conducted feeding trials and laboratory tests and will be happy to provide you with information on the results. Avoid brands that cannot or will not provide this information. Quality food contains minimum levels of carbohydrates, fats, and protein as well as minerals and vitamins essential to good canine nutrition.

In the United States, an excellent indication of quality is a statement on the label that the diet has been approved by the Association of American Feed Control Officials (AAFCO) protocol. An analysis of the ingredients in a particular food is not adequate because an element may be present but not in a form that the dog can digest and absorb. For example, chicken feathers are protein but are worthless as nutrition. Also, many nutrients, too numerous to itemize, are required. Toxic substances may be present in low-quality rations. Select a well-known manufacturer whose brand of dog food is recommended by your veterinarian and by other breeders. When you find a ration that maintains your Beardie in good condition, stay with it. Variety is not the "spice of life" when feeding your dog. In fact, changing his diet will often cause him to go off feed or have an upset stomach.

Types of Food

There are five basic types of diets. The first is the homemade diet. It *may* be nutritionally balanced, but because it rarely is, it can cause

"Is it dinnertime yet?"
Courtesy Artisan Beardies.

nutritional deficiencies, excesses, toxicities, and general imbalance

The second type, generally sold in grocery stores, pet shops, or feed stores, was referred to previously as "commercial" dog food, usually cereal-based. These brands are generally available in a maintenance ration but also may be obtained in a growth ration, which has a higher protein and energy content for growing puppies or lactating bitches.

The third type includes foods containing various drugs. These fairly recent products are usually available only through your vet or a specialty house. One type, called HRH, contains drugs to help control heartworms, roundworms, and hookworms. Another brand now being developed will contain a progesterone compound for birth control.

The fourth kind of diet is the prescription diet, especially formulated for use in the management of certain medical conditions and available only by prescription from a veterinarian.

The fifth type is the premium-food diet, usually based on chicken, beef, or lamb, and containing all of the essential elements, thus needing no additional supplementation of any kind except the possibility of oil for the coat. Most of these are sold only in feed or pet stores or by veterinarians. These rations are usually obtain-

able in formulations for maintenance, lactation, growth, and stress. They are highly concentrated and highly digestible, and feeding them will result in a lower stool volume.

Forms of Food

Three forms of dog food are available: dry, soft-moist, and canned.

Dry Food. Dry foods are cheaper, may be self-fed, and are abrasive enough to help prevent formation of tartar on the teeth. The disadvantage of this food is that it supplies a great deal of bulk. As a result, a Beardie under stress or with unusually high energy requirements may not eat enough to maintain correct weight. Also, dry food is sometimes deficient in the fatty acids, which aid in maintaining good coat and skin condition. This can be easily offset by adding one tablespoon of vegetable oil to each pound of dry food. Dry food loses its fatty acids to oxidation and becomes rancid if it is stored for more than six months (less than six months in extreme heat or humidity

Soft-Moist Food. Many brands of soft-moist (burger-type) foods are being marketed.

They are more expensive, cannot be self-fed, and contribute to tartar formation. They *may* contain a higher-quality protein or more energy per pound on a dry-matter basis. They definitely contain higher sugar and preservative percentages.

Canned Food. The advantages and disadvantages of canned food are similar to those of soft-moist food. Each can contains about 77 percent water, which means that more than three-fourths of the cost is for water. A dog must eat a much larger volume of canned food to obtain his daily nutritional requirements, and this makes canned food impractical for Bearded Collies.

Methods of Feeding

A dog may be either self-fed or individually fed. The only requirement for self-feeding is to leave food (dry food only) before your Beardie at all times. Self-feeding allows you more freedom to come and go, it is easy, and it requires no mixing, adjusting, or record-keeping. Each dog eats what he wants when he wants it. Self-feeding helps to discourage the eating of feces. The dog that likes to eat only small amounts at a time will often do best on self-feeding, but some dogs may overeat and get fat. Puppies that are self-fed may overeat, resulting in an overly rapid growth pattern and associated skeletal problems. A drawback to self-feeding is that the food can attract mice and insects, and even birds if fed outdoors.

A self-feeding program must be started slowly to discourage overeating. At first, feed the normal ration, then gradually increase the amount until some food is left at the end of each day. Self-feeding is not recommended for some Beardie puppies until they are at least six months of age. You may want to experiment to determine which of your dogs do best on self-feeding programs. If you have more than one Beardie, they all must do well on self-feeding unless they are kenneled separately.

If you feed your Beardies individually, any type of food may be given, and the amount of

food and supplementation should be balanced for each dog. Puppies less than six months of age and lactating bitches should be fed at least twice daily. In fact, evidence suggests that two feedings per day are better than one for all dogs, although many breeders feed adult dogs only once daily. A big advantage to individual feeding is that you can tell immediately if a dog is going off feed.

You can teach your Beardie to clean up his bowl by placing him in an area where he can eat alone and undisturbed. Pick up his bowl in about fifteen minutes whether he has finished or not. He will soon learn to complete his meal in the allotted time. Once-a-day feeding can be either in the morning or the evening, whichever fits your schedule the best, but it should be at approximately the same time every day.

Whatever type of food and method of feeding you select, avoid oversupplementing with vitamins and minerals. Supplements, when fed improperly, can do more harm than good, so use them only under your veterinarian's guidance. Avoid giving table scraps, sweets, or bones to your Beardie. You'll only encourage obesity, begging, or finicky eating. Knuckle bones of beef may be parboiled to kill parasites and can be given occasionally but are very abrasive to the teeth. Do not give your Beardie pork, steak, chicken, or other small bones. Many dogs have died from a bone-punctured intestine.

How much should you feed? This is difficult to answer, because each Beardie has a slightly different metabolism. Your best gauge is your dog's weight and condition. A dog that is too thin or too fat is probably eating too little or too much, respectively. Generally an adult Beardie can be expected to consume about four cups of dry food per day.

Food Supplements

Many food additives and nutritional supplements are available, but they are generally unnecessary if your adult Beardie is being fed a high-quality ration. It is safer, cheaper, and easier to buy a good-quality, balanced ration than to supplement a low-quality food. Vitamins, minerals, and nutrients must be supplied in balanced ratios to be effective, otherwise they can cause problems. It is difficult to duplicate scientifically balanced diets with home methods.

Beardie puppies between two and six months of age exhibit an unusually fast growth rate, and they may need added calcium and phosphorus unless they are being fed a premium-quality food specifically formulated for growth. If you must add these elements, the safest way to do so is by adding one tablespoon of bone meal to the food each day. It is inexpensive and can be purchased from pet supply or health food stores.

Beardies living in a dry climate, or those fed a dry kibble, may need a coat supplement to furnish additional fatty acids. Many commercial formulas are on the market, or you may simply add corn, vegetable, safflower, peanut, or soy oil at the rate of one tablespoon per pound of dry food. Fats from meat other than bacon supply only empty calories instead of the needed fatty acids and should not be used.

CONDITIONING THROUGH EXERCISE

Your conditioning program cannot be complete without planned exercise. The amount of exercise that your Beardie gets has as much control over his weight and bloom as does his diet. A fat, soft Beardie needs more exercise, perhaps accompanied by a more restricted diet. A thin or overmuscled dog usually needs less exercise along with, perhaps, a diet higher in calories. Exercise often improves appetite, and a thin dog that is not eating properly may be induced to eat more by increasing his activity.

Often, neither the kennel dog nor the house pet gets the right type of exercise. Both should have at least one hour per day of romping in a large yard or exercise area where they can move freely. The show or working Beardie needs additional exercise, and this is best achieved through road work. Road work means trotting your Beardie for a structured period each day, usually on a leash behind a bicycle or automobile, until he develops his maximum potential gait and endurance. With consistent road work, the Beardie that moves sloppily will tighten up, the good-moving dog will develop a gait that is effortless, smooth, and extended, and the tight dog will begin to move more freely. You can't correct real unsoundness through road work, but you can make the most of what your Beardie is capable of doing.

Adult Beardies should be initiated at about one-half mile per day, moving at a comfortable trotting speed on a loose leash. Do not allow your dog to gallop or pace—this develops entirely different muscles. The best surface for road work is dirt or cut grass. If you have only gravel or concrete surfaces, you will have to work shorter distances and check frequently for signs of sore pads or lameness. The surface should be level or slightly uphill. Never trot a dog downhill—it breaks down pasterns and shoulders.

Never work your Beardie until he is exhausted, stiff, or lame. If this occurs at any point, rest him for a day or two, then shorten the distance worked until it is comfortable for him. By the end of the first week, most Beardies will be ready to proceed to trotting one mile per day. Week by week, gradually lengthen the distance until your dog is easily trotting two or three miles daily.

After your dog has reached his maximum distance, it will take at least a month of consistent, daily road work for him to approach peak performance. After this point you can maintain optimum performance by working him only two or three times weekly. If you wish your dog to be at his best for show season, start his workouts about three months prior to the first show.

Puppies may be started on road work at about six months of age, but they should be worked much shorter distances and should progress more slowly from one distance to the next.

Never tie a Beardie behind a car. Instead, have someone drive while you sit on the tailgate

Four-month-old puppies exercise themselves by playing. Courtesy Michele Ritter.

of a station wagon and lead the dog (don't position him where he must breathe the exhaust fumes). Or, still better for you, ride a bicycle. You can buy a unit that attaches to your bicycle and holds the dog away from the wheels and that also has a spring to absorb any shock if the dog pulls away. A good trotting speed for an adult Beardie averages seven to eight miles per hour.

If you can't manage either of these methods, or if you have several dogs to work, treadmills are available for dogs. These have the advantage of being usable in any weather, although they don't give *you* any exercise. One dedicated Beardie owner set up a stationary bicycle beside the treadmill and pedaled while his dog trotted.

CARING FOR THE OLDER BEARDIE

Without your hardly noticing it, your Beardie will one day move a little slower and sleep a little longer. His body processes will slow, his resistance will be lower, and his digestion, sight, and hearing will not be as good as they once

were. But he will still be an important member of your family and can be depended upon to assist in training younger dogs. He will add an air of permanency and dignity to your household. He will be living proof of your healthy line of Beardies and will probably be a super-salesman besides.

The older Beardie requires little in additional care: a warmer, drier place to sleep; encouragement to exercise; and perhaps a special diet lower in protein to help keep his weight down and not overstress his kidneys. Loss of teeth may make food difficult to chew, so switch to a softer food and have his teeth cleaned regularly.

The older dog is often subject to cysts (which sometimes look like pimples on the skin), various infections, deafness, or blindness. In familiar surroundings, you may never know that your dog is blind, but he will become frightened and bump into things when taken to a different environment. A blind dog can be taught to respond to sound vibrations, and a deaf dog can respond to hand signals and still live a reasonably happy, comfortable life.

When the day comes that your Beardie can no longer lead a meaningful existence, or when his days are filled with suffering, you should consider ending his misery through euthanasia. No one wants to give up a friend, but it is often the best way for him. Your veterinarian will inject an overdose of anesthetic, and your Beardie will drift into a peaceful, permanent sleep. The process takes only a few seconds; there is no pain or fright, and no prolonged suffering.

Beardies enjoy sharing all aspects of your life. Courtesy Brigette Nowak.

Courtesy Diane and Dorine Wynen.

Willowmead Summer Magic takes a bow. Courtesy Collavechio.

8 *In Sickness and In Health*

You can protect your pet from many canine diseases by providing yearly vaccinations and preventive care. In addition, cleanliness and maintenance of a parasite-free environment will assure that your Beardie stays healthy. You are fortunate to have chosen a breed with relatively few hereditary problems or tendencies to illness. Yet, every dog owner at some point will be called upon to administer first aid or give medication for a minor illness. You will want to familiarize yourself with symptoms of illness, antidotes for poisons, and medical techniques so that you will be prepared.

IMMUNIZATIONS

Beardie puppies usually get their first immunization shot at five to seven weeks of age. Not all veterinarians agree on the schedule for vaccinating puppies, so it is best to follow your own veterinarian's advice. Puppies receive antibodies from their mother's milk, and immunization will not take effect until all of this maternal immunity has been lost. This can occur anywhere between six and sixteen weeks of age; therefore, the puppy should be protected from exposure to disease during his first three months, and the final immunization is given when he is three to four months old. Thereafter, yearly boosters are required. When you buy a puppy, the breeder should give you a record of the type and pharmaceutical of the shots and when they were given.

Rabies vaccinations are required by law and are given when a puppy is three to six months old. The same state laws also regulate the frequency of booster vaccinations. The American Veterinary Association recommends a booster vaccination for modified live-virus rabies one year after the initial shot, then boosters every one to three years. A certificate of rabies vaccination will be required when you apply for a city or county dog license or a health certificate for interstate shipping. Many localities require yearly boosters.

PARASITES

Parasites are dependent at some point in their life cycle on a host—your dog. They are common in almost any area of the world, and, while they generally do not represent a serious problem, they should be eliminated. They are often the cause of poor overall condition, thinness, dull, dry coats, and lack of vigor.

All parasites complete a life cycle, only part of which affects your dog. This cycle must be considered or you will continue to have the problem even after you have treated your dog.

Keep your Beardie puppy a picture of health by preventing disease and parasites.
Am. Can. Ch. Classical's Silver Cloud.
Courtesy Classical Kennels.

Internal Parasites

The most common internal parasites are roundworms, tapeworms, hookworms, whipworms, and giardia, all of which live in the dog's intestine. You may or may not see the worms or their symptoms. Microscopic diagnosis by a veterinarian is necessary. You will want to have your puppy checked several times the first year and every year thereafter by taking a small amount of fresh stool for an examination.

Roundworms or Ascarids

These white, cylindrical worms are the most common type seen in puppies. Puppies can be born with roundworms, or they can pick up the eggs from contaminated surfaces after birth.

Either way, it is safe to assume that almost every puppy will be infected with these worms.

Adult roundworms live in the small intestine, where they absorb nutrients from the digestive juices. The worms produce eggs that pass in the stool. The eggs become larvae, are ingested by either the same individual or another dog, and develop into worms to complete the cycle. Some of the larvae will not complete the cycle but will migrate into the lungs or other tissue to remain in a resting stage. When a bitch becomes pregnant, these resting larvae migrate into the fetus.

Beardies with roundworm infections may appear thin and potbellied. They may have dull coats or diarrhea, or they may vomit or cough. In young puppies, a heavy infection may cause death, but in adult dogs, the worms do not generally cause a serious illness. Roundworms are easily eliminated with a drug called piperazine.

It is safe and can be obtained from your vet or from a pet-supply store. It can be given to puppies as young as two weeks of age. The treatment should be repeated in two weeks and again in a month to make sure that all of the mature worms are killed.

The biggest problem with roundworms is that the eggs can remain alive and infective in the soil for months. Cleanliness is important. Remove the stool daily and control rodents, which serve as an intermediate host to the larvae. Treat the soil with salt or borax (*see* Chapter 5).

Tapeworms

This parasite attaches to the intestinal wall with suckers. The tapeworm's body is composed of a series of reproductive segments that look somewhat like grains of rice. They may sometimes be seen clinging to the hair or skin around the anus, or on the stool. The adult tapeworm produces eggs that pass in the feces and are eaten by an intermediate host, such as a rodent, louse, flea, or rabbit. The dog then eats the intermediate host containing the effective stage of the tapeworm, and the worm completes its life cycle by developing in the dog's intestine.

Tapeworms may cause digestive problems, weight loss, or poor condition. Avoid using tapeworm medication available in drug or pet stores, because it generally is ineffective and can be dangerous. Your vet can provide a safe, effective dewormer. Again, cleanliness and elimination of intermediate hosts, especially fleas, are required to prevent reinfection.

Hookworms

Hookworms are small worms that suck blood directly from the wall of the small intestine. They are one of the more tenacious and more damaging parasites. Dogs become infested by ingesting the larvae from the ground or by having their skin or pads penetrated by the infective larvae. Puppies are often infected before birth by the migrating larvae.

Symptoms include weakness, diarrhea, anemia, and blood in the stool. The stool is black and looks like tar with a distinctive odor. Heavily infected puppies may die before the worms are detected. Treatment must be administered quickly by a veterinarian, and blood transfusions may be necessary. All hookworm medications can be dangerous and should be used under the direction of your veterinarian. Do not use over-the-counter medications sold for these worms, because they can cause severe side effects.

Whipworms

These parasites live in the large intestine and may cause diarrhea or weight loss. They can be detected only by microscopic examination and require a specific wormer that your veterinarian can prescribe.

Heartworms

Heartworm disease is a very serious problem. The adult heartworms live in the right atrium and ventricle of the heart. The mature worms produce larvae called microfilaria, which circulate in the blood. When a mosquito bites an infected dog, that insect becomes the intermediate host for the microfilaria, which can be passed on when another dog is bitten. Once found mainly in the southern states, heartworm disease is now found throughout the United States

Infected dogs tire easily, cough, have difficulty breathing, and are generally in poor condition. Signs of heart failure may occur. However, heartworm may be present for some time before symptoms appear. Treatment can be long and difficult, and hospitalization is often required.

Fortunately, there is a very effective method of prevention. Two types of medication are available that will kill microfilaria before they mature into adult worms. Both medications come in pill form, and one type is given daily, the other once a month. It is necessary for a veterinarian to do a blood test before prescribing heartworm pills.

Protozoa

Protozoa are tiny, one-celled parasites that live in the intestines. Stools of an infected dog can be thin and watery, dark and loose, or covered in a thick mucus. A persistent diarrhea can occur that is resistant to the usual antidiarrheal drugs but that does not cause vomiting or lethargy. A protozoan infection can be very difficult to diagnose, because it requires immediate examination of fresh fecal matter and is easily missed unless looked for specifically.

Giardia. This parasite absorbs carbohydrates directly from the host. It was once thought to be rare but is found increasingly throughout the world. It is spread through contact with fecal matter, often in water in areas inhabited by wild animals. Dogs can be treated with drugs, or a mild infection can be left to run its course. Adult dogs build up a resistance to it, but once infected, they can carry encysted eggs that can become infective in a new host.

Coccidia. Coccidia is more common in puppies than in adult dogs. It is often characterized by yellow stools that have a distinctive, foul odor. Coccidia is found most frequently in filthy conditions, although a bitch that has been infected can carry it encapsulated in muscle tissue and this, in turn, can infect her puppies. It will usually run its course in a week or so, but young puppies can easily become dehydrated and may require treatment.

External Parasites

Fleas. Fleas are by far the most common external parasite found on dogs, cats, and other animals. The two kinds most often found on dogs are the fairly large, brown dog fleas and the much smaller, shiny black sand fleas. Fleas suck blood and therefore can significantly weaken the host as well as spread disease. Fleas deposit eggs about the size and color of a grain of salt on their host. The eggs drop off into bedding, into cracks in the soil or in buildings, into carpets, etc. In about two weeks, the eggs hatch into larvae, which then develop into adult fleas.

To control the parasites, you must eliminate them on your dog through the use of medicated shampoo or insecticide powders, then thoroughly clean all bedding and housing or kennel facilities. You may want to fumigate your house or kennel, or spray with lindane or malathion. Discard old bedding. A new pill administered once a month as a preventative has recently been released.

Lice. Lice are small, pale-colored, bloodsucking insects that are far less common than fleas. They are generally found only in extremely dirty conditions or around poultry facilities. They can be treated by the same methods used against fleas. Because lice die quickly once removed from their host, it is not necessary to treat the bedding.

Ticks. Ticks are a problem in some areas of the country. There are many different species, all of which attach themselves to the dog's flesh and engorge themselves with the blood of their host. They can cause anemia, weakness, or paralysis.

If your dog has only one or two, you can remove them by hand. Apply a little rubbing alcohol to the tick, causing it to loosen, then grasp the insect firmly as close to the dog's skin as possible and slowly pull the tick off. You can then burn it with a match.

If ticks are a constant problem, or your dog has picked up a number of them, purchase a good commercial tick and flea dip and spray, or fumigate bedding and kennel facilities. You may have to repeat the spraying several times before all ticks are killed.

Deer ticks that carry Lyme Disease are an increasing problem in many areas of the country. Lyme Disease is difficult to diagnose, because it mimics other conditions. Limping or arthritic symptoms are often the first signs. A vaccine is currently available but is not yet approved in all states, so check with your veterinarian.

WHEN YOUR BEARDIE IS NOT FEELING WELL

Once you have learned to observe the signs of good health in your dog and have become familiar with his habits and behavior, it will be easy to determine when he is ill. Any change in behavior or appetite can be a clue. He may be restless, depressed, or ill-tempered, or he may whine. His eyes may appear dull and uninterested, or they may water. He may vomit, have diarrhea, shiver, or appear to be uncomfortable. He may show signs of stiffness, or lameness, or he may urinate frequently. A fever is a definite indication of illness.

Any dog may have an off day, so don't panic at first. Just be observant. Take your Beardie's rectal temperature using any human rectal thermometer inserted about half its length. The normal temperature for most canines is 101.5 degrees, but be aware (and also inform your vet) that it is often normal for a Beardie to have a temperature of 102.0 or even 102.5. It will be highest in the afternoon or evening. Check your dog's temperature several different times while he is healthy to determine what is normal for him.

If your dog appears to behave abnormally for more than one day, or if acute symptoms or a high fever are present, take him to your veterinarian for a checkup, or call for advice. It is important for every dog owner to locate within close proximity a good veterinarian and establish a good relationship with him or her.

Giving Medication

With a little practice, you can give your Beardie a pill easily and quickly. To force your dog's mouth open, grasp his muzzle with your hand over his foreface and let your fingers press his upper lips over the tips of his upper teeth. Tilt his head upward slightly to encourage swallowing. With your other hand, place the pill far back in the center of the base of the tongue. Quickly remove your hand and close your dog's mouth, holding it closed until you feel him swallow. Rubbing the throat will sometimes encourage swallowing. If the pill is particularly large or dry, buttering it will help.

Liquid medication may be given from a spoon, but drawing it into a large syringe (minus a needle!), an eyedropper, or a kitchen

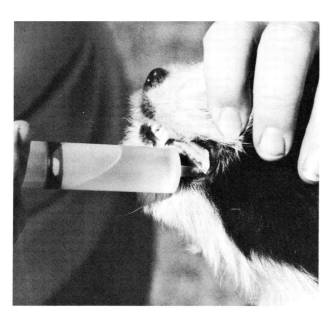

Giving liquid medication.

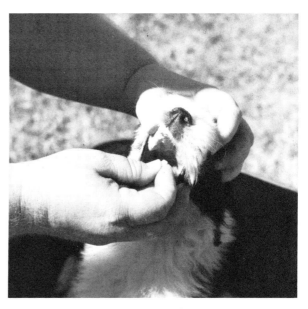

Giving a pill.

baster makes it easier to administer. Pull the corner of the lower lip outward and upward with one hand, forming a pocket. Keeping your Beardie's head tilted slightly upward, slowly pour the liquid into the lip pocket. Allow your dog to swallow as the liquid is given, but prevent him from shaking or lowering his head.

It is important when giving medications to administer the exact quantity specified. Pills should not be crushed into the food, because you can never be sure that they are being swallowed entirely.

Supplies

Every dog owner should have a medicine chest that includes the following: a rectal thermometer, a good liquid antiseptic, soap, cotton swabs, peroxide, gauze pads and a gauze bandage wrap, alcohol, clean towels, a blunt-nosed scissors for clipping around wounds, etc., styptic powder or silver nitrate to control bleeding of small wounds or bites, an old nylon stocking for use as a muzzle, Kaopectate, Milk of Magnesia tablets, a good antiseptic wound spray, a general purpose flea and tick dip or shampoo, Panolog dressing, Dramamine™, artificial tears for eyes, activated charcoal and a product such as Bitter Apple to prevent chewing.

Some Common Diseases and Problems

Arthritis. Properly called osteoarthritis, this is a disease in which the joints are affected by excess bone growth, resulting in pain and lameness. It can occur in young dogs due to trauma affecting a joint or from congenital joint defects. It more commonly occurs with aging.

Treatment is only symptomatic; there is no way to arrest the development of arthritis. Keep the arthritic Beardie warm and dry, and limit, but do not discontinue, exercise. Do not allow the dog to become overweight. Your vet may prescribe aspirin or Tylenol if the pain is severe, or in more advanced cases may suggest corticosteroids.

Conversion Table

16 drops = 1 cc = ¼ teaspoon
5 cc = 1 teaspoon
15 cc = 1 tablespoon = ½ ounce
30 cc = 2 tablespoons = 1 ounce
8 ounces = 1 cup
4 cups = 1 quart = 1 liter

Constipation. Constipation commonly occurs from lack of bulk in the diet but also may be caused by overlong confinement (especially while traveling), internal parasites, tumors, abscessed anal sacs, or old age. One day without a bowel movement is no cause for concern.

A mild change in diet or adding water to the food may help. Two tablespoons of Milk of Magnesia or one of the human laxatives designed to provide bulk may be given, or try a human rectal suppository.

Dermatitis. There are many kinds of dermatitis, or inflammation of the skin—some caused by allergies, some by contact with irritants, and some by infection. The symptoms are similar: red skin accompanied by hair loss in the area, and possibly bumps, scabs, dandruff-like scales, or oozing areas. The skin may feel hot to the touch.

Severe dermatitis requires veterinary attention. You may try treating small areas by bathing your dog frequently and rinsing him with one capful of Alpha-Keri per quart of water. Apply Furaspor or some other type of soothing, drying ointment to the area.

Diarrhea. Diarrhea may indicate a more serious disease or infection, or it may be the result of overeating, a change in diet, overexcitement, or the presence of parasites. The best initial treatment is to withhold food for twelve to twenty-four hours, then limit your dog to a light, bland diet containing broth, cooked eggs, cottage cheese, or rice for several days. Kaopectate can be given every four hours (two teaspoonfuls per ten pounds of weight).

Severe diarrhea, diarrhea accompanied by vomiting, or bloody diarrhea signals a trip to your veterinarian. Unchecked diarrhea causes dehydration, which can occur especially rapidly in puppies. Beware of administering some of the commercial products sold by pet-supply catalogs. They can be quite strong and possibly dangerous.

Distemper. Distemper is a highly contagious, infectious disease. The germs are airborne, so direct contact with an infected animal is not required. Distemper virus is everywhere; you can even carry the germs into your home on shoes or clothing. For this reason, and because the disease is generally fatal, every dog should be immunized with yearly boosters throughout his life

Symptoms are erratic. Often, the first signs include fever, listlessness, lack of appetite, stiffness, or vomiting. Later, the dog will probably develop diarrhea, nasal discharge, and coughing. Eventually, the nervous system becomes damaged.

Ear Inflammation. If your Beardie begins shaking his head and scratching at his ears, he may have an ear infection. The insides of the ear may be red or swollen, have large amounts of waxy discharge, or emit a strong odor. First, remove any excess hair from the ear canal by plucking. Try cleaning the ear with a cotton swab dipped in 70 percent isopropyl alcohol. Then place several drops of alcohol into the ear and massage the base of the ear to spread the medication. Severe or continued ear infectionsshould be treated by a veterinarian.

Ear Mites. These parasites are common in some parts of the country. They cause discomfort and scratching, accompanied by profuse amounts of dark reddish-brown to gray wax. If you live in an area where ear mites are common, your vet can give you drops containing lindane, rotenone, or some other insecticide. Clean the ear with a cotton swab dipped in isopropyl alcohol. You may be able to see the small mites. Drop the insecticide into the ears according to instructions.

Eye Irritations and Inflammations. Eyes are very delicate organs, and even the slightest irritation should not be ignored. Often, dust, pollen, or a foreign object or allergy will cause tearing or mild inflammation. Wash the eye area with a cotton swab dipped in a saltwater solution (one teaspoon salt per one cup water), or use artificial tears sold for humans. If the irritation continues, see your vet. Never use anything in the eye that is not specifically designed for ophthalmic use, and never use eye drugs prescribed for one problem to treat another case. Ophthalmic drugs are very specific; using the wrong one could cause blindness.

Conjunctivitis, or inflammation of the third eyelid, is a fairly common problem. The membrane appears red and swollen. Treatment with antibiotics is necessary.

Enteritis. Enteritis is acute, hemorrhagic diarrhea accompanied by cramping of the stomach, gas, and vomiting. The onset is sudden. Give your dog two tablespoons of Kaopectate to quiet his stomach and rush him to the vet. Causes of enteritis are varied, but sudden death can result unless treatment is begun immediately.

Heart Disease. There are a number of different heart problems that affect dogs, more commonly older dogs. All conditions generally progress from mild stages to more serious forms. Heart failure usually can be treated and controlled if discovered early. A Beardie suffering from heart disease may tire more easily. You may notice him coughing in the morning or evening, or after exertion. He may gag up mucus. In severe cases, you may notice an unusual arrhythmia, or murmur, in the heartbeat, or your dog may have difficulty breathing. Treatment for heart disease often involves regulation of the diet as well as administration of drugs.

Infectious Canine Hepatitis. Canine hepatitis is not the same as human hepatitis, although it is similar in that the disease primarily affects the liver. It is an acute viral disease characterized by high fever, bloody diarrhea, abdominal pain, and vomiting. Dogs may exhibit an intolerance for light, and occasionally a blue film will form over the cornea of the eye. This condition is known as "blue eye" and can occur from mild forms of the disease, or rarely, from a reaction to the vaccine. Hepatitis vaccine should never be given to a dog with an eye ulceration, because an extreme reaction and possible blindness may result

There is no cure for the disease. Hospitalization is required, but only the symptoms can be treated. You can protect your Beardie with vaccinations administered yearly in conjunction with distemper vaccine.

Kennel Cough. Tracheobronchitis, known as "kennel cough" because it occurs frequently in kennels, at shows, or anyplace where large numbers of dogs come together, is one of the most contagious of canine diseases. It is characterized by a dry, hacking cough or deep, harsh coughing often accompanied by gagging. The Beardie's appetite will remain good, and he will have no fever or other symptoms. Like a cold, kennel cough must run its course, and most dogs will recover with or without medication in two to six weeks if they are kept warm and relatively quiet. Occasionally, a stubborn case will hang on for several months. Over-the-counter cough suppressants marketed for humans may be given to mask the symptoms, and your veterinarian can prescribe broad-spectrum antibiotics.

A vaccine can immunize your Beardie against some forms of kennel cough. The immunization can be given separately or combined with the DHL vaccine. Be sure to request it if you have a number of dogs or plan to travel or show your Beardie.

Kidney and Bladder Infections. The most common problems affecting the urinary system are interstitial nephritis in the kidneys, or cystitis (bladder infection).

Nephritis is common in older dogs, but it can occur in conjunction with infectious diseases or be caused by the ingestion of poisons. An affected Beardie generally runs a fever, arches his back in pain, drinks increased amounts of water, vomits, and has strong body or breath odors. A urinalysis is required for diagnosis, and hospitalization may be required. Prompt treatment will usually prevent kidney damage in acute cases. Chronic nephritis is controlled by diet and medication.

Cystitis is generally caused by a bacterial infection in the bladder. Symptoms include frequent urination, cloudy or blood-tinged urine, and straining. Females may have a vaginal discharge and may lick themselves excessively. Treatment with antibiotics will be required for several weeks, and the dog should have plenty of water.

If you think that your Beardie has a kidney or bladder problem, collect a urine sample within an hour before you leave, and take it to your vet. Take your Beardie out on the leash and collect about one-fourth cup of urine in a clean container.

Leptospirosis. Leptospirosis is the third kind of infectious disease against which dogs are immunized, and it is the only one that is contagious to humans.

The disease primarily affects the kidneys, causing kidney failure. Germs are spread in the contaminated urine from affected dogs, rodents, or cattle. Rat- or mouse-contaminated foods are a prime source. The bacteria can enter a dog's system orally, through the skin, or during intercourse.

Symptoms include depression, loss of appetite, vomiting, fever, and constipation followed by diarrhea. The dog may be stiff and reluctant to move, often walking in a hunched-up posture with short, choppy steps. Occasionally, the infection is so slight that it is hardly noticeable; in other cases, it may cause death. Recovered animals may carry the germs for months afterward.

Vaccination will protect your Beardie from leptospirosis. The disease is more prevalent in some parts of the country than in others, and the vaccine, usually administered as part of the DHL package, may not be given routinely. Ask your vet for recommendations, and be sure to inform him or her if you plan to travel or ship your dog for breeding. The immunity is shorter-lived than other vaccines, and boosters every six months are required in high-risk areas.

Tonsillitis. If you open your Beardie's mouth wide, you can probably see his tonsils, which lie in a pocket on either side of the throat just behind the soft palate. Occasionally, they may become infected and may appear red and swollen. Your dog may refuse to eat or may have difficulty eating, or he may gag or vomit or have a slight fever. Tonsillitis is often caused by rapid changes in temperature, such as when a house dog is left in the cold too long, or a kennel dog is switched between the house and an unheated kennel in cold weather. Antibiotics are generally effective in clearing up the infection, but recurrent infections may lead to surgical removal of the tonsils.

Tumors. Older dogs are especially prone to abnormal tissue growths or tumors. Tumors may occur internally or on the outside of the body, commonly in the stomach or around the mammary glands of females. Tumors of the oil-producing glands are called sebaceous cysts. These are usually small, light-colored growths that somewhat resemble pimples. They may appear wart-like. They are usually benign and need no treatment but can be surgically removed if they become too large.

Vaginitis. Inflammation of the vagina is common in bitches. Young bitches may develop a type of vaginitis prior to their first heat. The condition is characterized by a mild irritation and discharge at the vulva, accompanied by an unusual attractiveness to male dogs. This form of vaginitis needs no treatment and will disappear with the first heat season.

Older bitches may exhibit a sticky yellowish, greenish, or gray discharge that will cause

them to lick the vulva excessively. The mucous membranes may be red or red-spotted. The symptoms may be accompanied by a bladder infection and should be watched carefully. Otherwise, a more serious uterine condition, such as metritis or pyometra, may develop. Vaginitis can be treated successfully with antibiotics.

Vomiting. Your dog will often vomit when nothing is really wrong other than an upset stomach or the fact that he ate something that he shouldn't have eaten. He may first vomit food, followed by a frothy clear or yellow fluid. If he vomits only once or twice and has no fever, pain, or other symptoms of illness, don't worry. Just withhold food for about twelve hours, then feed him lightly with soft, bland food for the next day. Don't offer large amounts of water. You can often soothe your dog's stomach by giving Maalox or Mylanta (one teaspoon per twenty pounds of weight).

Vomiting from car sickness usually ends shortly after movement has stopped. You can sometimes prevent this discomfort by giving Dramamine™ about one-half hour before leaving

Severe vomiting, vomiting of blood, or vomiting accompanied by illness or depression should be treated immediately by a veterinarian. Your Beardie cannot talk, and by the time symptoms are observed, the illness may be fairly well progressed.

FIRST AID

Applied quickly and correctly, good first-aid measures can save your Beardie's life. Use *them only as a temporary emergency treatment to maintain the life of your dog until professional medical help is obtained*

What Constitutes an Emergency

Severe (life-threatening)
Respiratory failure
Cardiac arrest

Massive hemorrhage
Multiple, deep lacerations
Anaphylaxis (reaction to drug or
    immunization)
Penetrating wounds of the thorax
    or abdomen
Coma and loss of consciousness
Spinal fractures
Rapid-acting poisons
Massive musculoskeletal injuries
Acute overwhelming bacteremia and toxemia
Continual convulsions (no letup)

Severe

Multiple, deep lacerations
Skull and spinal injuries
Thoracic trauma without respiratory
    problems
Multiple pelvic or long-bone fractures

Moderate

Simple fractures of long bones, ribs, and
    pelvis
Luxations and ligament rupture
Deep lacerations and abrasions
Bacterial and viral infection with no
    depression

Minor

Cuts, wounds, scrapes of minor nature.

Transporting an Injured Beardie

Unless broken bones are obvious, an injured dog may be carried by placing one arm under his body, supporting his chest with your hand, and cradling his body on your forearm. Steady his head with your free hand.

A badly injured dog must be placed gently on a solid board stretcher. Lacking anything solid, you can improvise by placing two sticks through the arms of a jacket or shirt to form a sling. Disturb the dog's position as little as possible.

Figure 8-1
*Right: Transport an injured dog
on a sling made from a blanket or jacket.*

Applying a Muzzle

A Beardie that is in pain or shock may bite at anyone who tries to handle him. To prevent this, fashion a muzzle in the following manner: tie the mouth shut with a piece of cloth or old nylon stocking, making two additional wraps around the muzzle with a hard knot under the chin. Bring the two ends of the material behind the ears and tie in a bow.

A properly applied muzzle.

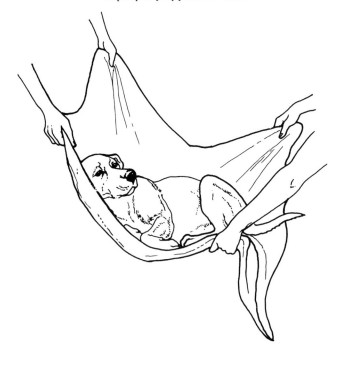

Checking the Pulse

The normal heart rate of a Beardie is 90 to 100 beats per minute. You can feel your Beardie's pulse by locating the femoral artery. Place your index finger inside the hind leg as closely against the body as possible. You can also feel the pulse by placing your fingers over the heart itself.

Artificial Respiration

If you find your Beardie unconscious and not breathing, but with a heartbeat still audible, you may be able to revive him with artificial respiration.

Place the dog on his right side with his head and neck extended so that the windpipe makes a straight line. Pull the tongue forward and outward. With the heels of your hands, press the chest moderately hard just behind the shoulder blade, forcing air from the lungs. Relax the pressure, count to five, and repeat. The rhythm must be smooth and regular. Continue until your dog is breathing at his normal rate (about

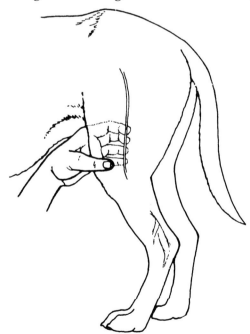

Figure 8-2
Hold your fingers over the dog's femoral artery and count the number of beats in six seconds. Multiply by ten to get beats per minute.

fifteen to twenty times per minute) without assistance. Then treat for shock.

You can also administer artificial respiration by placing your lips over your dog's mouth and nostrils, cupping your hands over them like a cone, and forcing air into his lungs.

Treating for Shock

A dog in shock appears depressed and has rapid heart and respiration rates, a rapid, weak pulse, and pale mucous membranes. He may shiver and feel cold to the touch. Breathing is slow, and the eyes are often glazed.

A dog in shock needs emergency veterinary treatment immediately. Wrap him in a towel or blanket for warmth, and if you are far from professional help, a tablespoon of whiskey may help revive him. Do not give water.

External Heart Massage

If your dog's heart has stopped, combine artificial respiration with external heart massage.

1. With the dog on his back, legs in the air, place the palms of your hands on his sternum, with your fingers on one side of the chest and your thumb on the other side.
2. Alternately compress and release the chest Compress the chest strongly between your thumb and fingers, pushing the ribs together. At the same time, press the sternum downward toward the spine. Release the pressure suddenly
3. Repeat the compression at the rate of seventy times per minute until the heart starts beating again. A dog can live about three minutes after the heart stops.

First Aid for Specific Conditions

Bee Stings. Apply an ice cube to the area and give your Beardie an aspirin tablet. If an allergic reaction sets in, consult your vet. Normally, the swelling will go down in forty-eight hours or less.

Bleeding. Cover the wound with sterile gauze and apply a pressure bandage by wrapping the injury tightly. Use a tourniquet between an arterial injury and the heart *only* if a pressure bandage will not control the bleeding. Tourniquets must be loosened every ten minutes.

Broken Nails. Apply a styptic powder or use powdered alum to stop the bleeding. Smooth the nail with a coarse file after bleeding has stopped.

Bruises. If the injury is recent and swelling has not yet begun, apply a cold compress. If the injury is swollen, apply a hot compress.

Burns. Run cold water over the area or apply an ice pack for about twenty minutes. Do not apply ointments of any kind. If a burn is serious, take your Beardie to the veterinary hospital immediately.

Cactus or Porcupine Quills. Remove them with tweezers or pliers. Treat with an antiseptic spray.

Cuts and Wounds. Wash with a 3-percent solution of hydrogen peroxide. You may pour the peroxide directly into the wound, use a cotton swab, or flush the solution into the wound with a syringe or baster. Repeat this procedure twice daily. Clip the hair around the wound to avoid irritation. Large tears or wounds will require sutures.

Dog Bites. Wash a dog bite with peroxide and treat with a topical antiseptic ointment. Deep puncture wounds or tears will need suturing.

Drowning. Hold your Beardie upside-down by his legs until water is drained from his lungs, then administer artificial respiration if needed. Keep your dog warm and rub his body vigorously. You may be able to revive an unconscious dog with spirits of ammonia held under his nostrils.

Frostbite or Chilling. Warm your dog slowly by wrapping him in warm towels. A puppy may be placed inside your coat. Apply tepid water to frozen feet, gradually increasing the temperature to 100 degrees. Do not apply dry heat. Give a tablespoon of whiskey as a stimulant.

Fractures. Move your dog as little as possible. Place him on a board or stretcher and take him to the veterinary hospital as soon as possible. Compound fractures, where bone has punctured the skin, require immediate attention. Other fractures that are not accompanied by shock can be treated within the day. Do not try to apply splints or bandages.

Heat Stroke. An overheated dog will pant, will have an increased pulse rate, and will appear anxious with a staring expression. He may vomit, or he may become unconscious. Immerse the dog in cold water, or if this is impossible, spray him with the garden hose. Massage the skin and legs to encourage circulation, and place ice cubes on his mouth and nose. Do not give stimulants or water. Immediate veterinary attention is needed.

Puncture Wounds. Remove small objects carefully and apply a pressure bandage. If the object is large or has punctured the eye or abdomen, let a veterinarian remove it.

Skunk Odor. Bathe your Beardie in tomato juice, followed by soap and water. Wash his eyes with a mild salt solution. If you cannot bathe him, you can make him a little more acceptable by rubbing him with a damp sponge sprinkled with baking soda. Commercial products are available for removing skunk odor.

Snakebites. Keep your dog immobilized as much as possible, with the wound at the same level as the heart. Use a snakebite kit or make a sharp cut at the wound to induce bleeding. If the bite is on a leg, apply a tourniquet loose enough to slip one finger underneath it, and leave it on the dog until you reach a vet. Get your Beardie to the veterinarian as soon as possible.

Swallowing a Foreign Object. Feed bread or other soft food that will wrap itself around the object. Check with your vet regarding further treatment.

Poisoning. Identifying the poison is of utmost importance. *Call a veterinarian.* If you *cannot* get a vet and you know what the poisonous material was, administer the antidote and then drive your dog to the clinic. *Do not treat for poisoning unless you are sure what material was ingested.* You can induce vomiting by giving one ounce peroxide in one ounce of water. Do not induce vomiting if the poison was corrosive.

If the poison was a contact poison, always wash the contact area with large amounts of water. If your dog goes into convulsions, try to keep him from injuring himself by muzzling him and holding him as still as possible until you get to the vet.

Some common household poisons include the following:

Alkalis: Household drain cleaner is the most common of this type. It causes profuse salivation, nausea, and sometimes vomiting. Give a neutralizing acid such as vinegar or lemon juice—two or three tablespoons should be enough.

Aniline dyes: Found in shoe polish, crayons, and other household dyes. The lip and oral membranes may turn brown, breathing is labored, and the dog is listless. Induce vomiting with peroxide and give coffee as a stimulant.

Aspirin: Too much aspirin will cause weakness, rapid breathing, stomach pain, and sometimes collapse. Induce vomiting. Then give the dog sodium bicarbonate (baking soda) in water

Bleaches: Cause a general upset stomach. Induce vomiting. Then give the dog an egg white or a little olive oil.

Cleaning fluids: Either inhaling the fumes or ingesting the substance may cause poisoning.

For inhalation poisoning, give artificial respiration if needed and move your dog to a well-ventilated area. Wash his eyes with water. If the fluid was swallowed, induce vomiting, and give a dose of olive oil. Be careful that the oil does not go down the windpipe and choke your dog.

Cyanide or phosphorus: Found in some rat poisons. These are fast-acting poisons and cause pain, convulsions, diarrhea, and odorous breath. Get a veterinarian. (Ordinary "strike anywhere" matches also contain phosphorus.)

Ethylene glycol: Radiator antifreeze contains this poison and is readily ingested by dogs. Induce vomiting at once, then give bicarbonate of soda.

Paint: Lead-base paint can cause lead poisoning, either when the liquid paint is swallowed or when excessive amounts of flaked paint are chewed from a painted surface. Symptoms include rapid breathing, restlessness, and collapse. Induce vomiting and give Epsom salts as an antidote

Pyrophosphates (Malathion, Parathion, Pestox, etc.): These are absorbed through the skin. Symptoms include pinpoint pupils, salivation, cramps, watery eyes, and muscular twitching. Bathe your dog with soap and water and get him to a veterinarian quickly.

Strychnine: The kind of poison people use to intentionally poison dogs or small rodents. Violent convulsions with the head and legs extended are a good sign of strychnine poisoning. *Do not induce vomiting.* Contact your vet immediately, and rush your dog to the hospital

If you know that your dog has eaten strychnine but symptoms have not yet begun, your vet may advise that you give your dog a sleeping capsule.

Warfarin: A common ingredient in rat poison. It is not supposed to harm dogs, but it sometimes does. The drug acts as an anticoagulant, causing death by internal bleeding. If your dog has eaten warfarin, take him to your vet for a shot that will cause the blood to coagulate. If you wait until symptoms appear, it may be too late.

Head study of Ch. Potterdale Privilege. Courtesy Mr. and Mrs. Lewis, England.

9 *Beardie Be Good*

THE PSYCHOLOGY OF TRAINING

Training is accomplished by teaching your dog to associate a verbal command or signal with an action. Once he makes this association, more complicated exercises can be easily taught.

The dog reacts much like a very young child; he will choose the path of least resistance, especially if it is reinforced by approval of his superiors. In the case of the dog, the natural pecking order is very pronounced, from the pack leader to the weakest member of the pack. In fact, only the most dominant animals are allowed to breed in the wild. The offspring are quickly relegated to their respective positions within the litter, and as they grow, they accept their placements within the adult community based upon their dominance and physical prowess. A submissive animal will not often challenge those above him in the pecking order, even if he could effectively do so. A dog's rolling onto his back is an indication of submissiveness in a particular situation. All dogs are dominant to some animals and submissive to others.

So it is with the domestic dog. However, if you want a successful relationship with your pet, you must establish yourself as a "pack leader" substitute. This allows you to have absolute authority in the eyes of your dog. This is especially important if you own a male Beardie, for if he feels that you are not assuming command, he will gladly challenge you for the position. You must know what you want the dog to do and decide on a reasonable approach to achieve those results. A Beardie is extremely intelligent and capable of acting independently; however, he has also been selected for reasonable submissiveness, which aids in trainability. Therefore, your dog will try to please you once he knows what you want.

The true pack leader is consistent, so you will get better results in your training if you behave predictably. A dozen halfhearted attempts at controlling a situation will never be respected, while a severe correction will only have to be given once. Always think before you react. If you are too emotional or inconsistent, your dog will become frustrated. Proper behavior for the Beardie conditioned by a particular stimulus must be reinforced by approval each time that it occurs if training is to be effective.

A dog's attention span is short, especially when he is a puppy. Therefore, he responds better to short, fast-paced training sessions. About ten- to fifteen-minute sessions either once or twice a day are best. Once you lose his attention, he is no longer able to learn, and you will find yourself vainly fighting with him. Also, if you ever lose your temper, the dog has won the battle. Stay cool, calm, authoritative, consistent, and worthy of your position as the pack leader. Do not underestimate your dog's ability; he will never overestimate yours.

TRAINING GUIDELINES

There are a few basic rules that apply to any form of training. Success is dependent upon careful attention to these details.

Be Consistent

Always use the same words for a particular command, and require the same response from your dog each and every time you use the words. Training is basically achieving a desirable conditioned response from your dog, and it takes repetition to condition him thoroughly. Eventually, his response to a particular command will become automatic.

Use Clear Commands

Keep your verbal commands short, make them distinguishable from other words, and give them in an authoritative (not loud) tone of voice. Allow a short but reasonable time for your dog to react. Say, "Dog, come," not, "There's a good boy, wouldn't you like to come here?" If you are casual or uncertain, your dog's response will show these same attitudes.

Use Plenty of Praise

Obviously, you should praise your dog whenever he obeys. Even more important is to praise him immediately after you have corrected an incorrect action. Praise is the only way for your dog to recognize acceptable behavior. He cannot understand your words, so make your tone of voice or your touch show approval. If your dog is really uncertain, a few food treats may reassure him. Never substitute food for praise—the incentive to work is much higher if your dog is doing it to please you.

Use Proper Equipment

Equipment does not need to be elaborate, but it must be functional. For most types of training, a medium-weight chain "choke" collar and a flat, six-foot-long leather or nylon leash are best. For herding or tracking, a fifty-foot "long line" (usually made of nylon webbing) is necessary. For tracking, the dog must also wear a properly fitted harness, and you will need a leather glove or wallet for him to find. Nylon choke collars or show leads may be used, or a light chain collar may be substituted for conformation showing of a well-trained dog or for leash-breaking a very young pup. Rolled leather

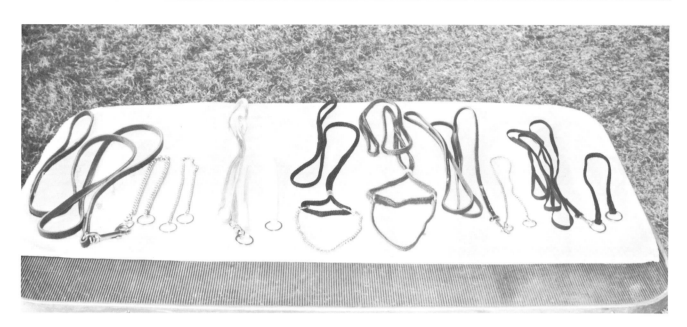

Above: Left to right: Obedience lead and collars, nylon choker and lead, two styles of martingales, fine choke chain and leather lead, and a nylon choker with web lead. The five styles on the right are suitable conformation leads.

Below: The correct way to put on a training collar.

collars are fine for yard wear and are a safety precaution while traveling. These are excellent for use in attaching ID tags, but they are unsuitable for training. Chain leashes are worthless, perhaps even harmful. They cut the handler's hands and hit the dog's face as he works. For this last reason, the metal snap on any lead should be reasonably small.

Use Aids Correctly

The choke collar must be put on the dog so that it tightens over the top of his neck when he is sitting at your left (*see* illustration). This allows the collar to release immediately after a jerk. If it is put on backward, the collar will remain tight, destroying its effectiveness as a training tool and perhaps choking the dog.

The lead should be held so that a slack loop appears at the collar. Fold the lead back and forth and hold the excess in your right hand. When you need to make a correction, quickly tighten and immediately release the pressure of the lead on the collar. Use a series of jerks if necessary, but never apply constant pressure to the collar.

When using a harness, keep your long line taut so that you can "read" your dog's responses to the track or livestock, but never allow a dog to lean into a collar. Correct him with quick jerks and praise. If you need a taut lead for any type of training, use the harness rather than the collar.

Never leave either a choke collar or a harness on a Beardie when you are not giving him a training lesson. He can easily hang himself if left unsupervised. Of lesser importance, but annoying nonetheless, is the fact that the collar will saw off the coat around the neck, leaving your Beardie with a short or bald area that can take months to grow back. If you must leave a collar on at all times, use a rolled leather or nylon collar.

Give Release Commands

Never leave your dog on a stay command without returning to release him. Many trainers use a separate command, "Wait," if they intend to give additional instructions. The dog is not allowed to move even one foot on a formal stay. By not returning to the dog, you teach him to break whenever he is tired of waiting. The dog cannot be blamed if you behave inconsistently in your demands on him.

When a lesson is finished, many trainers use "Okay" or "Free" to indicate that the session has ended and the dog is no longer expected to perform.

Encourage Your Dog to Challenge the Command

A dog that always performs perfectly does not truly know that he must respect the command. He has no idea that he'll be corrected, and therefore, he may be unreliable under a stressed condition. A dog that has lost a disagreement with the trainer over an exercise will be less likely to break later. Vary your training enough so that your dog respects the command in any situation. Distractions are vital in testing a

The proper heel position. Note how handler holds leash.

dog's training. The dog that will work only in a quiet, controlled environment is not really trained. He is only playing along because he has nothing better to do.

Vary Your Technique

If you experience continued problems with a specific exercise, go back to the beginning and retrain that exercise using a different approach that may be better suited to the individual dog. Seek professional advice if possible, or use some of the books listed in the bibliography for reference. Try to determine why your dog reacts as he does, and condition his responses accordingly.

TRAINING TIPS SPECIFIC TO BEARDIES

Beardies can be independent creatures. They are usually self-assured and sometimes strong willed. To train a Beardie successfully, you must establish yourself as the dominant personality so that your Beardie will respect you. Be consistent, but get tough if necessary to get his attention. Respect his intelligence, but demand his obedience. Use praise lavishly when he responds to you. You may think that he's hopeless at first, but after a couple of lessons, he will settle down and become much more manageable.

Beardies usually perform the worst on their "stay" exercises, which are taught first and require the dog to ignore distractions (nearly an impossibility for a Beardie on his first outing). Even if you are certain that your dog is the class dunce, keep working on this exercise (without losing your temper, or at least without letting your dog know that you've lost your temper) until he gives in. After that point, you will find him very quick to learn and rapidly passing his classmates in proficiency. The "stays" are very important for two reasons, so you must master them successfully. First, they establish your dominance over the dog, a condition that is mandatory for any further training. Secondly, the "stay" is fundamental to many future exercises that cannot be taught until the dog knows this step. It is the most useful tool in controlling your dog in everyday situations.

Beardies are very apt pupils, often learning their lessons as quickly as you demonstrate them. However, this same intelligence causes the dog to become easily bored and creatively defiant about performing by rote. You must work with enough speed and variety to keep your dog's interest, and whenever possible, show him a purpose for his actions. Alternate his lessons and create enough variations of each one to make them fun. You'll wind up with a better-trained dog that can perform all sorts of useful tasks.

WHAT EVERY BEARDIE SHOULD KNOW

A few basic concepts are necessary for every Beardie to learn for him to be socially acceptable. These are sometimes referred to as "yard manners" and constitute the very minimum of training that any conscientious owner should expect to do.

Training the dog to stand for examination.

Leash-Breaking

A young puppy can be started wearing a nylon choke collar or an English martingale. Older Beardies should be lead trained with a metal choke collar and leather leash. With the dog on your left side, start walking and encourage your dog to follow. Pat your leg and talk to him. This is not a formal "Heel," so don't use that command. If he follows along, stop after a few yards and pet him. Tell him how good he is, then resume walking. If he balks or runs the other way, give a snap on the lead, release the pressure immediately, and in a lighthearted voice encourage him to come with you. You may need to use several jerks in succession, each followed by praise.

Don't stop walking if your dog screams or throws himself; just ignore him and keep talking happily to him. Do not drag him along on a tight lead; rather, move him with a series of jerks and immediate releases of the collar. When he starts walking willingly, don't make him go too far at a time. A food treat may be offered to encourage him. If your dog forges ahead, jerk him back to your pace, but do not be too severe. Keep the lesson to about ten minutes and repeat once or twice a day until your dog trots along freely on a loose lead.

Sit and Lie Down

Give the verbal command "Sit," pull up on the collar, and push down on your dog's rear. As soon as he's sitting, praise him lavishly. Wait until he knows how to sit before you teach him to lie down. Start with him sitting. Say "Down," and step on his leash, forcing him quickly to the floor. Hold him until he quits struggling. If he resists, kneel beside him with one arm over his body and grasp one of his forelegs in each hand. Give the command "Down," and pull his legs toward you, moving your body into him and forcing him onto his side. Do this a few times, then return to stepping on the leash. Praise him immediately upon his response or your correction.

Stay

Sit your dog at your left side with the collar and leash on. Tell him to stay, and hold your open palm in front of his nose. Step in front of him and face him. If he moves, replace him and jerk up on the collar, repeating the command. Gradually increase the distance between you and your dog until you can walk across the room with him off lead. Always return and give a release command ("OK" or "Free") before allowing him to move.

Play is an important part of training. Ch. Walkoway's Frosted Flakes UD, HC, a BCCA HIT winner, "just having a ball." Owners: Linda and Jim Leek.

Not Jumping on People

Bump your dog's chest with your knee every time he jumps up, and say "No." This should discourage him if you are consistent and correct him *every* time. If you still have problems, grab your dog's front feet and run him backwards like a wheelbarrow. Flip him backward after about ten feet. Pretend that you're having a great time, and he'll soon decide that he doesn't like your game. Do not use the down command, because that should be used to tell your dog to lie down.

A big problem is that many dog-loving visitors will encourage your dog to jump up on them. By using a command such as "Feet" and pulling him off whenever he jumps on anyone, he can learn that jumping up is permitted unless specifically forbidden. If you are expecting visitors, put your Beardie on a leash and have him sit until the first excitement wears off.

Stop Biting

No dog should *ever* be allowed to bite unless he is badly injured and in shock. Stress or fear are not adequate excuses. Some Beardies tend to be "mouthy"—they nibble or grab with their mouths at every excuse. This must be discouraged. A slap on the muzzle and a sharp "No" may be adequate, but if your dog actually snaps, grab him and run your hand down his throat. This renders him unable to bite, but will gag and frighten him. Use your advantage to scold him and exert your dominance. Once your dog backs down, reassure him that you are still friends.

Come When Called

The biggest secret is to always praise your dog when he comes, regardless of how long it takes or what he has done. *Never* call him to you and punish him, or he will have second thoughts about coming the next time. He will think that he has been punished for coming and not connect the correction with any previous action. At three months of age, he will run away, but given another month to develop emotionally, he should come eagerly. Make sure that he trusts you and that you don't grab or frighten him every time he comes within reach. If your dog does not come willingly, he must be insecure about your reaction or motives. Loosen up, and so will your dog.

If your dog continually runs away, attach a long lead and correct him every time he fails to come when called. Follow the correction with a great deal of praise and reassurance.

Five-month-old future Ch. Chantilly High Stakes at Highlander, CGC, practicing the Come.

Coax the dog into show stance using bait.

The puppy should stand still, yet look alert.

SHOW TRAINING

Training a Beardie for conformation showing is simply a matter of keeping him under control. Most Beardies are cheerful extroverts and enjoy showing once they understand what is expected of them. Start training pups between ten weeks and five months of age. Puppies of this age are ready subjects and need to gain confidence in a show atmosphere before they enter adolescence. Keep training sessions short and fun, with a play period as a treat at the end. And remember to praise, praise, and praise.

The first thing that your puppy needs to learn is to trot freely on a loose lead. He should move in a straight line without weaving or crabbing. Use quick jerks and talk to him to bring him back in line. Speed up a bit to get your dog moving with his body in a straight line. When the pup has learned to move smoothly both in a straight line and as you circle the ring, practice making smooth turns (*see* gaiting patterns, Chapter 16) and walking smoothly into a stop as you face an imaginary "judge."

Your puppy must also learn to be friendly and relaxed while being examined by a stranger. Kneel beside your pup and hold his collar with your right hand, steadying him with your left hand resting under his flank. This way you can talk to the puppy and hold him while the judge examines him. Keep the training casual so that your puppy feels that it is a game. Do not worry at this point if he does not position his feet properly or if he does not stand still for more than a few seconds, and always give him plenty of praise.

Practice is required if you hope to obtain perfection. If a conformation training class is held in your area, make use of it. If not, or for additional exposure, take your puppy to shopping centers, parks, or wherever people congregate. Ask people to pet your puppy while you stack him. They will generally be happy to oblige if you explain what you are doing.

As the pup gains proficiency, begin "stacking" him for more control. Lift your puppy by the chest (*see* illustration) and set him down so that his front feet are positioned squarely and

naturally under his body. Hold him steady by placing your right hand under his chin. With your left hand, set his hind feet individually. Position them so that the metatarsus is vertical and slightly behind the line of the hip and about as far apart as the height of his hocks.

Some people continue to show adult dogs in this manner. However, it is most impressive if you can walk the dog into a natural stance and train him to stand squarely while he is "baited" to show expression. Of course, the dog must be constructed properly to be shown naturally, and many structural deficiencies can be minimized by clever stacking. Any knowledgeable judge is aware of this, however. Ch. Shiel's Mogador Silverleaf won a Best in Show because he was stepped forward several times at the judge's request and set himself up perfectly each time.

Right: A Beardie should gait freely on a loose lead.

Bottom Left: Lift the dog to set the front legs.

Bottom Right: Steady the pupy with a hand on his flank.

His closest competitor required constant stacking, and in the final evaluation, the handler had him slightly overstretched. A good Beardie with correct temperament looks better in a natural, alert pose than he does if artificially stacked.

CANINE GOOD CITIZENS

The Canine Good Citizen Test gives dog owners an opportunity to prove that their dog is a well-behaved member of society. It involves a non-competitive pass/fail test that demonstrates the dog's behavior in practical situations in the presence of unfamiliar people and other dogs. Your Beardie will be asked to accept a friendly stranger, walk on a loose lead, sit for petting, walk through a crowd, and respond to the commands Sit, Down, and Stay.

Local dog clubs and dog trainers offer the test. Watch your newspaper or ask a veterinarian or local pet-supply outlet for information. After he successfully completes the test, your Beardie will receive a certificate stating that he is a Canine Good Citizen. Some owners have found this helpful in obtaining rental housing that permits a dog, or admittance to public places where a dog might otherwise be prohibited.

OBEDIENCE TRAINING

Obedience training begins with the same exercises used to teach yard manners but demands more precise reactions and continues into more advanced work. Each exercise has practical applications, and there are three levels of proficiency, each level adding new and more difficult exercises (*see* Chapter 17). The first stage can earn a degree called the Companion Dog (CD), which is indeed descriptive. Any obedience-trained Beardie makes a superior pet, and obedience lessons are highly recommended for any dog. They will enhance your relationship with the dog and benefit him in nearly any capacity. Obedience-trained dogs are often welcomed where other dogs are not allowed.

Ch. Daybreak Storm at Candelaria, UD, HC demonstrates the high jump.

All obedience work is started with your dog in the heel position (sitting at your left with his front legs even with your legs). Once your dog is trained, hs is expected to perform with each command spoken only once. A dog that has been formally trained will work in a precise, efficient manner, which is exciting to watch.

Beardies are excellent workers as long as the routine is varied during training so that they do not get bored. Most Beardies enjoy advanced work if you can struggle through the initial stages of training. The sport of obedience is fun and constructive because it encourages individual achievement. Most communities offer training classes, at least on the beginning level. If you live where classes are not available, consult one of the many fine books on the subject. Be sure to work your dog where there are distractions so that he will be reliably trained for any situation.

OTHER ACTIVITIES FOR BEARDIES

Like other herding breeds, Bearded Collies are happiest when they have something to do. Obedience and show training are just a few of the activities in which Beardies successfully participate. Following are a few others you may wish to consider.

Agility

This exciting sport is rapidly becoming one of the most popular activities for dog owners. Anyone can do it, and Beardies, with their enthusiasm and high energy, are especially well suited to the sport. The agility course originated as a take-off on equestrian grand prix. The dog is required to navigate a series of obstacles and assorted hurdles. The course usually includes scaling an "A" frame, navigating both open and collapsible tunnels, crossing an elevated ramp, a seesaw or sway bridge, jumping, and a course of weave poles. Agility is a timed event that tests the willingness, athletic ability, and training of the dogs. The training also helps to mentally and physically prepare a dog for all types of work, and adds an element of freedom and fun that is lacking in structured obedience exercises.

Backpacking

While not a structured sport, you may find that you enjoy your Beardie's companionship more if

Ch. Walkoway's Frosted Flakes UD, HC crossing the ramp in agility.

you take him with you on camping and day hikes. Doggie backpacks are readily available, and it is easy to train a dog to carry a pack. Just be sure you start out slowly and build up his strength very gradually, and don't try it with your show dog — the pack may ruin his coat for showing. An adult Beardie can pack up to one-third of his body weight, which means he can easily carry his own food and supplies, plus some of yours. You'll be amazed at the bonding

Ch. Highlander Wildest Dreams HCT, CGC, in agility training with owner Beth Tilson.

that takes place when you share a wilderness adventure with him.

Flyball

This is another exciting spectator sport at which some Beardies excel. Teams of four dogs run in relay fashion over a course of jumps to a flyball box, where they must eject and catch the ball and retrieve it back over their jumps to their handler. The event is timed, with the fastest teams in a playoff for championship points. Obedience clubs often organize flyball teams, or you may find an unaffiliated group in your area.

"Catch that Flyball!" Courtesy of Alice Bixler.

Frisbee

Frisbee fetching is a perfect activity for the backyard, but it has also evolved into local, regional, and national competition. Besides being great exercise, your Beardie could win some impressive trophies.

Tracking

Tracking tests are held regularly in almost every location. Sponsored by AKC and UKC obedience and tracking clubs, they allow dogs to qualify for two different levels, Tracking Dog (TD) and Tracking Dog Excellent (TDX). The dog learns to rely on is natural scent discrimination and to work independently.

A tracking dog follows a scent along a track until it leads to a person or article bearing his scent. A well-trained dog can advance to search-and-rescue work or find your lost car keys in heavy underbrush. Either task is infinitely useful and satisfying and is within the reach of any Beardie owner who pursues training his dog to track. Several Beardies have competed in tracking, and the breed seems to excel at it.

A dog must be "certified" by a licensed tracking judge before he can enter a tracking test. The certification involves an informal test given to assure that the dog is qualified to compete. It helps to avoid unnecessary expense and time required to set up a test for dogs that are not ready. A great deal of space is needed, so most tracking tests limit the number of entries. The certification is usually somewhat easier than the actual tracking test, but individual

Jumping for a stick. Ch. Caldelaria Glengarry O'Riley CD, HC, owned by Laura Price and Judith M. LeRoy.

requirements are at the discretion of the judge. Only one tracking test must be successfully completed to obtain a TD.

Complete rules concerning tracking tests may be obtained by writing to the AKC. These rules are updated periodically, so it is wise to obtain a current set of regulations for either tracking or obedience before you start training. Professionally supervised classes in training a tracking dog are held in many areas of the country, or you can attempt training on your own with the help of a good book on the subject (*see* "Other Sources").

Service and Therapy Work

The ability of dogs to bring joy and companionship, as well as to assist, those in less fortunate situations knows no bounds. It takes a mature, somewhat quieter-natured Beardie to function in these roles, however. He must be trainable, intelligent, able to work independently, and have a certain degree of courage or boldness.

Therapy dogs visit the ill, handicapped, or those with learning disabilities. Because of their enthusiasm, Beardies may be too much for an elderly person, but they could excel with youth.

Service dogs assist people who are in wheelchairs, serve as hearing dogs for the deaf, or perform other helping tasks for the disabled.

Can./Am. Ch. Classical Mystique. Courtesy Brigette Nowak.

Ch. Highlander Spellbound HC, ROM, CGC.

Ch. Parcana Silverleaf Vandyke ROM.
Courtesy Mrs. Richard S. Parker.

10 *Building a Better Beardie*

Breeding dogs is not something to be taken lightly. With the breeder rests responsibility for preserving the unique characteristics shaped in the past and the creation of all the breed can become. As the sculptor manipulates his marble, so does the dog breeder express him or herself in canine flesh and blood, and in his or her hands rests the future, good or bad, of the breed.

There are no shortcuts to becoming a successful breeder. The initial building blocks include a thorough understanding of the breed Standard, the dog's anatomy and structure, the laws of inheritance, and the practical applications of genetics. Knowledge of the history of the breed and of the various types and bloodlines provide necessary guidelines in making breeding choices. Through experience, the breeder begins to develop that "sixth sense" seemingly used by all good breeders in choosing the two individual dogs for producing this ideal.

Both science and art are involved. The successful breeder has a comprehensive knowledge of the breed and the tools (genetic principles) that can be applied to produce a better Beardie. Artistically, the breeder forms a mental picture of the ideal Beardie according to his or her interpretation of the Standard and develops a certain "eye" for picking out those individual Beardies that best contribute to this ideal.

THE BUILDING BLOCKS

The science of breeding is based on an understanding of genetics embodying the laws of Mendelian inheritance. The principles are complex and fascinating and can be applied to the reproduction of all living organisms from virii to human beings. When enough data on a particular species are collected, theoretical genetics can be practically applied to increase the chances of obtaining the desired results from a planned breeding.

However, learning to understand and use genetic theory is not easy. With each possible inherited characteristic are many considerations, such as: mode of inheritance of the particular trait; number of genes controlling that trait; whether the trait is inherited from one or both parents; whether there are nonvisible, hidden variations; what possible combinations of the trait can be passed on to the offspring, etc. Several sets of genes may control a single trait, and more than one trait may be inherited at one time. When you begin asking questions about a topic as complex, yet relatively unstudied, as the Bearded Collie, the lack of available documentation becomes frustrating. There are no easy answers to the question, "How do you build a better Beardie?" But perhaps as breeders supply the needed data, the pieces will eventually fall into place if the following basics are understood and applied.

Every body is comprised of cells. These are the smallest living units, and although there are many specialized types of cells, nearly all share a similar structure. The outer layer, called the cell membrane, holds the unit together and conducts the inward progress of building materials and disposing of wastes. The membrane contains a jellylike substance known as cytoplasm. Within the cytoplasm float several specialized units that carry on the chemical processes and life functions of the cell.

In the center of the cell is a smaller body known as the nucleus. Its function is to control the inheritance and the implementation of that inheritance within the cell. The nucleus has a nuclear membrane, nucleoplasm, and the colored threads known as chromosomes. These contain the genes that make an organism unique from all others. The chromosomes, which usually appear as identical pairs, are different in number in every species. Fruit flies are often used for study because their cells contain only four chromosomes, each of which is large and easy to see under a microscope. The complexity of the organism is not determined by how many chromosomes it has. Humans have forty-six chromosomes; dogs have seventy-eight. In the cell, these are long, tangled, and impossible to separate.

On each chromosome are found the genes, or building blocks, for that organism. A gene is thought to be only a point or "locus" on a chromosome. The actual genetic material is the substance that comprises the chromosomes: the long, spiraled, extremely complex molecules known as DNA. DNA contains the "blueprint" for all parts of an organism. Chromosomes from cells in your dog's tail contain genes determining his eye color, controlling the aging process, and perhaps triggering a dreaded disease. The chromosomes that are matched pairs are called "alleles." They can be aligned together, with matching points representing genes for the same trait. One allele is inherited from each parent, and only one can be passed on to the offspring. The infinite reshuffling of these genes makes every organism unique.

The messages and timed releases in the DNA are transmitted throughout the body to the proper place by a substance in the cytoplasm known as RNA. RNA serves as a messenger between the nuclear membrane and the rest of the body. The DNA never leaves the nucleus except during cell division (reproduction).

Cell Division

Normal cell division is called mitosis. It occurs during growth of the organism and continues to replace old cells throughout the life of the organism. During this process, the chromosomes duplicate themselves, separate from their newly formed twins, and become two sets of chromosomes, each set identical to the original. The cytoplasm pinches in two, and the cell membrane closes around each new nucleus. Two identical new cells now appear where formerly there was one.

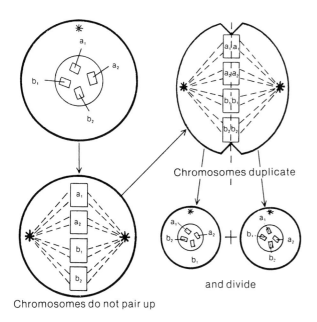

Above: Mitosis, or normal cell division.

Below: Meiosis, division of the reproductive calls.

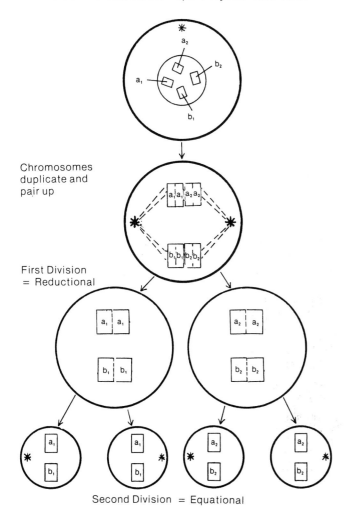

The only exception to mitosis occurs in the "gametes," or reproductive cells. These cells contain only one allele from each set and therefore have only half the normal number of chromosomes. Their sole function is to supply DNA from a parent to an offspring. It is purely chance which of the two alleles transfers to which gametes, and no two gametes will be alike for all traits. These gametes will combine with equally random gametes from the other parent to produce a new entity. This is why no two puppies, even littermates (except identical twins), are exactly alike in either appearance or producing ability.

The division of the sex cells to form gametes is known as meiosis. During this process, the alleles come together in a complicated dance but do *not* duplicate themselves. The corresponding alleles move to opposite sides of the cell, and the cytoplasm divides between them. The result is two new cells, each containing half the genetic material of the original.

Assume that each parent has the following pairs of traits (eye color, tail length, size of spinal column, or what have you). Each gene will be expressed in a slightly different manner, but these alleles all control the same traits.

AaBBcc is the genetic makeup of the father.

aaBbCC is the genetic makeup of the mother.

Their gametes will contain only one allele for each trait, but the possible combinations are numerous.

The father can produce these combinations:

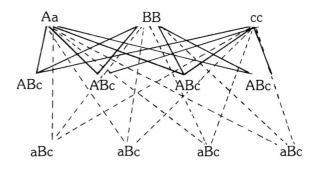

equal chances of ABc, ABc, ABc, ABc, aBc, aBc, aBc, and aBc

or: ½ ABc and ½ aBc

Combine these with the eight possible choices from the mother which are:

aBC, aBC, abC, abC, aBC, aBC, abC, and abC

or: ½ aBC and ½ abC.

To determine the possible combinations of offspring, form a genetic box:

Parent #1	ABc	aBc
aBC	AaBBCc	aaBBCc
abC	AaBbCc	aaBbCc

(*Parent #2* labels the left column pairs aBC and abC)

There is an equal chance of each result shown within each square. Multiply these by as many traits as you can imagine, and you'll have some idea of why there will always be an element of chance in breeding. Breeders can only improve the odds for a certain result.

Dominant and Recessive Characteristics

In the simplest form of inheritance, a dog carries two genes for a trait (one inherited from each parent). If they are the same, the dog is said to be *homozygous* for that trait. If they are different, he is *heterozygous* for the trait.

When the alleles (pairs of genes) are homozygous, the genotype (genetic makeup) for that trait is obvious in the phenotype (the dog's appearance). However, when the heterozygous condition occurs, only *one* gene is apparent in the dog's phenotype. He may be identical to the homozygous dog for that trait (in which case the gene is dominant), but he may carry the opposite trait (if the gene is recessive). When the dog displays the dominant trait, it is impossible to tell just by looking at him whether he is homozygous or heterozygous. However, if he produces a puppy exhibiting the recessive trait, it can be determined that the parent is heterozygous. The dominant gene will completely mask its recessive counterpart, but either one (not both) can be passed on to the offspring. When a recessive trait is expressed, the dog must be homozygous, or "pure," for that trait. A homozygous dominant individual will always produce his own likeness in the next generation, because the dominant allele will mask a recessive that may be inherited from the other parent.

Applicable Facts

1. Each parent contributes half of the genetic makeup of the offspring. *Both* parents must be of good quality before success can be expected.
2. The first two generations contribute most of the genes to a puppy. Dogs more distant in the genetic line have less influence unless they are repeated in the pedigree several times.
3. Littermates may be virtually unrelated genetically and therefore may not produce alike.
4. A recessive trait can be masked completely by its dominant allele. Therefore, the genotype (genetic makeup) must be considered as well as the phenotype (appearance).
5. A dog carrying a hidden recessive is heterozygous for that trait. He can pass on one allele or the other, but not both, to any given puppy.
6. A dog pure for a trait is homozygous for it. He can only pass on the trait as he shows it.
7. A dog that exhibits a recessive characteristic must be homozygous for that trait.
8. A dominant trait cannot be present unless at least one parent shows it.
9. Many traits are polygenic (controlled by more than one pair of genes) or are influenced by modifiers, so they are not inherited in simple dominant/recessive patterns.
10. Genes located near to each other on a chromosome tend to be inherited together as one unit and are difficult to separate in controlled breeding.
11. Mutations do occur but are very rare. Recessive genes carried by both parents usually account for unexpected results.

GENETICS AND HEALTH

Some health and structural problems can be considered genetic, and a judicious application of basic genetic knowledge to a breeding program can help prevent their occurrence. About one hundred diseases or defects in the dog are known or believed to be hereditary. Some, such as heart, eye, and hip abnormalities, affect the health and usefulness of the dog. Others, such as dewclaws on all four feet, blue eyes, etc., are simply undesirable.

Raising an otherwise promising Beardie only to find that he has a hereditary defect is one of the most devastating experiences that a breeder has to face. It is always a difficult problem, and the temptation is to ignore or disbelieve the diagnosis. The most harmful thing that a breeder can do is to mislead others with related stock about the nature of the condition. When a serious genetic defect occurs with a high degree of frequency in a line, its impact can be serious, and, if uncontrolled, it can ruin a breed. Once a defect becomes widespread, it may take generations of carefully selective breeding to eliminate it, if, indeed, it can even be eradicated. Also, many hereditary problems are not easily discernible, especially to the novice; therefore, they go unnoticed and are perpetuated.

Beardies came to America as a relatively unspoiled breed. They are among those breeds that display the least tendency toward hereditary defects. However, there are isolated instances in *every* breed, and several closely related breeds already have seen the devastating effect of breeding afflicted dogs. The only way to avoid problems is to be aware of the possible threats and to be thorough in checking all breeding stock and their offspring.

What is a Hereditary Defect?

A *congenital* defect is present at birth. It may be inherited or be the result of intrauterine factors such as nutritional deficiency, toxicity, or the effect of a drug administered to the bitch during pregnancy. An *inherited* defect is transmitted on the genes. It is possible for a defect to be *both* hereditary and congenital. Unfortunately, not all inherited defects are visible at birth. A dog with progressive retinal atrophy may be normal at weaning and develop clinical blindness by six months of age, while another dog may not develop signs of diminished vision until he is six years of age or older.

Gene combinations that produce defects take many forms. They may be dominant, recessive, or incompletely dominant. They may or may not be sex-linked (i.e., perpetuated by or affecting only one sex because the gene for the defect lies on the sex chromosome). If only one pair of genes is responsible for the defective characteristic, the fault is said to be *autosomal*. This is the ideal genetic situation and can be eliminated most easily. However, if more than one pair of genes is involved, as is often the case, the defect will be much harder to breed out. This occurrence is referred to as *multisomal* inheritance.

To further complicate the problem, not enough is known about many defects to enable researchers to accurately determine which type of inheritance pattern is involved. In addition, a breed may be predisposed to a problem even though direct inheritance cannot be demonstrated, as in the case of "Collie nose."

A discussion of some of the more common hereditary defects found in Beardies follows. There are, of course, numerous others.

Eye Defects

Eye defects, which have plagued dog breeders for years, may also be present in Bearded Collies. Although veterinarians report that the incidence of eye anomalies in Beardies affects only a small percentage of the total Beardie population, there is adequate cause for being alert.

The Eye Structure. The colored portion of the eye is called the iris. In the center of the iris is the pupil (the dark area), through which light enters the eye.

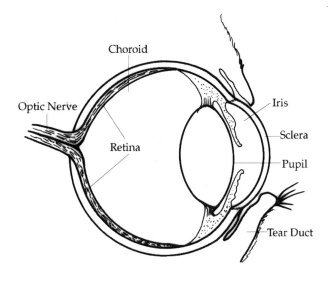

Structures of the eye.

Basically, the eye is constructed in three layers. The outer layer—the sclera—coats and protects the entire eyeball. A middle layer, called the choroid, lies between the retina and the sclera and is a highly vascular structure. The inner lining of the eye—the retina—is a neural, light-sensitive layer.

Light enters the eye through the pupil, then reaches the retina. Here, the light is converted to nervous impulses which are then transmitted to the brain by the optic nerve. This process produces sight. The area on which the image is projected is called the fundus. The fundus consists of the tapetal, or reflective part, and the nontapetal, or nonreflective area. The tapetal portion of the fundus has the texture of fine, granulated beading, literally a projection screen. In the center of this area is the optic disc, where the optic nerve and the blood vessels enter the eyeball.

Progressive Retinal Atrophy. Two hereditary retinal atrophies have been identified, and they affect many breeds. One is generalized atrophy, referred to as PRA. The other is central progressive retinal atrophy, or CPRA. Both diseases are progressive and eventually result in blindness. Retinal atrophy may not appear until the dog is two years of age or older, making him difficult to eliminate from breeding stock.

PRA is generally attributed to a simple autosomal recessive; thus, both parents may have normal eyes but harbor the damaging recessive genes. PRA advances in stages. Initially, the pupils are semidilated and respond sluggishly to light. There is increased tapetal reflectivity and some loss of granular beading, and the small blood vessels are diminished in size.

Next, the pupils become dilated and have little response to light. The granular beading nearly disappears, along with the smaller vessels. As the disease progresses, the disc becomes pale and the nontapetal fundus grows lighter in color, developing a mottled appearance. In the final stage, the pupils become fully dilated and have absolutely no response to light. All of the vessels may disappear from the fundus, and the dog becomes totally blind. Both eyes are usually affected equally.

The first warning of PRA that you may observe is night blindness. Initially, the dog will show signs of reduced vision only in darkness or diminished light. Later, he will become day blind as well. Many owners see this as a personality change and wonder why their dog reacts differently in low-light situations. They may not realize that the dog is blind until some time after total blindness has occurred.

Central progressive retinal atrophy (CPRA) seems to be less common in most breeds related to the Bearded Collie. Research directed toward how the disease is inherited is being conducted but is inconclusive at this time. The initial signs of CPRA differ from those of PRA. In PRA, night blindness is the first clinical sign, whereas this symptom occurs late in CPRA. In CPRA, the owner first observes that his dog has difficulty picking out objects directly in front of him but still has good peripheral vision. Because the central portion of the retina is affected initially, the outer portions continue to function, and the dog does not become totally sightless until a later stage of the disease.

At this time, there is only one positive diagnostic method capable of detecting PRA in puppies, and it can only be done by competent specialists. This method is not yet widely available.

It is called the electroretinograph, or ERG. The puppy is anesthetized, and a special contact lens is fitted over each eye and connected to an electrical recording device. A strong source of light is then flashed in the pup's eye, and the reaction is recorded. This gives a clear, positive evaluation and saves years of waiting until the disease can be detected by ophthalmic examination. Under regular ophthalmic examination, the disease cannot be recognized until the dog is mature, and it may not appear until he is five years old. By this time, he will, if used for breeding, have children and grandchildren also being used for breeding. *All* offspring of an affected dog will be carriers of the defect.

Cataracts. Although little information is available concerning cataracts in Beardies, a related breed—the Old English Sheepdog—is plagued with a hereditary form of this problem. The type affecting sheepdogs is called juvenile cataracts and usually appears after six years of age. The condition exists in many breeds and is dominant in some, recessive in others. The mode of inheritance in sheepdogs is undetermined at this time.

In severe cases, juvenile cataracts progress to blindness. In milder afflictions, they can advance to a certain point, then remain static, causing some sight impairment. Occasionally, a cataract will go into remission and sight will improve.

If the cataract is unilateral (in one eye only), no treatment is recommended. If both eyes are affected (bilateral cataracts), surgical removal of the cataracts is indicated. No early diagnosis is available, and the first positive sign of the condition may be the appearance of a cloudy spot on the eye. Ophthalmic diagnosis is possible at a slightly earlier stage.

Hip Dysplasia

Hip dysplasia is a hereditary, developmental condition caused by several different genes (polygenic). It occurs in both humans and animals. It occasionally shows up in puppies as young as eight weeks of age but more commonly cannot be detected until somewhere between the ages of four months and two years. A Beardie may go through life with a very mild degree of dysplasia that is noticeable only as a sort of hitch in his rear gait, or he may be severely affected and have a great deal of pain. If your dog falls easily, sways from side to side when walking, or has noticeable difficulty getting up, suspect dysplasia.

The hip joint is a ball-and-socket joint. The thigh bone of the dog has an offset protrusion at the top in the shape of a ball. Normally, this ball fits into a socket in the pelvis and is held firmly in place by muscles and ligaments. The hip joint of newborn puppies is reported to be normal, but then the initiating genetic factors begin to cause a poor fit or function. The socket may not be deep enough, or it may be improperly formed. Or the ball is not properly formed and may not fit well into the socket. Either condition is diagnosed as hip dysplasia.

Diagnosis and the OFA. The only positive method of diagnosing dysplasia is by radiography (X-ray). This should be done when the dog is in good health. Bitches should not be in season or have recently whelped, nor should the dog have had a prolonged period of inactivity, because these situations can affect the radiographic appearance of the hip joint. Proper positioning and radiographic technique are essential. Obtaining the correct position may require restraint. The type of restraint—physical, sedative, tranquilizer, or general anesthesia—is best left to the veterinarian.

The Orthopedic Foundation of America (OFA), a not-for-profit organization, was established to check and certify dogs of all breeds for freedom from hip dysplasia. Your veterinarian will send the X-ray, the application form, and the fee to the OFA. The X-ray is then sent to three different radiologists for evaluation. The results are sent to the owner and to the veterinarian.

The OFA classification, based on comparison with other dogs of the same breed and age, are as follows:

1. Excellent conformation
2. Good conformation
3. Fair conformation
4. Borderline conformation (a new X-ray is recommended in six months)
5. Mild dysplasia
6. Moderate dysplasia
7. Severe dysplasia

Only the first three categories are considered normal and assigned an OFA number certifying freedom from dysplasia.

Inheritance — Being polygenic in mode of inheritance, hip dysplasia is difficult to breed out of a line or breed of dogs. Many genes are involved, and all must occur in a dog before the condition is expressed. Nondysplastic Beardies may not have any of the genes for dysplasia, or the genes may be present but not in the right combination for the defect to be expressed. The latter may produce dysplastic puppies if mated with another carrier.

In 1989, the OFA published tables ranking breeds with 100 or more submissions of X-rays according to the frequency of dysplasia. Beardies were fifty-fifth lowest out of eighty-two breeds. The percentages out of 1,085 Beardies evaluated were: excellent, 10.0; good, 67.3; fair, 11.6; borderline, 0.8; mild, 4.3; moderate, 3.8; severe, 2.1. (These figures do not reflect the actual frequency of dysplasia, because the more obvious cases are usually not submitted.)

Selectively breeding for normal progeny is the only effective method for controlling the frequency of hip dysplasia. The following guidelines are suggested:

1. Breed only normal dogs to normal dogs.
2. The normal dogs should come from normal parents and normal grandparents.
3. The normal dogs should have greater than 75 percent normal siblings. A dog rated fair with more than 75 percent normal siblings is a better prospect than a dog rated excellent but with more than 25 percent of his siblings dysplastic.

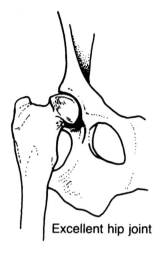

Excellent hip joint

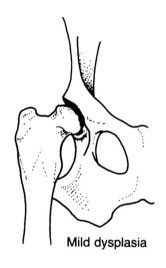

Mild dysplasia

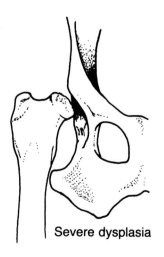

Severe dysplasia

Excellent hip joint, mild dysplasia, and severe dysplasia.

4. Choose replacement bitches that have better hips than their parents.

This, of course, is a tremendous undertaking, and without the cooperation of breeders in obtaining certification and making this information available, it is impossible. The American Kennel Club is helping by putting the OFA number of certified sires and dams on the registration certificates of their offspring.

Skin Disorders

There is a tendency for Beardies to develop sebaceous cysts, especially as they age. These are lumps in the skin that move freely with the skin. They are virtually always benign and rarely cause any problems unless they are in an area that is easily irritated, in which case a veterinarian can easily remove them. Cysts, as well as a tendency to warts, may be associated with the graying factor.

Pink skin on the bridge of the nose, often occurring with a white blaze, may be easily sunburned and may lead to "Collie nose" (solar dermatitis).

Autoimmune Problems

Autoimmune (immune-mediated) disease has been increasing in recent years in both humans and animals. This has been attributed to factors such as genetic and sex predisposition, nutritional influences, viral infections or frequent use of modified live-virus vaccines, and pituitary-thyroid imbalances.

Addison's Disease. A number of cases of Addison's Disease have been reported in Beardies recently. Some breeders believe it to be hereditary, but this has not been proven. Most cases are believed to be idiopathic (cause unknown or uncertain) but probably immune-mediated. Two facts suggest an environmental

factor. First, there are more immune-mediated diseases in some states than in others, and second, in humans there are cases of identical twins raised in different environments, one contracting Addison's, the other not. Possible environmental factors that may initiate the disease are infections, drugs given for other diseases, steroids added to feed, arsenic or steroids given for coat growth, and the large number of vaccinations given to puppies, which may overwhelm their immune systems. Environmental factors could mimic hereditary factors when dogs are raised in the same environment.

Addison's Disease is the failure of the adrenal glands to manufacture sufficient cortisol-glucosteroids, which relieve stress, and mineralosteroids, which control the sodium/potassium balance. It is probable that the destruction of the adrenal cortex occurs gradually over a period of time without noticeable symptoms and that stress precipitates the acute condition known as Addison's.

The onset of Addison's Disease is characterized by lethargy and weakness with the avoidance of exercise, loss of appetite, and a significant increase in water intake and urination. Unfortunately, these symptoms also can indicate several other conditions. However, *any* marked increase in water consumption and urination is a danger signal and should be checked immediately by lab work. A physical examination may reveal a low pulse rate and mild anemia, and an EKG or ultrasound may show heart abnormalities. Lab work will indicate low sodium and high potassium. For a definitive diagnosis, this *must* be followed by taking a baseline blood sample and then giving an injection of ACTH to see if the adrenals will respond and make more cortisol.

Drugs are available for maintenance therapy but must be continued for the lifetime of the dog. Once your dog is stabilized and dosages are adjusted to individual needs, he can be expected to live a full, normal life. Neutering is generally recommended as well as helping your dog to avoid unnecessary stress.

Heart Defects

Twenty-five distinct forms of congenital heart disease have been found in dogs. Some are rare, while others are fairly common. Together, they form one of the more common types of hereditary defect.

One form, patent ductus arteriosus (PDA), is fairly common. It is believed to be hereditary and of a polygenic nature. Test matings conducted with mixed breeds show that when a normal dog is mated with a known carrier of PDA, nearly 59 percent of the puppies are affected; when two defective dogs are mated, the ratio increases to 68 percent.

Prior to birth, a blood vessel in the whelp, called the ductus arteriosus, allows blood pumped from the right side of the heart to bypass the nonfunctioning lungs. At birth, as soon as the puppy starts using his lungs, the ductus normally closes and blood circulates through the lungs for proper oxygenation. The term "patent ductus arteriosus" refers to a condition in which the ductus fails to close after birth, allowing blood to recirculate through the lungs. This overworks and enlarges the heart. If the patent ductus arteriosus is large, the volume of blood shunted to the pulmonary circulation will be correspondingly great and may result in congestion of the lungs and heart failure. This can be evidenced by shortness of breath, rapid, labored breathing, coughing, and, occasionally, collection of fluid in the abdominal cavity. If the ductus is small, the dog may appear normal for years.

PDA is generally accompanied by a heart murmur, which usually can be detected by a veterinarian when a puppy is two to three weeks old. Severe cases develop signs of heart failure before weaning, and it is often possible to feel the throbbing heart vibrating in the chest. Most affected dogs will present signs of cardiac insufficiency before maturity. Chest X-rays and an electrocardiogram are beneficial in establishing a positive diagnosis. The condition can be corrected surgically by tying off the ducts, thus eliminating the abnormal pattern of blood flow, and the dog can usually then lead a normal life. If a corrected dog is bred, however, *all* of the puppies will be carriers of the defect.

Monorchidism or Cryptorchidism

When a male Beardie is born, the testes will not be easily felt. As the puppy grows, the testes descend into the scrotum. Sometimes this does not happen, and either one or both testicles remain in the abdominal cavity or do not completely descend. A dog with one testicle descended is called a *monorchid*; one with neither testicle descended is commonly referred to as a *cryptorchid*. The condition is hereditary, probably in a simple recessive form. Occasionally, testicle descent can be delayed or prevented by the administration of antibiotics to either the dam or the puppies at critical stages of development.

AKC regulations for conformation showing state that testicles must be normally descended. Therefore, it is unethical for a veterinarian to do surgery to a show dog or give medications that might cause the testicle to come down. When testicles do not descend properly, they are held at a higher body temperature, which has been related to an increased incidence of testicular tumors. Therefore, the best procedure is to have the dog castrated.

In Beardies, both testicles have usually descended by eight weeks of age. Sometimes, the testicles do descend into position, but the puppy may be able to pull them up into the abdomen so tightly that they cannot be palpated. You can be sure that both testicles are descended properly only when they grow large enough to prevent their being pulled out of reach. It is not uncommon for a veterinarian to advise that a Beardie male three months of age without both testicles in position be discarded as a show or breeding prospect. This is a bit harsh, but a male whose testicles cannot be found at least most of the time by four months of age is a questionable risk. Be aware of the evidence supporting the claim that dogs with testicles descending late tend to produce monorchid or cryptorchid puppies with greater frequency than normal males.

Although monorchids are usually fertile, they should never be used at stud.

Epilepsy

One of the oldest brain diseases affecting man—epilepsy—also occurs in dogs. There are many kinds of epilepsy and many causes, including tumors, post-traumatic scars, inflammation, and lesions due to infectious agents such as viral infection, mycotic substances, and bacteria. The distemper virus is a very common cause. Only when all other causes have been ruled out should a dog be considered to have idiopathic (cause unknown, possibly hereditary) epilepsy. Most cases have specific acquired causes. The idiopathic form has been suspected by some breeders to affect Bearded Collies, because it seems to reappear to a small extent in certain lines. Expert neurologists are clearly skeptical but allow the possibility of this occurrence. No clinical evidence, however, supports such claims. It is also possible that an inherited predisposition makes certain lines more susceptible to outside influences and, therefore, to increased epilepsy.

The inherited form of grand mal epilepsy is characterized by recurring seizures during which the dog may be unconscious. Alternating muscular contractions and relaxation occur, followed by running movements. Profuse salivation, urination, and defecation often occur. Sometimes the dog will howl, become restless, or show marked behavioral changes just before a seizure. After a seizure, the dog usually is physically exhausted for varying periods of time and may be temporarily blind.

Typically, in the inherited form of grand mal epilepsy, seizures begin when the dog is in his second year of life, although they may occur earlier. The convulsions are recurrent, with few, if any, other physical signs. The seizure pattern becomes progressively more severe, with seizures occurring more frequently and with greater intensity. Single seizures are not life-threatening; however, if several occur in a series with little or no time interval (status epilepticus), the dog could die from hyperthermia and electrolytic imbalances. Seizures can usually be controlled somewhat by the use of anticonvulsant drugs.

If a Beardie is known to have epilepsy and all physical causes have been ruled out, the inherited form of the disease should be suspected. Because the cause is difficult to determine, dogs with epilepsy (or ones producing it frequently) should not be kept in a breeding program.

Solar Nasal Dermatitis

Solar nasal dermatitis is referred to as "Collie nose" because it is most commonly seen in Collies and related breeds. It is found in many breeds, usually in ones that have white blazes and a corresponding tendency to have light spots of unpigmented skin on the bridge of the muzzle. Essentially, the condition is an inflammatory reaction of the skin on the nose, and occasionally around the eyes, to sunlight. Studies have been unable to pinpoint the cause. Beardies are slightly predisposed, but inheritance studies have been inconclusive.

The first sign of Collie nose is loss of pigment at the junction of the haired and nonhaired tissue of the nose and sometimes around the eyelids. The hair will drop off; a lesion will develop, then crust, and finally scale. When the scale is rubbed off, the area will bleed. The lesions may spread up the nose to the eyes, into the nares, and possibly onto the upper lip. If the eyes are affected, conjunctivitis may develop. Untreated Collie nose can result in cancer of the nose. Lesions similar to Collie nose can be caused by infections or neoplasia. Therefore, a positive diagnosis should be made before any treatment is started.

Keeping the affected Beardie out of sunlight, and sometimes out of all light, is beneficial but impractical. Topical applications of sunscreen preparations or medicated ointments may help somewhat. Corticosteroids may be prescribed orally. Tattooing the affected area works in many cases but is expensive and usually only temporary. The condition tends to become more severe in summer with increased exposure to sunlight. Beardies with Collie nose should only be bred very judiciously, and careful records must be kept.

Smooth Coats

The very occasional occurrence of smooth-coated specimens in Bearded Collies causes concern to breeders. Some claim that it is the result of impure breeding (probably crosses with Border Collies) during the formative years of the breed. This statement, plus the use of the term "Border Collie throwbacks" instead of "Smooth Beardies" by some breeders, has brought unfortunate and unwarranted attention by the AKC to this problem in the breed. Smooth specimens occur in many breeds, and breeders simply eliminate and don't register them knowingly. A dog that produces large numbers of smooths (or any other undesirable characteristic) should be retired from breeding. The only reason for panic is that breeders in the United States chose for several years to hush up the topic and not admit its existence. This, in turn, created panic when novices accidentally produced smooths and did not know what they were. Open communication of any problem is the only way to solve it.

Many English breeders are aware of the problem, and apparently, specimens have appeared in very small numbers in most lines. Because most modern dogs trace to the same ancestors, this is not surprising. Inheritance is inconclusive, but the trait may be a simple recessive. In many breeds, smooth coats are dominant, but this cannot be the case in the Bearded Collie breed. Multiple gene control or variable expressivity are likely. No line can be completely free of the possibility of producing a smooth, and the only sensible approach is to eliminate smooths and avoid breeding dogs that are known to engender this fault.

Some breeders claim that the temperament (wouldn't *you* become shy if you were a freak kept around just to demonstrate a point?) and structure of "smooth Beardies" are different from normal Beardies. The differences, however, are no more than those that occur from one individual Beardie to the next. The impression made by coat changes the entire look of the dog.

Just be aware that the condition exists, and try to avoid perpetuating or increasing its incidence in your breeding program. You will probably never encounter a smooth individual even after several years of breeding.

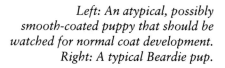

Left: An atypical, possibly smooth-coated puppy that should be watched for normal coat development. Right: A typical Beardie pup.

Other Defects

Many defects occur in dogs. Distichiasis, a condition in which the eyelashes turn inward, is sometimes seen. Hemophilia—the inability of the blood to clot properly—is a recessive, sex-linked, hereditary defect. A normal male will not be a carrier, but a normal bitch can carry the disease without exhibiting signs of it herself.

There is a small incidence in some working breeds of patellar luxation, a condition in which the stifle joint slips out of position, creating a hopping motion in the gait. This defect is rare if angulation is adequate in the rear. Over- and undershot jaws are hereditary in nature, as are other conditions.

CONTROLLING GENETIC DEFECTS

The sensible approach to genetic defects is to be aware that they exist in Beardies and to strive to eliminate from breeding all known or suspected defectives. If a Beardie develops *any* serious structural or physical defect that your veterinarian cannot attribute to injury, illness, or other environmental conditions, suspect the fault to be genetic in nature.

Telling someone not to breed their defective dog is easy. Observing that rule when the defective dog is your own champion or prospective champion is something else. And there's an old saying among dog breeders that the pick of the litter always seems to have the defect. The only real answer, then, is to weigh what this dog can contribute to the breed against the disadvantages of breeding him.

Using the symbol "N" to represent normal, and assuming that it is dominant, and using the symbol "d" to represent a simple recessive defect, the expected inheritance patterns can be charted. Keep in mind that many defects involve more than one pair of genes, which makes the situation much more involved.

Assume that you have a defective dog and you mate it. You probably have no way of knowing if your dog's mate is also a carrier for that defect. But assume that the mate is *not* a carrier, making the dog "NN." The results would be:

Parent #2 | Parent #1

	d	d
N	Nd	Nd
N	Nd	Nd

dd plus NN = all puppies Nd, or all carriers

If you breed the defective Beardie to a known carrier:

Parent #2 | Parent #1

	d	d
d	dd	dd
N	Nd	Nd

dd plus Nd = 50% Nd (carriers), 50% dd (defective)

Now, look at what happens when you breed just the carriers—the pups that you produced when you bred your defective Beardie to a Beardie not carrying the defect at all (provided you were able to determine this). You will have:

Parent #2 | Parent #1

	N	d
d	Nd	dd
N	NN	Nd

Nd plus Nd =
25% normal puppies (NN)
50% carriers (Nd), and
25% defective puppies (dd)

The only way to prove that a dog is not carrying the genes for a defect is to test-mate him with a known defective dog. Outside of the laboratory, test matings are generally inconclusive and only add to the number of carriers being produced. It takes many litters with different combinations of parents to definitely establish that a dog is a noncarrier. For your protection, and for the protection of the Bearded Collie as a breed, it is far better not to use any Beardie known to have a hereditary defect or known to be a carrier for a genetic defect.

Endnotes

[1] Donald F. Patterson, DVM, D.Sc. and R. L. Pyle, VMD. "Genetic Aspects of Congenital Heart Disease in the Dog," in *The New Knowledge About Dogs.* Papers presented at the Twenty-First Gaines Veterinary Symposium, Octobe 20, 1971. Ames, Iowa.

[2] "Congenital Heart Disease in the Dog," in *Circulation Research*, XX, August 1968.

[3] Leon F. Whitney, *How to Breed Dogs.* New York: Howell Book House, 1971, p. 33

[4] *Ibid.*, p. 316.

Ch. Osmart Smoky Blue Parcana, ROMX.

11 *Color Schemes*

Coat-color inheritance in Bearded Collies is one of the few areas in which breeders can reliably apply their knowledge of genetics. Even this concern, however, poses some unanswered questions.

Beardie pups are born one of four colors—black, brown, blue, or fawn—with or without white and/or tan markings. Genetically, there are just two basic colors in Beardies—black and brown. Anything else results from modifications of these colors or from factors added to them. Black is the dominant color, and brown is recessive to it. Blue and fawn are the results of a modifying gene that dilutes black to blue and brown to fawn. Nondilution is dominant over the recessive dilution. A dog must be pure for any recessive to exhibit that trait.

The standard symbol designation for genetic characteristics is the first letter of the word representing the *recessive* of a trait and would appear in lowercase. The corresponding dominant would use the capital of that letter. Therefore, any dog with a symbol "B" would be black. Because it is dominant and can carry a hidden recessive, a black dog could be either homozygous BB (pure for black) or heterozygous Bb (brown-factored). A brown dog would be a homozygous recessive and would be designated "bb." The symbol for dilution will be "d"; the symbol for the dominant nondilution, "D." A black or brown dog can be either DD or Dd. A blue or fawn dog must be dd. **Two pairs of** genes (two for color and two for dilution) determine a dog's color at birth and the color combinations that he can pass on to his offspring.

GENETIC PROFILES

Considering only the color at birth, the following genetic makeups are possible for Beardies:

Black (must have one "B" and one "D")
    BBDD—not carrying brown or dilution
    BbDD—carrying brown but not dilution
    BBDd—carrying dilution but not brown
    BbDd—carrying both brown and dilution

Brown (must be homozygous brown and carry one "D")
    bbDD—not carrying dilution
    bbDd—carrying dilution

Blue (must have one "B" and be pure for dilution)
    BBdd—not carrying brown
    Bbdd—carrying brown

Fawn (pure for both recessives)
    bbdd

Because each parent can contribute only one gene from each pair (randomly combined), the following are the possible combinations from each of the above genetic makeups:

Blacks
    BBDD—only a B and a D
    BbDD—BD or bD
    BBDd—BD or Bd
    BbDd—BD, Bd, bD, or bd

Browns
    bbDD—only bD
    bbDd—bD or bd

Blues
    BBdd—only Bd
    Bbdd—Bd or bd

Fawns
    bbdd—only bd

The possible results of breeding any two individuals can be determined by constructing genetic squares. Make a chart with the possible combinations of the sire across the top, and the possible combinations of the dam down the side. Then fill in the squares with a combination of one set from each parent. This gives the possible colors as well as the statistical probabilities. These odds might not hold true for any given litter, only over a very large number of litters. You might not get each possibility, but you will *not* get any that are not on the chart.

Example: Breeding a black dog carrying brown but not dilution to a fawn bitch.

Parent #1

Parent #2		BD	bD
	bd	BbDd	bbDd
	bd	BbDd	bbDd

The results would be one-half black and one-half brown, all carrying dilution.

Example: Two black parents, both carrying brown and dilution.

Parent #1

Parent #2		BD	Bd	bD	bd
	BD	BBDD	BBDd	BbDD	BbDd
	Bd	BBDb	BdBd	BbDd	Bbdd
	bD	BbDD	BbDd	bbDD	bbDb
	bd	BbDd	Bbdd	bbDd	bbdd

If you had sixteen puppies, your odds would be:

    1 BBDD black
    2 BBDd blacks
    2 BbDD blacks
    4 BbDd blacks
    2 bbDd browns
    1 bbDD brown
    1 BBdd blue
    2 Bbdd blues
    1 bbdd fawn

You cannot tell by looking at a dog if he carries a hidden recessive, but you do have some clues. If one parent is a recessive, all the puppies will carry that recessive. If one of the grandparents is a recessive, there is a 25-percent chance that a puppy carries it. If one grandparent on each side is the same recessive there is a 50-percent chance that a puppy will carry that recessive. If one parent has produced a recessive in a prior litter, there is a 25-percent chance. If both parents have produced the recessive in prior litters, there is a 50-percent chance. You can make charts like the ones above for any possible breeding combination.

White should not surround the eye at the skin.

WHITE MARKINGS

White markings are the result of a factor added to rather than modifying the base colors. The white markings characteristically found on Beardies are derivatives of the "Irish" pattern. In its full expression, this pattern superimposes itself on the base color as a white shawl collar, front legs, chest, hind feet, and tail tip. A face blaze may accompany the Irish body pattern.

White found on any part of the Bearded Collie may be broken into three separate inheritable patterns. None have any bearing on the presence or absence of any other white pattern factor present in a given individual. A dog may carry any or all of these factors.

One factor determines the markings on the head and is inherited separately from the white body patterns. On Beardies, anything from a plain face to a wide, white blaze connecting to

Unacceptably marked "white" puppies.

the collar is acceptable. Predominately white heads or markings at the skin line that extend onto the ears or surrounding the eyes are considered undesirable. While a full blaze can contribute to a pleasing expression, a plainer face must not be discriminated against. Acceptable full blazes seem to be inherited as incomplete dominants. The excessively white and asymmetrically marked heads are relatively uncommon and are probably recessive in nature.

The white appearing anywhere behind the head can be divided into two factors. The Irish pattern fully or partially expressed is acceptable. It ranges from minimum white points, to a partial collar, to full markings. Any combination is considered acceptable. The full pattern tends to be dominant but is probably caused by more than one set of genes; therefore, it can be inherited unexpectedly in certain combinations.

There is another unacceptable white body pattern which, when fully expressed, creates a white dog with colored spots. This pattern is also responsible for white body spots or any white extending past the normal Irish pattern. The genes accountable for this condition are referred to as "white factor," and a predominately white dog is called "white." Whites can have completely colored heads because, as mentioned before, the white on the head is inherited separately. Full white markings are not an indication that a dog carries white factor. However, white markings up the stifle connecting with the white on the belly usually denote white factor.

White factor is inherited as a recessive. Two whites bred together would produce all whites, and *all* offspring of a white would be white-factored regardless of their individual markings. Dogs carrying the white factor are not undesirable, but you will be more limited in selecting a suitable mate for them. Whites are unacceptable in England and by the majority of breeders in the United States, which means that it would be best *not* to breed a white dog.

TAN MARKINGS

Occasionally, a puppy will appear with tan markings on the cheeks, eyebrows, and legs and under the tail. These markings can appear on all four colors. The markings generally lighten as the Beardie matures and disappear completely by the time the dog is one year old. Occasionally, they may reappear in a vague suggestion of the original pattern when the dog darkens into his adult color. Generally, the tan remains indistinguishable in the adult Beardie, so unless breeders note which puppies are tricolors at birth, it is impossible to guess at a later time.

Tan is inherited by one set of genes. In most breeds, the tan markings are dominant. If tan is dominant, one parent must have exhibited the trait at birth. If a tri puppy has two parents, neither of which are tricolors, then the tan markings must be assumed to be recessive.

It is possible that the tan will disappear because it is masked by the graying factor. If so, the tan might remain rich and noticeable on a dog that matures almost completely black.

GRAYING

All factors mentioned so far are present at birth. The most unique and confusing trait in Beardies is the way in which they gray as they mature. This graying factor is a modifier, and it works on all four colors. Nearly all Beardies possess the graying factor to some degree, and no two individuals show identical expression of the trait. Some remain almost the same color as at birth, with a few salt-and-pepper hairs appearing and increasing in number with age. Most individuals gray astonishingly as puppies and at one year of age become a nondescript silver or cream color. At this time, the difference in coat color between a blue and a black or

Graying starts around the eyes. Nose pigment will color later.

New color continually grows from the roots outward.

between a brown and a fawn may be indistinguishable. Only the nose color will make the distinction, and sometimes even this variation is subtle enough to cause confusion. This is why it is *essential* to register a Beardie with his birth color, rather than try to guess how he will look as an adult.

Changes in color first become evident at the roots of the outer coat and become more noticeable as the coat grows. The old color moves toward the tips of the hair and eventually disappears, suggesting that the outer coat continuously grows and breaks off at a certain length.

Coat color usually darkens (sometimes drastically) by the second year, but it always retains some of the frosted, graying effect. Color will change slightly with each new coat; changes past the second year will be very gradual. Rarely does a Beardie come along that does not gray at all. Solid-colored Beardies are uncommon, because the graying factor is dominant and widely spread throughout the breed.

Many other breeds possess a graying factor (Kerry Blue Terriers, Shih Tzus, and Yorkshire Terriers, for example). However, in these breeds the coat lightens to a certain color, then remains constant. Beardies are unique in their redarkening of the adult coat color. Old English Sheepdogs and Soft-Coated Wheaten Terriers may come closest to the Beardie in this respect, but even they do not show the variety and changeability of colors seen in the Beardie.

PREDICTING ADULT COLOR

Many people ask how to select a puppy that will mature to a specific shade of color. This is virtually impossible to do, but there are a few hints. The puppy that grays earliest will probably be lightest in color. As the pup lightens, check the color of his ears and tail. The dog will usually darken to match these points.

Because of the variations in graying, it is possible (although rare) for a born-black dog to mature a lighter color than a blue dog. The term "slate" or "grizzle" is used to describe any gray dog that is born black. A black *never* turns into a blue, even if the coat color appears to do so. A blue is born a chinchilla-gray color and must have a dark gray nose and eye rims at maturity. A slate will have black pigmentation.

Graying also varies in browns and fawns, and a brown may occasionally mature lighter in color than a fawn. The adult color for both browns and fawns may be called "sandy." Adult color is more easily predicted in browns than in blacks. The shade will vary with graying, but the color—be it chocolate, red, or honey gold—will be evident at birth. A washed-out or muddy brown will lighten but will remain unattractive. A rich, dark brown or red is desirable.

Blues and fawns appear dull in color at birth but become more attractive within a few weeks. Blacks and browns are usually very rich and shiny at birth, but this intensity never remains even though the coat may have minimal graying.

EYE COLOR

One set of genes determines whether eyes will be blue or brown (brown is dominant), but these colors are subject to four different modifiers that produce infinite variations of shade. Most Beardies have brown eyes, ranging from golden to almost black. Although a gray or brown eye is preferable, blue eyes are permissible with a blue coat color. The blue-white "china eye" can distort expression and is disliked by most breeders. Fawns may have very light-colored eyes, usually hazel, which can still impart proper expression. Browns often have amber eyes, the shade varying with the intensity of coat color. Any eye color that is a soft shade of a color blending with the coat will always contribute to proper expression. Because the coat constantly changes, there will be periods in a Beardie's life when the eyes appear too light or too dark. Most people prefer the appearance of a darker eye, but a light eye cannot be faulted in a light-colored dog. Coat and eye color tend to be inherited together. In fact, a very dark eye in a fawn or a blue dog could look piercing and unnatural.

Can H. Raggmopp Gaelin Image, Raggmopp, showing color progression as she grows.

At age twelve weeks.

At age four months.

At age five months.

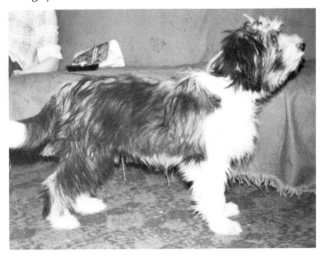

At one year of age.

At two years of age.

At three years of age.

The eye that changes from baby blue to brown at the earliest age will be the darkest color. Because their adult color will be lighter, brown puppies almost always retain their blue eyes longer than black puppies. A light eye usually indicates that the coat will lighten accordingly. However, some dogs simply have a light eye, and if it accompanies a dark coat color, it is to be faulted. A black dog with yellow eyes looks very harsh in expression.

In many breeds, dark eyes are always preferable. The preference of eye color to follow the coat color is another unique trait in Beardies, and one that necessitates educating the public (including show judges and new breeders).

PIGMENTATION

Pigmentation usually refers to the color of nose and eye rims in a dog. It also should include the lip color and skin color, but these areas are not as obvious at first glance. Beardies are "self-pigmented," meaning that the nose, the eye rims, etc. are the same as the birth color of the coat. A well-pigmented blue nose may appear to be black, but if the nose is held next to a black nose under a strong light, the difference becomes obvious. Most blues will have an easily discernible Maltese gray color to the nose. Browns will have brown pigment—the darker the better. Fawns will have noses a shade lighter than browns, actually tending to a rather mauve tone.

At birth, most puppies have entirely or partially pink noses. These should color in by a few months of age. Puppies that are fully pigmented at birth or as early as four weeks of age are the safest to select for breeding. As a rule, puppies with white blazes will take longer to reach full pigmentation than plain-faced ones. Also, those with white faces will be more likely to have broken pigment on the bridge of the muzzle. A pink spot above the nose should not be faulted, but it will be more sensitive to sunburn and possibly even to Collie-nose syndrome. Some pink skin is inevitable when a

Left: A fawn showing correct light pigmentation and eyes.

Right: Incorrect unpigmented nostril. Light eyes — faulted with a black coat.

dog has white markings, but this is of far less importance than the pigmentation of the nose leather itself.

The lips should fill in to a solid color. Spotted lips or pink on the inside of the nostrils indicates poor pigmentation, which in breeding should be compensated for by selecting a strongly pigmented animal as a mate. Nails will usually be pink, because Beardies have white feet. Either light or dark nails are acceptable.

In certain individuals, pigment seems to "fade," and pink spots appear around the eyes and muzzle. This can be caused by vitamin deficiency, by allergy, or by hereditary. The hereditary form of pigment loss is usually permanent, and care should be exercised if the dog is bred. If your puppy has light-colored eye rims, try exposing him to more sunlight. This condition is often due to a lack of certain vitamins or the inability to assimilate them. Sunlight can correct the problem if this is the cause.

ACCEPTABLE COLOR BREEDINGS

Acceptable theory suggests that one parent in every breeding should be a black to ensure good pigmentation. Many breeders have shied away from breeding dilute (blue or fawn) to dilute, or even from breeding dilute to brown.

Results will vary depending on the genetic makeup of each individual as well as on the dog's obvious color. In all cases, try to avoid breeding together two white-factored or poorly pigmented individuals, and select only acceptably colored stock for breeding. Recommended color combinations include:

1. black to any color
2. brown to black
3. brown to brown (if colors are rich)
4. blue to black
5. fawn to black

If a breeder wants all fawn or blue puppies, two Beardies pure for the dilution factor must be bred. If pigment is good and colors do not tend to degenerate, nothing is wrong with breeding two dilutes. A well-pigmented dog from one of these combinations is no different genetically from a blue or fawn from any other combination and can be perfectly suitable for breeding. It has not been determined if the dilution creating blues and fawns is a constant or if it is accumulative. If the latter is true, breeding blues to blues might increase the chance of pale color, light pigmentation, light eyes, or a host of possible defects. Based on observations, the dilution is not accumulative and therefore is safe to double, but it is probably wise to avoid doubling up for several generations in a row. Possible combinations that *may* be suitable include:

1. blue to brown
2. fawn to brown
3. blue to blue
4. blue to fawn
5. fawn to fawn

It is recommended that these breedings be left to the more experienced breeders who will be able to recognize if color is degenerating. To be perfectly safe, it is advisable for one parent to be black or brown and that at least one (preferably both) be well pigmented (including inside the nostrils). Even blacks can exhibit poor pigmentation. Certainly some lines and individuals produce better pigmentation than others. It would seem that this concern becomes a problem only when breeders quit using pigmentation as one of the considerations in selecting breeding stock.

12 *Laying the Foundation*

With well over one million purebred dogs registered each year with the American Kennel Club, dog breeding is not an avocation to be undertaken lightly. It implies taking responsibility for the puppies that you produce and being obligated to breed only because you love the breed and are committed to its preservation and improvement. Moreover, since the Bearded Collie is a relatively new breed rapidly growing in popularity, the Beardie breeder is charged with the awesome tasks of preventing overproduction and its accompanying deterioration of quality, of avoiding fads, and of protecting the breed from loss of the original, unique Beardie characteristics.

If you are willing to accept this charge, there is much to be done. Memorize the Standard. Go over as many Beardies as you can, rating them against the Standard. Your eyes must be able to see and your hands be able to feel the details that create the perfect dog. Visit other breeders. Ask questions, even those "dumb" ones that the novice is afraid to ask. Watch all of the shows in the area. Study the great producers and the various lines and subtypes within your breed. Obtain the pedigrees of Beardies that interest you and research them. Find out what their parents and grandparents looked like and whether they were from top-producing lines. Almost every name on the pedigree should eventually call up an image of that dog.

After a while, you will begin to form a mental picture of how your ideal Bearded Collie should look and act. You must have this ideal clearly in mind before you can progress toward breeding it.

Only when you are thoroughly familiar with the breed, when you know what is available, and when you have decided upon your ideal are you ready to begin to create with canine flesh and blood.

FINDING YOUR FOUNDATION STOCK

Selecting the foundation of your kennel should be one of the most important and careful decisions that you make. These Beardies cannot be compromises—they must be as close to your ideal and as good in overall quality as you can obtain. Never settle for mediocre stock, thinking that you can upgrade it with successive generations. That path is long and rocky and filled with stumbling blocks. It is also uneconomical and contributes to overproduction of pet stock.

Conformation, pedigree, and producing record weigh almost equally in importance in selecting your foundation Beardies. A lovely

Eng. Ch. Andrake Persephone, Andrake. Top-winning English bitch.

animal without a solid lineage of good Beardies behind it will be unlikely to reproduce its own quality. The great winner may or may not be the great producer. Ideally, your foundation Beardies would be exquisite show specimens with a solid, linebred pedigree of top producers behind them. However, you may not be able to purchase such an animal, in which case you should choose either the proven producer of winners or the best youngster that you can find with a history of top producers behind him.

A primary consideration in your foundation stock, or for that matter in any Beardie, should be sound structure. Structural faults in general are much more difficult to improve than such obvious characteristics as coat, pigment, size or shape of eye, or showmanship. Another consideration, if you plan to use your Beardies for work, is herding instinct. If lost from a line, this instinct may be nearly impossible to revive later. Dogs do not inherit the ability to herd, but they do inherit the instinct and certain traits that, with training, enable them to excel in this work.

The Foundation Bitch

The timeworn advice to new breeders has been "start with a bitch," and this is still very valid. A good bitch is a wise investment. If you can improve upon her with each succeeding generation, keeping a daughter each time, you will soon have the beginning of your own line. Keep no pup unless he is better than his parents, at least in some small way, and sell any bitch that, when bred to carefully selected studs, does not produce well in two litters.

Your foundation bitch should have exceptional quality and a solid pedigree. Look for a bitch with a long line of top-producing bitches behind her, and you can be reasonably assured that she, too, may produce well. Select a bitch that is not only healthy herself, but that has healthy parents and grandparents. Be sure that her dam was an easy breeder and whelped without problems. These considerations may seem minor, but every experienced dog breeder knows that the bitch that is difficult to breed,

First-place brood bitch at 1976 National Specialty — Shepherd's Help from Shiel CD, second from left, and progeny.

that has difficulty whelping, or that is sickly (even though not with a hereditary disease) has a great tendency to produce daughters with the same weaknesses.

Wait for the right bitch. It may take many months to find her, but when you do, it will be worth the time and effort. If you cannot obtain a young bitch, start with an older, proven producer and breed her to the best male available. Hopefully, she will produce a daughter to carry on for you. If you cannot find the perfect bitch, choose one with at least one great virtue. The mediocre bitch with no major faults but also with no major virtues will be less likely to produce the outstanding Beardie than will the bitch excelling in certain qualities but exhibiting a more serious fault. If you must compromise on a bitch with obvious faults, do make sure that the defects can be bred out easily. Also, be certain that you can find a complementary mate. It would be a mistake to begin a breeding program with an individual having faults so common that the correct trait cannot be found.

The Stud Dog—Asset or Liability?

Owning a stud dog can be very different from maintaining a small kennel of bitches. If selected and handled properly, a stud may become your most valued asset. In reality, however, most studs become a severe liability to the small kennel—and sometimes it takes the owner several years of mistakes to realize it.

First, a male can be a nuisance. He will undoubtedly become the most dominant dog in your kennel and will not always be a gentleman in proving so. He will harass your bitches, jump on your guests, eat up any profits that you may have anticipated, drown your flowers, become hysterical whenever a bitch comes in season, and demand more grooming and training than the girls. And, by far, the most devastating effect will be to your breeding program. The cost of any decent male will exceed that of the stud fee for the best dogs in the country. Especially if you buy a puppy, the chance of his actually producing well with your bitches is slim. Only a very special few meet the requirements of being both an outstanding individual (and a male that is anything less should be totally eliminated from breeding) and a consistent producer of his best points. Some combine well only with a limited few bitches, and no dog can suit every bitch. Even if you are lucky enough to find a dog that produces well, what about all of his lively daughters that you keep? They will have to be bred to a different dog

*Ch. Stonehaven's Trevor McGregor, CDX, HC, ROM.
Owners: Robin Stamm and Irene Carson*

when the time comes, yet you will still be feeding, grooming, and picking up after papa. It is not cheaper to own your stud. Unless you have a dog that is truly outstanding in some area, it is preferable that you breed your bitches to established stud dogs.

On the positive side, a male is often your claim to national recognition. He can be your top show dog, an ambassador with the public, and generally your most effective advertisement. He stays in coat more months of the year than a bitch, and he usually is larger and flashier in showmanship. He will have greater potential as a top winner in most cases (although a few notable bitches would call exception to that statement). If you want a show dog, a male is heartily recommended. If he turns out to be a good producer as well, so much the better. Just don't expect all good males to become good stud dogs!

If a promising male is the result of your own breeding, you may wish to keep him to guarantee that he is promoted properly. If you desire a potential stud, you will find it advantageous to purchase a male that possesses virtues needed throughout your bitch line. Just remember that promotion of a stud dog is absolutely necessary if he is to stand to the public. Yet, this promotion can run into thousands of dollars with no assurance of any return.

An adult male that has proven his worth is not likely to be for sale, but he is the best bet if he can be obtained. The price of such a dog may be prohibitive; at best, he will not be cheap. Occasionally, an older dog can be obtained reasonably on the condition that the buyer provide him with a retirement home after he quits siring. This can give a beginner an excellent start, because the dog will already be trained and will have acquired his reputation. Another possibility is to obtain a young dog (sometimes even a champion) that is surplus to the program of an active kennel. He may be as good and as well bred as their top dogs but too closely related for them to use. Make sure that such a dog is really good and is not just being culled.

Beardies have the advantage over some breeds of developing consistently; therefore, they can be selected fairly predictably at an early age. Although there is still significantly more risk than with a puppy, it is better to buy a top puppy than a mediocre adult. It may require growing out two or three puppies to get just the right one, but do not settle for less. A male that is not quite show quality is not suitable to breed. He will only set your program back several generations behind other breeders. Even his best offspring will inherit the ability to pass on his mediocrity.

If you decide to risk acquiring a puppy, select one that is sound, outgoing, and reasonably typey. He should come from a very solid pedigree of quality individuals and preferably be linebred to dogs that are known to produce consistent quality. Expect a reasonable guarantee of quality and fertility to accompany such a puppy. The more you demand in a guarantee, the more you must expect to pay. Select a deal that sounds fair to both buyer and seller.

DEVELOP A PLAN

Breeders who follow a plan will progress at a steadier rate than those who consider each mating individually. Your goal is to retain the virtues of your foundation stock while improving the faults. The plan, then, becomes a deliberated method for accomplishing this goal.

Suppose you obtain a typey bitch with excellent structure and angulation, good temperament, and natural herding ability. However, she lacks coat and is only mediocre in head qualities. Your plan, then, might be to select males that have superior heads and hopefully somewhat better coats but that are not significantly lesser in quality concerning structure. You hope to improve the head, obtain moderate improvement in coat, and retain the structure, temperament, and type. In the second generation down from the foundation bitch, you may try for more improvement in head or hope to hold the head qualities that you have gained while going after better coats. In the successive generation, you might want to try setting both of these improved qualities aside while breeding for more elegance and style. Your progress may be slow, but it will be steady. You will generally find that it is better to select one improvement at a time and try to retain the good qualities that you have already obtained than to go after too many new virtues at once and risk, in the process, losing those strengths that you are beginning to establish.

Selecting for specific qualities is sometimes done irrespective of pedigree, but if many different and unrelated lines are involved, the results may be unpredictable and inconsistent. Therefore, most breeders plan their matings by considering both individual qualities and pedigree. This combination of breeding for a specific sub-type, improving faults one at a time, and planning a genetically sound program is the surest road to success as a Bearded Collie breeder.

UNDERSTANDING PEDIGREES

Basically, there are three types of genetic programs: inbreeding, linebreeding, or outcrossing.

A breeder may use one or all of these forms in a breeding plan, but each of them must be understood and used appropriately.

Linebreeding

Linebreeding is the safest and most widely recommended long-term program. Linebreeding involves breeding two individuals that have common ancestors on both the top and the bottom of the pedigree. To be considered linebred, a dog should have from half to three-quarters of his ancestors from one bloodline (not necessarily one individual). Anything closer than grandsire to granddaughter is considered inbreeding.

In linebreeding, both desirable and undesirable traits are concentrated gradually over several generations. Because all of the faults in the line don't surface at once, they can be dealt with in stages. Uniformity is usually achieved by the second or third generation, and linebreeding can be continued indefinitely provided the line has individuals that offer correction for the particular faults encountered.

The linebred individual is generally most valuable for breeding. This Beardie will be a much more consistent producer than an outcrossed individual. He can be linebred, inbred, or outcrossed to achieve your desired results. You have the choice of linebreeding on an established strain or linebreeding to a certain individual to form a new strain. The linebred Beardie will also usually bring a higher price and be more saleable, especially if he is from a popular line.

Linebreeding encompasses variations from breeding a bitch with her grandsire or grandson to breeding third cousins. Preferably, three or four of the grandparents come from the same general family, with at least one individual appearing several times in a four-generation pedigree.

Inbreeding

Inbreeding involves the mating of two closely related individuals, such as brother to sister, father to daughter, mother to son, or half-brother to half-sister. Inbreeding is the fastest way to establish uniformity in a line because it concentrates the genes of a few individuals and will sometimes set type in one generation.

Inbreeding can only concentrate the qualities already existing in a line; it cannot add new characteristics. It can bring to the surface recessive traits that you did not know existed in the line; these traits will also be concentrated in the genetic makeup of the dog that exhibits them. The poor inbred specimen will be just as prepotent for his qualities as will the good inbred Beardie. Therefore, if you inbreed, you must be prepared to cull your breeding stock ruthlessly.

Inbreeding is successful only if the dogs used are outstanding representatives of the breed and have very few inheritable problems in their background. It is not recommended when there is insufficient knowledge of the dog's pedigree.

After World War II, when the Bearded Collie was being reestablished as a recognized breed, inbreeding was used excessively because so few good individuals were available, and many foundation dogs in the United States had either inbred or linebred pedigrees. Do not be afraid of this or be hesitant to use the good inbred dog. A really fine inbred Beardie can have tremendous influence on the breed. However, we should be concerned with establishing more distinct linebred strains as well. Continued inbreeding leaves no place to go for improvement and tends to reduce size and vigor and concentrate undesirable recessives.

Outcrossing

Outcrossing technically means breeding two totally unrelated individuals. This is a nearly impossible feat with Beardies. Probably the best that you can find are two individuals with no common ancestor in four generations and hopefully with at least two lines that are not closely related. Breeding two inbred individuals from different lines produces what is know as a first generation outcross. A resultant offspring bred back into either line would produce linebred puppies.

A linebred pedigree

Breckdale Pretty Maid
— Braelyn Broadholme Crofter
— — Ruairidh of Willowmead
— — — Wil O Wisp of Willowmead
— — — Sweetheart of Willowmead
— — Bobby's Girl of Bothkennar
— — — Int.Ch. Bobby of Bothkennar
— — — Beauty Box of Bothkennar
— Breckdale Cala Sona River Danube
— — Alastair of Willowmead
— — — Ruairidh of Willowmead
— — — Ch. Willowmead Barberry of Bothkennar
— — Ch. Willowmead My Honey
— — — Wil O Wisp of Willowmead
— — — Merry Maker of Willowmead

An inbred pedigree.

Ch. Criterion Silverleaf Rascal

Ch. Shiel's-Mogador Silverleaf C.D.

Eng. Ch. Sunbree's Magic Moments of Willowmead

Yager Aplomb at Osmart
(c. c. winner)

Eng. Ch. Broadholme Cindy-Sue of Willowmead

Misty of Mogador

Eng. Ch. Osmart Bonnie Blue Braid

Glendonald Gladsome

Ch. Thaydom Silverleaf Cinnamon

Ch. Shiel's Mogador Silverleaf C.D.

Eng. Ch. Sunbree's Magic Moments of Willowmead

Misty of Mogador

Hyfield Hyteeny

Eng. Ch. Wishanger Cairnbahn

Wishanger Bluebell

An outcross pedigree.

Ch. Cala Sona Westernisles Loch Aber

Alastair of Willowmead

Ruairidh of Willowmead

Wil O Wisp of Willowmead

Sweetheart of Willowmead

Ch. Willowmead Barberry of Bothkennar

Ridgeway Rob

Bra' Tawny of Bothkennar

Westernisles Wishanger Beechmast

Cannamoor Bailie

Swalehall John Scrope

Brasenose Annabelle

Wishanger Wysteria

Ch. Wishanger Barley of Bothkennar

Wishanger Jessica of Multan

Outcrossing as a general practice is not considered planned breeding unless selection for a specific type is made for several successive generations. Most outcross matings are specifically made to introduce into a line some positive qualities that are weak or nonexistent in the major line. This may be achieved in one outcross breeding or in a series of crosses. The offspring of these outcross matings are usually inbred or linebred into one or the other of the original lines. Outcrossing for several generations becomes a hit-and-miss proposition, and the outcrossed individual is unpredictable as a producer.

PRACTICAL APPLICATIONS

Breeding for the sake of pedigree or type alone is risky; the dogs must complement each other as individuals and combine well on paper. The line must be worthy of concentration or the breeder will magnify his problems.

In selecting individuals for mating, most breeders consider the pedigree of the dog and whether he will fit into their program. Then, by a process known as cross faulting, they will arrive at the individual that best suits a particular bitch. In cross faulting, remember your ideal Beardie. This is your goal. A good match will double the outstanding traits as well as compensate for each fault. Any time that a fault is doubled (both dogs exhibiting the identical fault), the percentage of offspring that will inherit it is high.

When you cross fault, look for the ideal characteristic in the mate to offset the fault. Never breed a Beardie with a fault at one extreme to a mate with faults at the opposite extreme—for example, short back to long back—hoping for a compromise. The genetic process does not work that way. In the above example, you would get approximately half of the puppies with long backs and half with short but none with the desired moderate length.

Instead, breed either the overly short- or overly long-backed dog to one with correct proportions. The same is true of every other characteristic. If your Beardie has a fault, seek a mate that is most correct for the trait.

A good breeder always keeps the overall dog in mind and breeds for balance in all characteristics. If you become overly concerned with one trait (for instance, good angulation), you will tend to develop a line with faults in areas where you have placed less emphasis (heads, for example). You may not want poor heads, but the trend will develop because you ignore the total dog. Keep in mind that you may sometimes have to compromise on your most valued qualities in order to attain quality in other areas. The most talented breeders continually keep the overall ideal Beardie in mind.

Establishing a New Line

The breeder becomes truly creative when he or she contributes to the breed a unique gene pool of individual dogs prepotent for certain exceptional qualities. It is far better to maintain a line that is high in overall quality and that has at least one outstanding characteristic than it is to maintain a kennel of good Beardies having no major faults but also no outstanding virtues. Always consider this when selecting your foundation Beardies and making those important first matings.

If you really want to make a mark on the breed, count on spending many years in developing your goal. Select as your foundation the best individuals available, and work with existing lines until you are familiar with their genetic makeup. Avoid, if possible, concentrating on only one dog, because no Beardie is perfect. Assess each litter carefully, and when you have made progress, try to determine how it was achieved and how it can be maintained. This is the challenge of establishing a new strain.

13 *Planned Parenthood*

The most exciting aspect of dog breeding for many breeders is the planning of future matings. Selection of the right mate for each dog requires creativity, common sense, and a knowledge of genetics, breed characteristics, and the genetic makeup of the individuals involved. But there is more than art to raising consistently healthy, quality litters. Considerable care and effort must be given to establishing an effective conditioning program and preventing the spread of infection, disease, or parasites in the kennel environment. The wise beginning breeder will devote equal attention to each of these factors.

Popular opinion to the contrary, breeding dogs is not a profitable business; more often, it becomes a rather expensive hobby. The first litter may seem a cinch, but with time, the probability of losses and problems increases. The following are average costs that you can expect when breeding a litter of Bearded Collies, providing there are no complications.

Cost of bitch ($1,500 purchase price divided by
average of four litters produced)................................$375
Pre-breeding exam and tests...90
Stud fee (average) 500
Shipping for breeding (average)....................................400
Feed and vitamins for bitch and litter...........................200
Puppy vaccinations & worming ($25 ea. x 8 pups).....200
Advertising...100
AVERAGE TOTAL..$1,865

Actual costs could be nearly double this amount.

You also need to consider the cost of facilities. While most Beardie bitches are pets whose litters are whelped in the house, a four- or five-week-old litter may be too much for the corner of your kitchen or laundry room. Some type of large puppy crate or an exercise pen is a necessity. The problem compounds if you are contemplating establishing your own bloodline, in which case you may start with more than one bitch and will probably be growing out some of the youngsters. In this case, a kennel may be needed. It must comply with city or county zoning and sanitation requirements, and you may find such plans hampered by increasingly stringent laws and regulations governing kennels.

There are personal and emotional considerations, too. Even the best planned litters may produce a high percentage of pet puppies. Will they find loving homes? Can you accept the fact that defective or unwanted puppies may need to be humanely destroyed? Will you resist the temptation to breed a favorite animal if it carries a hereditary defect or is lacking in quality even though exceptional in disposition? If, having considered all of these factors, you still want to breed your Beardie, there is no time like the present to begin making preparations.

THE BROOD BITCH

About the only difference between keeping a bitch for breeding and keeping one for a pet or for showing is the need to be a little more meticulous about her condition. The prospective brood bitch should be kept in hard, firm, lean condition by feeding her a well-balanced diet (supplemented with vitamins and minerals if these are not adequate in the feed) and by giving her daily exercise. Road work is the surest method of conditioning the muscles, and bitches should be kenneled in large runs or yards with one or more other dogs so that they are encouraged to run and play. A fat or soft bitch often has trouble conceiving or whelping.

Brood bitches must be kept free of parasites. Worm checks should be performed at least twice yearly and immediately prior to breeding. Immunizations should be current, and, because they cannot be administered while a bitch is in whelp, they should be given early if you anticipate breeding her during the time she would normally be scheduled for a booster shot. Every bitch should be checked and certified clear of hip dysplasia, hereditary eye problems, or other inherited defects before she is mated.

Beardie females generally have their first heat when they are about six months old, and most cycle regularly every six months thereafter. To be certain that a bitch is mentally as well as physically mature before breeding, she should be at least eighteen months of age, but preferably two years old. If a bitch is on a six-month cycle, she should be bred no more often than every other season, but bitches that cycle less frequently may occasionally be bred on successive heats without harm. Most bitches will continue to produce through their eighth year.

The Estrous Cycle

When your bitch comes in heat, a complex series of events takes place within her reproductive organs. The sequence of events leading to heat, ovulation, and possible pregnancy is governed by four hormones—estrogen and progesterone from the ovaries, follicular stimulation hormone (FSH), and luteinizing hormone from the pituitary. Depending upon the influence of these hormones at any particular time, the sexual cycle can be divided into four stages—anestrus, proestrus, estrus, and diestrus.

Anestrus is the period of rest between reproductive cycles and lasts an average of three to six months. Hormonal activity in the bitch's system during this time is low and steady.

During proestrus, the first stage of heat, the ovaries are stimulated by FSH, which causes the follicles containing the eggs to grow. The growing eggs produce estrogen, which causes the vulva to swell, stimulates a red discharge, and increases the bitch's sexual interest. This signals

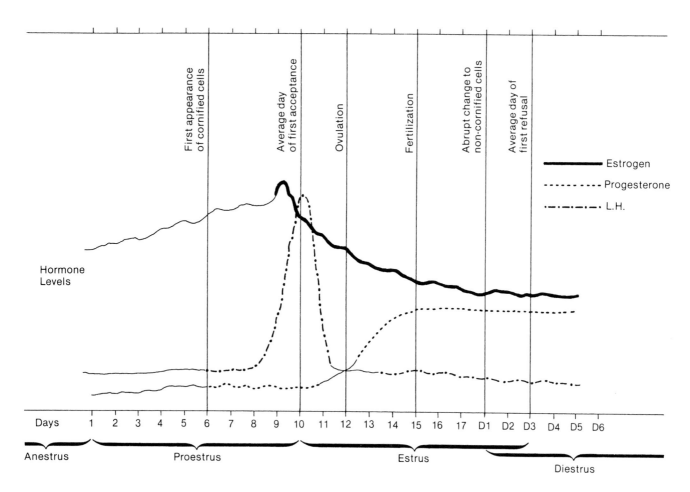

The estrous cycle of the bitch.

the beginning of the heat cycle. At this time, the bitch will not stand for the male dog, although she will probably flirt.

About the ninth or tenth day of heat, the estrogen level peaks, and the bitch will willingly accept the male. This marks the beginning of estrus. At this time, the discharge turns from pink to a clear color, the vulva becomes soft and more swollen, and the bitch will usually "flag" (hold her tail to one side). Shortly after the estrogen peak, the luteinizing hormone also reaches a peak. It is believed that this action triggers ovulation, or the releasing of the eggs. All of the follicles discharge their eggs at approximately the same time, but the eggs are immature and cannot be fertilized for three more days.

The follicles that formerly contained the eggs now become a new gland—the corpus luteum—which produces progesterone. The rise in progesterone and the corresponding lowering of the other hormones stimulate the beginning of the third part of heat, called diestrus. Diestrus occurs about six days after ovulation and marks the end of the heat cycle. The bitch refuses to stand, the discharge becomes brownish and then decreases, and the swelling leaves the vulva. Somewhere between the eighteenth and twenty-first day, the bitch will normally be completely out of heat. However, the progesterone level in her system will remain high for about two more months, whether or not she is pregnant. It is impossible to tell at this stage if a bitch is pregnant.

When to Breed

Bitches are unique in that their eggs are released in an immature state. Bitches will accept the dog some five to nine days prior to the time that the eggs can be fertilized. However, the spermatozoa of the dog are remarkably long lived and can remain fertile for up to eight days. Therefore, breeding any time from the day of first acceptance to the day of first refusal to breed generally results in pregnancy. The highest rate of conception usually occurs from matings on the day of ovulation and for up to three days thereafter. Because ovulation generally occurs on the twelfth or thirteenth day of the season, with fertilization taking place three days thereafter, the normal optimum breeding pattern would be on the day of first acceptance (approximately day ten) and again four days later (day fourteen). If only two breedings are made, they should occur three or four days apart. A few bitches are missed because they accept early and are bred on the first day of acceptance, then again two days later. If the bitch happens to ovulate later than normal, she may not conceive because the sperm will have died before the eggs matured.

Most Beardie bitches have normal seasons in which the outward signs of heat and acceptance correspond with what is happening inside the reproductive tract. Hence, the success of breeding when nature says "breed." A few bitches, however, will accept on the first or second day of heat or throughout the season. Other bitches may never want to accept at all and will have to be forcibly held for mating. Still others will have silent heats and will show almost no swelling, discharge, or other visible signs of being in season, even though they will ovulate.

The Use of Vaginal Smears

Scientific research has provided a valuable aid for breeders by discovering that vaginal smears may be used to pinpoint the exact time of ovulation. This is especially useful in unusual cases such as just described or in helping to determine the cause of a bitch "missing."

During her season, three kinds of cells may be found in the vagina of the bitch—red blood cells, white blood cells, and epithelial cells. Numerous red blood cells are present during the early part of the season, but normally there will be only a few white blood cells. (A high white cell count on a slide generally indicates that an infection is present.) It is the epithelial cells that are of interest. As estrogen levels rise, the vaginal lining (epithelium) thickens. Cells are sloughed off the surface of this lining and carried away in the discharge. The epithelial cell is larger that the blood cells and resembles a fried egg in appearance. Each cell has a nucleus (yolk of the egg) surrounded by a wide, translucent rim. These cells, which vary in appearance under the influence of estrogen, provide an accurate picture of how the bitch is being influenced by estrogen at this particular time. As her season progresses, the slides will show fewer and fewer blood cells and a gradual progression in the changing shape of the epithelial cells, from the more regular egg shape to an irregular shape resembling a potato chip or a taco. The edges begin to turn up so that the cell looks like a deep "U" and the nucleus is almost, if not completely, invisible. Such cells are referred to as "cornified."

If the bitch is in proestrus when you begin taking smears, you will notice a progression toward the cornified state. The day on which nearly 100 percent of the epithelial cells are cornified marks the beginning of true estrus, whether or not the bitch will stand for breeding. Ovulation occurs approximately six days later. The cells will remain cornified for a total of ten to fourteen days. About the sixth day after ovulation, the cells will change abruptly in appearance as they return to their former, noncornified state. This marks the onset of diestrus. After this point, the eggs cannot be fertilized.

If smears reveal cornified epithelial cells, breed the bitch regardless of the outward signs or the day of her season. If you know the date on which the cornified state first predominated, you

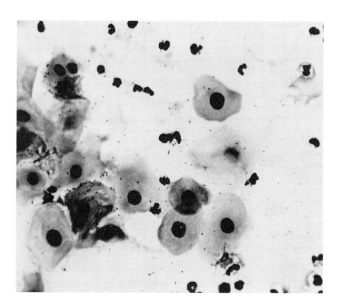

Noncornified epithelial cells and a few blood cells.

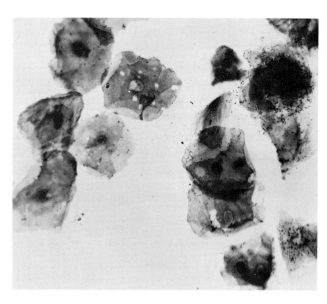

Fully cornified epithelial cells.

can be sure that ovulation will occur six days later and that the bitch should be bred at that time. If a bitch comes in heat but no cornified cells appear during the season, ovulation has not occurred; therefore, the bitch cannot conceive.

To prepare a smear, insert either a pipette or a cotton swab about one and one-half inches into the vagina to collect the material. Transfer this onto a slide and let it set for several minutes before staining. Fill a small bottle with Wright's stain (or substitute) and two bottles with distilled water. Follow the instructions that come with the stain. The usual procedure is to dip the slide into the bottle of stain for a specified number of seconds, then into the first water bath for several more seconds. Finally, rinse the slide in the second water bath and prop it on end to dry. When dry, examine it under a microscope that gives good resolution at 100 power.

Progesterone Testing

The level of progesterone in dogs is very low during proestrus and begins to increase gradually about four days prior to the luteinizing-hormone (LH) surge. It then increases dramatically and remains high during estrus and diestrus. Your veterinarian can do this testing by drawing blood samples. Begin testing every other day at the first signs of heat (as determined by either smears or discharge). When the tests show that the LH surge has occurred, breeding should take place within four days.

How Conception Takes Place

A bitch will ovulate about one and one-half times as many eggs as she will actually produce puppies. Providing that live sperm are present in the oviduct, fertilization takes place as soon as the eggs mature. Research has proven that all eggs mature and are fertilized at the same time; therefore, all puppies in a litter are the same age. Size differences in puppies are due to genetic makeup, positioning, and the nutrition that each receives, not to age difference, as is commonly imagined. Puppies lower in the uterine horn tend to be larger and better nourished than those farther up.

It takes only a few seconds for the ejaculated sperm to find their way to the oviduct. If the ova are mature, they will be fertilized immediately. If they are immature, the sperm will surround them and remain motile (alive and able to move) for several days. Once a sperm has fertilized an egg, that egg becomes impervious to other sperm even though it may be surrounded by millions of them. Thus, an individual puppy can have only one sire. It is possible, however, for a litter to have two or more sires if all of the matings take place prior to the time that the eggs mature. In this case, all of the sperm would surround the eggs and wait for them to mature, at which time it becomes pure chance which dog's sperm fertilizes which eggs.

Caring For the Bitch in Heat

A Beardie bitch in season is anything but modest, and often she is an escape artist par excellence, as are most males. Therefore, keep her closely confined, preferably in a crate in the house or in a covered chain-link run until she is ready to be bred to the dog of your choice. Be sure to confine her throughout her season until all signs of estrus are gone. The urine odor from a bitch in heat will attract males from great distances. If you absolutely must take her for walks, take her in the car far from your house. You can give your female certain products that help to neutralize the scent, but it is preferable not to use these if you plan to breed her later in the season. Furthermore, these products are not always successful. Chlorophyll pills are safe and will decrease odor, but the bitch will still be attractive upon close inspection by the male.

Sperm remain alive for up to two weeks, which means that a mismating even early in your bitch's season will probably result in pregnancy. If a mismating occurs, do not breed her to another dog. An estrogen injection given immediately after the mating will prevent conception, but it can also cause serious side effects and is not recommended. Birth-control pills that prevent heat, injections that stimulate heat, and hormones given to effect an abortion can all upset the delicate working of the reproductive system, in some instances to the point where a bitch will never again reproduce. Hormones sometimes cause extreme allergic reactions.

Formerly, if a bitch was bred by more than one male, the offspring could not be registered. Recently, the use of DNA testing to determine parenthood has been allowed by the AKC. If the bitch was bred to more than one male, this test could determine which male sired each puppy. This test is extremely expensive, so it is better to be careful and be sure that there is only one sire.

SELECTING A MATE

Undoubtedly the most critical part of breeding is selecting the right mate for your bitch. Your search will be long and probably continuous as you watch the young stud dogs appear on the scene each year. Don't wait until your bitch is ready to mate to decide on a stud. Your search should begin almost the day that you bring her home, far in advance of mating.

Most of the basics of selecting a mate apply similarly to selecting an individual (see Chapters 4 and 9). The only additional factor that you must keep in mind is "cross faulting," or selecting a mate that does not double on one of your bitch's prominent faults in either genotype or phenotype. He must be strong in the virtues that she lacks and hopefully also strong in some of her virtues so that these may be set. He should not bring in any major new faults, although you may have to compromise and accept a few minor faults along with the needed virtues. To ascertain the faults and virtues that the dog carries but may not exhibit, study his pedigree, his bloodline, and especially his parents and his progeny.

Select a male that is a proven producer of quality and that seems to impart some of his strong points to most of his offspring. Beware of a male that has produced well from one bitch but poorly from several others. He should be structurally sound, healthy, and certified clear of hip dysplasia and eye defects. Avoid like the plague any dog that is producing puppies with genetic defects or health problems. Even though he may be clear, he must be a carrier in order for the puppies to exhibit the defect.

Am. Can. Ch. Britannia Love Me Do ROM HC

Study the dog's pedigree. A good pedigree will have the superior dogs on the left side. All of those "greats" in the fifth generation will have little influence on your puppies. Look very closely at all four grandparents, because the puppies often will more nearly resemble the grandparents than the parents. The influence exerted by even these four dogs, or the parents, is not equal, however, and a puppy may closely resemble one grandparent and exhibit none of the traits wanted from the other three.

Unless you can see and go over a stud in person, the selection of a good mate becomes more difficult. Correspond or talk with the owner of a prospective stud at length, and ask all of your questions. (Be aware that breeders who spend all of their time writing books are likely to be lousy correspondents!) Ask to see photos from several angles, and try to obtain action photos. A good action shot is worth a thousand words, because it will tell you much about the dog's structure and angulation. Ask the opinion of a trusted breeder, judge, or handler of your

acquaintance who has seen the dog. Then, since opinions vary and are quite subjective, make up your own mind about the dog.

Contacting the Stud Owner

Your initial inquiries are made before your bitch comes into season, so your final step is to contact the stud's owner to let him know that your bitch has come into heat and will be arriving for breeding on a specified date. If you are shipping the bitch, have the airline flight numbers and times of departure and arrival handy when you call so that you and the other party can mutually decide on a convenient flight.

If she is leaving your state of residence, your bitch will need a health certificate. In addition, the stud owner may ask for a vaginal culture to determine that the bitch is free of infection, for a brucellosis test (this blood test usually takes several days, so do it early), and possibly for copies of her eye and hip certifications. Now is the time to double-check to make sure that your bitch is free of parasites and that her immunizations are up-to-date. Injections and worm medications may be given while she is in heat but must be administered prior to breeding.

Expect your bitch to stay at the stud owner's kennel for several days while she is being bred. In order for her to settle in before the mating, plan for her to arrive a day or two prior to the day of first acceptance, or about the ninth day of heat.

The stud fee is always paid in advance. You are paying for the dog's service, not for puppies. Some breeders will guarantee two live puppies or a free return to the male, while others may guarantee one puppy. The guarantee is a courtesy, not an obligation. In no instance can you expect your fee to be refunded if your bitch fails to conceive. Most stud owners use a contract such as the one displayed later in this chapter to spell out these conditions in writing. Your "letter of introduction" accompanying the bitch should contain her name, registration number, age, number of previous litters (if any), and the date that her current season began. She should be returned to you with a contract or letter stating the number of breedings and the dates.

THE STUD DOG

As a stud owner, your first responsibility is to be totally honest about your dog. You must have him tested and certified free of any common hereditary defects. In Beardies, it is recommended that you get both a hip X-ray by a qualified radiologist to test for dysplasia (studs older than two years of age should have an OFA number) and an eye examination by a qualified ophthalmologist for progressive retinal atrophy and cataracts. If there is any question, the dog should not stand at public stud; using him may also hurt your own program. The dog should have no known serious health problems in his immediate background.

No one owns a perfect dog. It is your responsibility to know your dog's faults as well as his virtues and to be sure that the latter outweigh the former. An honest evaluation of the dog and his suitability for a particular bitch must be given to the bitch's owner. After a few litters, you should recognize which traits your dog produces in a majority of his offspring and which faults he will not correct. This is almost as important as the traits he possesses. You must be firm in refusing to breed any bitch that is substandard in quality and in referring those unsuitable for your dog to a more compatible male. It takes effort to do this tactfully, but most people respect an honest effort to preserve quality in the breed.

The owner of a popular stud generally refers puppy buyers to breeders who have mated their bitches to the dog. Are you willing and able to provide this service? This by no means implies that you are responsible for selling the puppies—at times there is no market for anyone. Yet, there is a greater chance of selling puppies sired by a well-known champion rather than by an unknown dog. However, if an unfinished less-known dog appears to be a better

*Ch. Stonehaven's Super Trooper, HC
Owned by Irene and Ralph Carson*

choice for a bitch, you shouldn't hesitate to recommend him.

If you are a stud owner, you must have adequate facilities to care for visiting bitches, you must be able to handle the breeding efficiently with no danger to any of the parties involved, and you must have reasonable transportation connections with the rest of the country. You should have a good veterinarian close at hand and good public relations with your neighbors so that they won't object to the extra barking dogs coming and going. You also must be willing to put the time and money into showing and advertising your dog fairly extensively. This is not only for personal publicity but is an obligation to the people who have used the dog.

Most adolescent males will begin mounting other dogs. This is normal and should be corrected only if carried to excess. While most Beardies are eager breeders, it is important that your young stud not get the idea that he will be punished for mounting a bitch. Try to separate him or distract him rather than correct him for mounting. Do not let him be dominated constantly by an older male during adolescence. The youngster is insecure enough during these months and needs to feel that he is "top dog" at home.

From the time you acquire your puppy, you must establish yourself as the dominant personality. If you are firm, yet consistent, in requiring that he must do what you tell him when you tell him, he will become a delightful, well-mannered Beardie. If you let him "get the upper hand," he can become unmanageable when mature. Males will challenge you more than most bitches. However, if you do not let him get away with the first few things, he will accept you as his boss and try very hard to please you in the future.

Conditioning the Stud Dog

Conditioning of a male can begin when he is very young. During the growth months, he should receive the best nutrition possible for full expression of his genetic potential. He should be fed a balanced diet with adequate protein and calcium for optimum growth. A fat puppy is not necessarily a healthy puppy. The best condition is hard and muscular with just enough weight to cover the ribs. Encourage your male puppy to get plenty of exercise and make sure that he receives all of his vaccinations and checkups on schedule. Take note of the age at which both testicles descend. It is preferable that they be normally descended by eight to twelve weeks of age.

Keep your stud dog healthy and in hard condition. If he is used heavily, a slight increase in protein in his diet may be warranted. Stick with a good, balanced ration as a basic diet. Your male should also be periodically checked for evidence of brucellosis or infections. You will probably want to require his bitches to be examined as well. You must be particularly careful to elim-

inate parasites in a stud dog, because he can contaminate the bitches with whom he comes into contact. Treat any problems immediately, and do not allow your dog to breed any bitch while he has a communicable problem.

A common problem found in breeding-age males is sheath infection. Check the penis for signs of discharge or inflammation. If this exists, work some topical antibiotic into the sheath and repeat twice daily until the condition corrects. If your dog is subject to recurring infections, have him examined by a veterinarian for possible cause. Clipping some of the hair around the penis and keeping the area clean may help.

Handling the Mating

Never leave your dog alone with a bitch in season or allow him to breed her unassisted. The possibility of injury to the male is great, and you will not know if the bitch has actually been bred and, if so, when. Plan to conduct a mating in a quiet place with good footing. The procedure can take from ten minutes to an hour, so use a place that is comfortable for this length of time. Rough concrete, carpet, or rubber matting provide good footing. Keep both dogs under control at all times, and wait a few hours if they are uncooperative. Some bitches need restraining, while others are eager to stand for the male. An experienced male will usually know when to breed a bitch. Believe him, even if the timing seems odd. You may miss a bitch with an unusual cycle if you breed her strictly according to the charts.

Check the bitch for any obstructions that will require veterinary attention. If she has an excessive amount of hair around the vulva, comb it aside or trim a small area immediately surrounding the vulva. Check her discharge. It should be light pink or clear, and she should flag her tail to one side if you touch her hindquarters. If you are unsure about correct breeding time, have a vaginal smear taken. The first breeding usually takes place between the tenth and twelfth days of estrus, with a second breeding occurring two to four days later. If smears have not been taken and the bitch still stands willingly, a third breeding can take place. One breeding is all that is necessary if the timing is right. Do not routinely breed your male at less than thirty-six-hour intervals. Repeated daily use will deplete his sperm count, because sperm need approximately thirty-six hours to mature.

Whenever possible, have two people assist with the mating. This minimizes the potential of injury to either dogs or people. One person will hold the bitch's head. Put a choke collar on her and attach a six-foot leather lead. Wrap the leash firmly, but not tightly, around her muzzle and behind her neck. If you prefer, you may use a muzzle made of an old nylon stocking (see Chapter 8). Few bitches actually need to be muzzled, but even the gentlest bitch may bite if she becomes frightened. Have the bitch's handler place one hand on each side of the bitch's neck just behind her ears and firmly grasp the wraps of the muzzle, talking reassuringly to the bitch and holding her steady throughout the mating. This person may sit in a chair and hold the bitch's head on his or her knees if preferred.

The second person assists the stud. Kneel or sit beside the bitch and place a hand under her flank to steady her. If she tries to lie down, you may have to support her weight on your knee. Hold her tail to one side as the dog mounts. If he penetrates and forms a "tie," help him turn so that the two dogs stand tail-to-tail until the tie breaks (usually ten to fifteen minutes). If the dog has trouble penetrating, place one hand under the bitch's vulva and guide her against the dog as he thrusts. Try to guide him into the proper position without dampening his enthusiasm.

Once the dog has tied and turned, hold him steady with the collar so that he doesn't pull. Restrain the bitch from throwing herself to the ground or jumping. In this vulnerable position, the male can be badly injured, which is why no one should allow a dog to breed unassisted. It is usually the male that is damaged, often ruining a valuable animal for future breedings.

After the dogs break apart, confine them separately in a quiet area for half an hour.

Financial Arrangements

The stud owner is not required to guarantee live pups, but most breeders do. The usual guarantee is either one or two puppies alive to a specified age, or else the bitch may be returned for a free service at her next heat. These arrangements are individual and may be altered to suit both parties. The only requirement is that both parties clearly understand the terms and that the agreement be recorded in writing. A young, unproven dog may have a lower fee or delayed payment for stud fee. The owner of a very old dog may allow him to be used for a partial fee with the remainder due when the bitch is determined to be in whelp.

When drafting your stud contract, consider as many contingencies as possible. Will you charge for transporting the bitch to and from the airport? Will you charge board for any days over a certain minimum? If you take a puppy as stud fee, is it first or second choice, who chooses it and at what age, who pays shipping, if any, and whose kennel name can be used? These special provisions could be added to the sample contract shown.

BREEDING DIFFICULTIES

It would be impossible to cover in this book all the reasons why a bitch fails to conceive or carry a litter to term, or why a stud quits siring. Every breeder at some time or other will be confronted with a problem of this kind. About half of the problems are freakish, onetime occurrences. Others include:

Abortion

Until the emergence of canine brucellosis, abortion was considered to be rare in bitches. The death of one fetus will not cause a bitch to abort. Rather, she will resorb or partially resorb the fetus. If a problem occurs very early in pregnancy, the bitch will probably resorb the entire litter. Fetuses that die in the last week of pregnancy will most likely be delivered along with

STUD SERVICE CONTRACT

The Bearded Collie stud dog, (name) _____ ; (color) _____

registration # _____ owned by XYZ Kennels was bred on (date) _____ to the

bitch (name and reg.#) _____

owned by (name) _____

of (address) _____

Phone: _____

Color: _____

POLICY FOR APPROVING BITCHES: Bitches must be approved before being accepted. Bitch must be in good health and condition at time of breeding and must be free of hereditary defects, parasites, or infections. She must be of good conformation and temperament and must be physically suitable for breeding to the selected male. Recent negative culture and brucellosis test may be required at the owner's expense.

The owner must be willing and able to provide proper care for the litter and agree that no puppies from the resultant litter will be sold to pet shops or other wholesale outlets. If the owner does not have a statement from a veterinarian that the bitch has a recent negative culture and brucellosis test, or if the bitch is so uncooperative that a natural breeding is not possible, the stud owner reserves the right to breed by artificial insemination at the owner's expense.

STUD OWNER'S RESPONSIBILITY: The best possible care and handling will be given to visiting bitches. However, we cannot accept responsibility for accidents which happen while a bitch is in our care. Our stud dogs are guaranteed to be in the same good health that we require of a bitch.

GUARANTEE: XYZ Kennels guarantees at least two living puppies to the age of three weeks. If less than that number result, the owners of the bitch are entitled to a free return service to any male owned by XYZ Kennels, subject to the availability of the dog requested. This guarantee applies to the above named bitch only, unless otherwise agreed upon. No other guarantee is given or implied.

The stud fee is due and payable at time of service and is not refundable.

STUD FEE: $ _____ Paid in full?   Yes   No

SPECIAL PROVISIONS: Signed _____
                                       (owner of bitch)
Airport pickup and delivery fee: _____
                                       _____
                                       (owner of stud)
Board after _____ days $_____
                                       _____
                                       (address)
Other:
                                       _____
                                       (phone)

the rest of the puppies. Abortion, therefore, is only recognized during the fifth to eighth weeks.

Beginning about 1962, an infectious disease characterized by abortion and by infertility in males and females occurred in epidemic form in all regions of the United States. By 1968, the disease had been diagnosed in more than eight hundred bitches in thirty-eight states.

The most striking characteristic of brucellosis, B. canis, is that abortion usually occurs between the forty-fifth and fifty-fifth days of gestation, without any forewarning and without fever or illness in the bitch. Most aborted litters are stillborn or die shortly after birth.

Bitches commonly exhibit a vaginal discharge for several weeks, and most fail to conceive thereafter. A few, however, may deliver normal litters a year or so later.

In males, this infection may be accompanied by scrotal dermatitis and painful swelling of the scrotal sac, which often is followed by testicular atrophy and sterility.

At present, no known cure or immunization exists, although research is currently underway. The disease is detected by testing for elevated serum antibody titers with a standardized tube agglutination test. Dogs should be checked two times, thirty days apart. Suspect brucellosis when a bitch aborts late in pregnancy or fails to conceive twice in a row. Suspect any male that has associated with a bitch that has aborted or failed to conceive. The bacteria remain active for at least a year, and the infection is spread through the urine as well as by genital contact. When one dog in a kennel is infected, the Brucella generally spread rapidly throughout the entire kennel. At this point, the infection can only be controlled by isolating all new dogs and eradicating all infected dogs.

Failure to Conceive

Inability of a bitch to become pregnant when bred at the correct time by a fertile male can result from infection in the uterus, a hormonal imbalance, or disease. A bitch that has had dis-

temper, leptospirosis, or other serious infectious disease may never come in heat. Other bitches come in heat quite often, yet never conceive. Generally, this situation is caused by ovarian cysts or by overproduction of one of the hormones, which prevent ovulation. A tumor or infection in the reproductive tract will often prevent conception.

Some veterinarians induce heat by giving pregnant-mare serum to bitches. This is a dangerous practice, because horse serum contains large amounts of protein that can cause extreme allergic reactions in dogs. If you wish to artificially stimulate your hormone-deficient bitch to come in season, request that the vet use pure FSH (follicular stimulating hormone), not pregnant-mare serum. FSH in its pure form should not cause allergic reaction.

False Pregnancy

Occasionally, bitches, bred or not, will have all of the symptoms of pregnancy—the uterus will enlarge under the influence of progesterone, and the mammary glands will fill with milk. At about the time that they would be due to whelp, these bitches may go through the process of nesting and, in rare cases, even labor. It is difficult at first to determine whether such a bitch is really pregnant. The only difference is that the whelps cannot be felt. False pregnancy ends at about the time that a normal pregnancy would terminate. It does not harm the bitch, and little is really known about what causes the condition. Some bitches with a history of false pregnancy never conceive. Others conceive normally when bred.

Obstructions in the Bitch

A bitch may have a stricture or a hymen that prevents penetration by the male during the breeding. This must be broken or dilated or in severe cases corrected by surgery. To examine the bitch, wear a thin rubber glove and lubricate a finger with surgical jelly or petroleum jelly. Insert the finger about three inches into the vagina of the bitch. Any obstruction should be obvious within that distance. If the vagina is too small to penetrate, the bitch may be too early in her season, but more likely she will need to be dilated or bred artificially. It is best not to breed a bitch that cannot be bred naturally, because this condition tends to be hereditary. You may find a bitch that is difficult to breed because the vulva is lower than the vaginal canal and the male is unable to penetrate. Try lifting the vulva between two fingers so that the male has an unobstructed passage.

Resorption of Whelps

If a bitch conceives and something goes wrong—hormonal imbalance, injury, toxicity from medication or poison—before the sixth week of pregnancy, she will simply resorb the dead puppies or those that her body cannot sustain. Resorption sometimes occurs so early in the pregnancy that one may never know if the bitch was actually pregnant. In some cases, this problem can be corrected by giving repositol progesterone after breeding and repeating the treatment at two-week intervals through about the sixth week. The injections will have to be given with each breeding, because the deficiency does not correct itself.

Sperm Counts

A sperm count is a microscopic examination of a dog's semen. It will determine if sperm are present, if they are in sufficient quantity for the dog to be a reliable sire, if they are motile, and if the sperms' morphology (form) is normal. A semen sample must be collected from the male immediately prior to examination. The container must be heated to body temperature and held inside an insulated sleeve to keep the sperm motile. It is easier to stimulate the male if a bitch in season (any breed) is present to excite him. Morphology of the sperm is more easily determined if the slide is stained.

Sterility of the Stud Dog

There are two primary reasons for a stud to quit siring besides brucellosis or infection. One is the inability to produce live sperm. This problem is usually caused by a hormonal change within the body (sometimes a hereditary concern) which, if complete, will eventually lead to testicular atrophy. A biopsy of the testicle can tell if the dog is producing semen, but unless it is done properly, the scars from this operation can guarantee permanent sterility. A series of hormone injections may temporarily restore fertility, but excessive use of hormones will cause the body to quit producing them altogether, and result in testicular atrophy. A change in diet and exercise may be beneficial.

The other cause of male sterility is a blockage preventing sperm from being ejaculated. In this case, a biopsy will reveal that the dog is producing viable sperm, but a check of the semen finds only carrying fluid present. In this case, hormone injections are detrimental. A blockage may be helped surgically depending upon its location. Seek help from a specialist in breeding problems if you decide to attempt this procedure.

Occasionally, a dog becomes sterile for seemingly no reason, then suddenly begins siring again. This may be due to overuse, condition, diet (hormones in some commercial feeds and from poultry used in animal feed can be harmful), or a temporary hormonal reversal. A dog that has not been bred for some time should be bred at least twice to his next bitch, because the first ejaculate may contain aged or dead sperm.

The recommended procedure in determining sterility in a stud is to take a sperm count and a brucellosis test. If these are normal, the fact that a bitch missed is not the males's fault. If sperm are nonexistent, even after a change in environment, a testicle biopsy should be conducted and treatment scheduled accordingly. Prognosis is usually poor for correcting male sterility.

Thyroid Imbalance

An over- or underactive thyroid can cause failure to conceive. If enough thyroid hormone is not produced, the bitch will not ovulate. She will tend to be overweight and lazy and have a greasy-looking coat.

Thyroid malfunction can easily be detected through blood tests and corrected by the administration of the hormone, but it is one conception problem that few veterinarians consider. If your bitch will not conceive and you suspect thyroid deficiency, request a blood test for thyroid level. This problem is usually hereditary but may be aggravated by living at high altitudes. Consider carefully before perpetuating the tendency.

Uterine Infections

While the uterus of a nonpregnant bitch is remarkably resistant to infection, the pregnant or pseudopregnant uterus is quite susceptible to infection from a variety of bacteria. Therefore, the period between breeding and whelping, and immediately after the birth of a litter, are key times to check your bitch for vaginal discharge, odor, or other signs of infection.

There are a host of potential low-grade uterine infections. Most are characterized by some type of discharge and may be treated with antibiotics. Several more serious types also exist.

Acute Metritis. This infection occurs from bacteria introduced during whelping or, less commonly, during breeding. The chances of metritis are increased in cases of abortion, retained whelp or placenta, or lacerations of the uterine wall. Bacteria isolated from infected bitches include staph, strep, and E. coli.

The bitch appears depressed and has a foul-smelling, dark reddish discharge. She is feverish and does not want to eat. Neither will she care for her litter if she has one. Treatment with antibiotics is required immediately, and spaying is sometimes necessary.

Pyometra. This is by far the most serious uterine infection. The cervix closes under the influence of progesterone after the end of estrus, and the infected uterus fills with pus that cannot drain. The bitch may be depressed and may have an odorous, pus-filled discharge. She will want to drink unusually large amounts of water and may run a temperature. If not treated immediately, she will become very ill. The infection does not respond well to any drug, and the only hope of saving the bitch is immediate removal of the uterus.

CULTURING AND TREATING INFECTION

Any time that a colored or foul-smelling discharge is noticed, that a bitch aborts or fails to conceive, or that uterine infection is suspected, a uterine culture should be taken. If infection is present, the veterinarian can learn from the culture what organism is causing the problem. Common infections include staph, strep, and E. coli. A culture to determine sensitivity to specific drugs should follow any positive growth. A culture from a bitch is more accurate if taken while she is in season. Semen from a male can also be cultured.

14 *The New Generation*

During the first few weeks after a bitch has been bred, no dependable signs of pregnancy appear. Occasionally, you will observe a slight change in the bitch's behavior, or her nipples may appear pinker and the vulva softer than normal. There may be a clear discharge from the vulva. None of these signs are reliable clues, however, so feed and condition any bitch as if she is pregnant until proven otherwise.

If the eggs were fertilized, they will move from the oviduct down to the uterus, where they will implant themselves into the uterine wall about twelve days after the onset of diestrus. As the whelps grow in size, the horns of the uterus, normally about seven inches long, will also increase in length, often to several feet by the end of gestation. By the twenty-fourth to thirty-fifth days of pregnancy, the whelps will have grown to about the size of a ping-pong ball and can often be palpated with your fingertips. The two horns of the uterus generally lie below the intestines. Sometimes they rest along the abdominal wall, while at other times they lie well up in the abdomen just behind the rib cage. Take the bitch's abdomen between your thumb and forefinger and gently, but firmly, palpate from the rear toward the rib cage. The fetus at this stage will feel like a small lump. It is impossible to tell how many puppies the bitch will have, because some of the fetuses will be carried high and out of your reach. After the thirty-fifth day, the fetuses will be surrounded with fluid and will be impossible to feel.

Date bred	Date due to whelp	Date bred	Date due to whelp	Date bred	Date due to whelp	Date bred	Date due to whelp	Date bred	Date due to whelp	Date bred	Date due to whelp	Date bred	Date due to whelp	Date bred	Date due to whelp	Date bred	Date due to whelp	Date bred	Date due to whelp	Date bred	Date due to whelp	Date bred	Date due to whelp
January	March	February	April	March	May	April	June	May	July	June	August	July	September	August	October	September	November	October	December	November	January	December	February
1	5	1	5	1	3	1	3	1	3	1	3	1	2	1	3	1	3	1	3	1	3	1	2
2	6	2	6	2	4	2	4	2	4	2	4	2	3	2	4	2	4	2	4	2	4	2	3
3	7	3	7	3	5	3	5	3	5	3	5	3	4	3	5	3	5	3	5	3	5	3	4
4	8	4	8	4	6	4	6	4	6	4	6	4	5	4	6	4	6	4	6	4	6	4	5
5	9	5	9	5	7	5	7	5	7	5	7	5	6	5	7	5	7	5	7	5	7	5	6
6	10	6	10	6	8	6	8	6	8	6	8	6	7	6	8	6	8	6	8	6	8	6	7
7	11	7	11	7	9	7	9	7	9	7	9	7	8	7	9	7	9	7	9	7	9	7	8
8	12	8	12	8	10	8	10	8	10	8	10	8	9	8	10	8	10	8	10	8	10	8	9
9	13	9	13	9	11	9	11	9	11	9	11	9	10	9	11	9	11	9	11	9	11	9	10
10	14	10	14	10	12	10	12	10	12	10	12	10	11	10	12	10	12	10	12	10	12	10	11
11	15	11	15	11	13	11	13	11	13	11	13	11	12	11	13	11	13	11	13	11	13	11	12
12	16	12	16	12	14	12	14	12	14	12	14	12	13	12	14	12	14	12	14	12	14	12	13
13	17	13	17	13	15	13	15	13	15	13	15	13	14	13	15	13	15	13	15	13	15	13	14
14	18	14	18	14	16	14	16	14	16	14	16	14	15	14	16	14	16	14	16	14	16	14	15
15	19	15	19	15	17	15	17	15	17	15	17	15	16	15	17	15	17	15	17	15	17	15	16
16	20	16	20	16	18	16	18	16	18	16	18	16	17	16	18	16	18	16	18	16	18	16	17
17	21	17	21	17	19	17	19	17	19	17	19	17	18	17	19	17	19	17	19	17	19	17	18
18	22	18	22	18	20	18	20	18	20	18	20	18	19	18	20	18	20	18	20	18	20	18	19
19	23	19	23	19	21	19	21	19	21	19	21	19	20	19	21	19	21	19	21	19	21	19	20
20	24	20	24	20	22	20	22	20	22	20	22	20	21	20	22	20	22	20	22	20	22	20	21
21	25	21	25	21	23	21	23	21	23	21	23	21	22	21	23	21	23	21	23	21	23	21	22
22	26	22	26	22	24	22	24	22	24	22	24	22	23	22	24	22	24	22	24	22	24	22	23
23	27	23	27	23	25	23	25	23	25	23	25	23	24	23	25	23	25	23	25	23	25	23	24
24	28	24	28	24	26	24	26	24	26	24	26	24	25	24	26	24	26	24	26	24	26	24	25
25	29	25	29	25	27	25	27	25	27	25	27	25	26	25	27	25	27	25	27	25	27	25	26
26	30	26	30	26	28	26	28	26	28	26	28	26	27	26	28	26	28	26	28	26	28	26	27
27	31	27	May 1	27	29	27	29	27	29	27	29	27	28	27	29	27	29	27	29	27	29	27	28
28	Apr. 1	28	2	28	30	28	30	28	30	28	30	28	29	28	30	28	30	28	30	28	30	28	Mar. 1
29	2			29	31	29	July 1	29	31	29	31	29	30	29	31	29	Dec. 1	29	31	29	31	29	2
30	3			30	June 1	30	2	30	Aug. 1	30	Sep. 1	30	Oct. 1	30	Nov. 1	30	2	30	Jan. 1	30	Feb. 1	30	3
31	4			31	2			31	2			31	2	31	2			31	2			31	4

Whelping chart, courtesy of Gaines.

The pregnant bitch must be kept in good muscular condition so that she will have plenty of strength to expel the whelps. During the early weeks of pregnancy, her regular routine or training need not be discontinued. The house dog should have several hours of free exercise in fresh air each day, or at least half an hour daily of road work on leash. During the last two or three weeks of pregnancy, the bitch that is heavy in whelp will not be inclined to run or work. She should be prevented from jumping, herding, or doing any strenuous work and should be encouraged to exercise freely in the yard or taken for long walks on leash. A bitch that is closely confined is prone to whelping difficulties.

About the fourth week of pregnancy, your bitch's appetite may increase. If she is self-fed, just make sure that she is not becoming obese. If you feed her individually, change to two meals per day and increase her food intake as she requires, making sure that she does not overeat and put on unnecessary fat. Providing you feed a premium ration, simply switch over to the "lactation" or "growth" formula during the fourth or fifth week of pregnancy, and continue this diet until her litter is weaned. Additional supplements are not needed. However, if you continue to feed a standard maintenance-type food, your bitch will need additional protein, calcium, and phosphorus during the final weeks before whelping. Small amounts of liver, lean beef, or cottage cheese are excellent sources of protein, and bone meal supplies the best and safest calcium/phosphorus supplement. Calcium and phosphorus must be balanced at a ratio of 1.2 to 1. An unbalanced mixture can be harmful.

As whelping approaches, your bitch will appear quite obviously pregnant by her enlarged abdomen. About a week prior to whelping, the puppies "drop," leaving the bitch with a sunken-in appearance in the loin areas. Her nipples will enlarge and turn pink in color, and the mammary glands generally fill with milk. The bitch should now be kept in the house, where you can keep a close watch on her condition. She will need to go outside frequently because her bladder will be crowded by the growing puppies.

About ten days before the litter is expected, move the bitch to her whelping box. This will give her time to get used to sleeping in a new area, and you will be prepared if the litter happens to come early.

WHELPING BOX

The most commonly used whelping box is a wooden box with the addition of a "pig rail" to protect the puppies from being laid on by the bitch. But there is a far better way that imitates nature. Wild mothers, or even the stray that crawls under a porch to have her litter, will dig a hole that has a rounded bottom. This has a distinct advantage other than just a place to whelp.

If there is a rounded bottom instead of a flat one, the puppies all gravitate to the bottom center, where they stay in a bunch. When the dam gets in with them, it is easy for her to lie down around them without stepping on or lying on a puppy. If one pup gets isolated, gravity guides him downhill so that he quickly finds the other puppies instead of crawling aimlessly around and crying. Because the puppies stay bunched together and no pup is isolated for long, the puppies easily keep each other warm while the bitch is away for short periods, and supplemental heat is not needed in normal room temperatures of sixty-eight to seventy degrees. (If the room is colder, the litter is very small, or the pups are delicate or orphaned, extra heat would be needed. Just be very careful to avoid overheating the puppies or the bitch.)

There are commercial whelping "nests" available that are built on this principal. However, it is easy and far less expensive to build your own. This box is easy to clean, provides excellent footing, and is easy to store between litters. A good size for a Beardie is twenty-seven inches wide by thirty-seven inches long.

Do not make this box too large, because the puppies should stay in it just until they are getting up on their feet and moving to the edges to eliminate. At this time, move them into a pen so that they can have sleeping quarters in one area and be able to move away to eliminate. This preserves their instinct to stay clean and makes them far easier to housebreak later on. The pen should be as large as possible, and should have wire it so that they can see out easily.

Materials Needed for Whelping Box

1" x 2" boards
1" x 12" boards
Sheet of heavy corrugated cardboard (large packing cartons are good—just cut out one side to the needed size)
Sheet of vinyl leatherette (the cheaper grades are best because they will stretch more readily)
Lightweight canvas or heavy duck material (cut to size after washing because they will shrink a lot)
Tools—saw, either hammer and nails or screws and screwdriver; either 1" carpet tacks or a staple gun.

Assembly Instructions

1. Cut and assemble the 1" x 2"s into a rectangle, 26½" by 36½" outside dimensions .
2. Trim the cardboard to fit out to the edges.
3. Cut the vinyl so that it overlaps the cardboard on all sides by 1½ to 2 inches.
4. Cover the cardboard with the vinyl and fold the edges of the vinyl under the cardboard, then tack (or staple) to the top of the frame, spacing the tacks every ½ inch all around.

Assembling a whelping box.

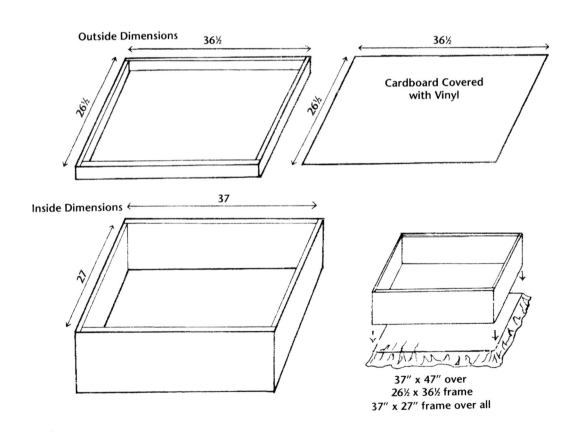

Outside Dimensions   36½

26½   26½

Cardboard Covered with Vinyl   36½

Inside Dimensions   37

27

37" x 47" over
26½ x 36½ frame
37" x 27" frame over all

5. Using the 1" x 12"s and either nails or screws, assemble another rectangle, slightly larger than the first so as to fit around it, 27" by 37" inside dimensions.

6. Cut the canvas or duck into at least three pieces, each measuring at least 37" x 47".

7. Place a canvas sheet over the bed, then lower the 1" x 12" frame over it. The weight of the frame holds the canvas snug so that the bitch can't scratch it up. The weight of the bitch will cause the bed to sag, giving the rounded bottom. For the first use, you might place some weights in the bed for a week or so to start the stretching. Prior to and during whelping, you will put plenty of newspapers in the box, but afterwards use just the canvas. To change the bedding, just tip the frame up on end and put down another piece of canvas.

Pig Rail

If you feel that you absolutely must have a pig rail, it could be attached to the inside of the 1" x 12" frame without losing the other benefits. In this case, the bed dimensions should be enlarged to allow for the rail. Also, if you like to sit on the edge of the box (it is amazing how much time you can spend watching puppies do nothing but eat and sleep), you can nail a triangular board across one corner for a seat.

Storage

To store, you can either leave the 1" x 12" frame assembled or take it apart and tape the boards together. If you do the latter, it is best to assemble the box with screws. This pen will last indefinitely because it is easy to replace the cardboard and vinyl if necessary. Try this design and you will be amazed at how quiet and contented the babies will be.

WHELPING SUPPLIES

You will also need to assemble a few supplies near the whelping box. The list might include a large stack of newspapers, several towels, sterilized scissors, and a hemostat, dental floss, and several plastic garbage bags. You might also want to have on hand a can of bitch's milk replacer, a feeding tube, and some liquid glucose. If you are experienced at whelping, your vet might also supply you with some oxytocin to keep on hand for uterine inertia. He will instruct you in its use, and you must follow these directions explicitly.

Accustom the bitch to the whelping box.

SIGNS OF APPROACHING LABOR

All Beardie bitches are individuals, and it is difficult to predict just how they will behave prior to whelping. Some announce the event by nesting for several days in advance; others nonchalantly go into labor and whelp their puppies without so much as a murmur. The surest clue that whelping is imminent is a drop in the bitch's temperature. Start taking her rectal temperature morning and evening about ten days prior to her due date. At first, it will hover in the neighborhood of 101.5 to 102 degrees Fahrenheit. A few days before she whelps, it will drop slowly to around 100 degrees, and just before the onset of labor, her temperature will drop abruptly, usually to 97 or 98 degrees. If no signs of labor occur within twenty-four hours of this drop, have your bitch examined by a veterinarian.

The bitch will usually have a clear, profuse discharge from the vagina at this time. The young bitch having her first litter will probably show only slight enlargement of the mammary glands, but the older, proven brood bitch may be heavy with milk. The bitch may refuse to eat during the day or so preceding whelping, but again, each bitch is an individual and may not

Restlessness marks the start of prelabor.

follow the expected pattern. She will probably seem restless and uncomfortable, and the young bitch, not knowing what to expect, may be a bit nervous.

Make your final preparations now. Bathe the bitch, or at least wash her hindquarters and stomach with an antiseptic soap. Keep the discharge cleaned up as much as possible to prevent the hair from matting. Finally, clip the hair around the vulva. This will keep the area clean and prevent a puppy from becoming entangled in the long hair. Also comb the hair away from the breasts. Most of it will be loose and will come out as you comb. Clip the feathering at the sides of the belly and any hair that still remains around the breasts.

Prelabor

This is the early stage of labor during which much is happening inside the bitch's body to prepare the puppies for birth, but outward signs may be difficult to detect. This stage lasts from two to thirty-six hours.

During this time, various hormones effect a series of events. The whelp, which has been attached to the uterine wall by the placenta (through which the whelp receives its nourishment and oxygen supply), prepares to detach. The cervix and birth canal dilate to allow for the passage of the puppies. The contractions at this time are weak and cannot generally be seen or felt. The bitch, however, becomes increasingly uncomfortable. She may scratch feverishly at the newspapers in her box, pant, or possibly vomit. Between these fits of activity, she will probably lie quietly asleep in her box. As time passes, she may begin to lick vigorously at her rear parts or sit and watch her sides with much curiosity.

You should not interfere at this stage, but do keep an eye on your bitch. Note how long the prelabor stage is lasting and be concerned if it continues much longer than twenty-four hours. If the bitch wants to go out, let her relieve herself, but make sure that she does not whelp a puppy in the yard. If you think that whelping is progressing abnormally, or if it has been more than twenty-four hours since the bitch's temperature dropped or she began prelabor, take her for an examination. If a puppy is stuck or an obstruction exists, the bitch may not go into labor at all. Excessive nervousness, pain, bleeding from the vulva, or a foul-smelling discharge at this time all warn of problems that should be dealt with by your veterinarian. Also have your bitch checked if she goes past the sixty-third day with no signs of going into labor.

Some vets will advise you to wait if you just call and consult them on the telephone. If you are concerned, insist on an examination. Most Beardies are easy whelpers, and if problems arise, they usually are serious enough to require veterinary assistance.

WHELPING

During labor, the contractions increase in intensity and can sometimes be seen as the abdominal wall hardens and then relaxes. The bitch may be seen straining as though she is having a bowel movement. By now the whelps have begun to detach from the uterus and move into position in the birth canal. Puppies at the base of the uterine horns will be whelped first. The whelp, the cord, and the placenta are all contained in the outer sack. This sack is filled with amniotic fluid, which acts as a cushion for the whelp. A second sack covers the whelp itself. The whelp and the placenta are connected by the umbilical cord, which contains two umbilical arteries and one vein. As the puppy, enclosed in this double-layered sack, moves down the birth canal, the water bag is forced out in front, where it helps to soften and dilate the passage. It finally bursts during a contraction and the fluid lubricates the vagina, making the way easier for the whelp.

Watch for the breaking of the water bag. If you notice fluid or see wet papers in the whelping box, you can be sure that the first puppy is on the way. If the water bag ruptures and no puppy appears within an hour, or if the bitch goes into hard labor and suddenly stops having contractions, there may be complications. Sometimes a puppy gets jammed at the junction of the uterus and the birth canal; if so, you will need veterinary assistance. Do not give oxytocin before the first puppy has arrived, because the contractions stimulated by the shot could cause the uterus to rupture.

The Puppy Arrives

Puppies are born either head first, which is preferable, or hind feet first, which is known as "breech." In the head-first position, the sack is filled with a dark fluid that you see first. A young bitch may become frightened and try to bite at the sack as it appears. If this happens, prevent her from tearing at the sack or the puppy by grasping the hair at each side of her neck just behind her ears, holding her head rigid. Lift her completely off the floor so that she cannot struggle against you. Don't bend recklessly over her head—you could be bitten accidentally. The next contraction should cause the puppy to come free and drop to the floor of the whelping box. You can then release the bitch and let her get back to the work at hand.

The puppy will generally still be enclosed in the translucent sack; he will be attached to the placenta by the umbilical cord. Occasionally, the placenta will not come out with the puppy, and the bitch will sever the cord, leaving the placenta in her body. It should be expelled with the next puppy. Be observant of this and ask your veterinarian to check any bitch that you suspect has retained a placenta, because this condition can cause infection of the uterus.

The pressure encountered during birth will stimulate the puppy to start breathing, and if he is not removed from the sack within a minute or two, he could suffocate. Most bitches will instinctively begin cleaning the sack off of the puppy. If she does not get the puppy out, you will have to take over for her. Grasp the sack between folds of a clean washcloth and pull for-

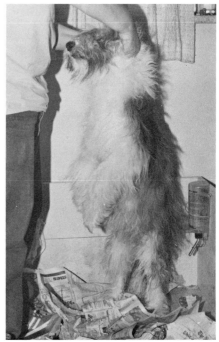

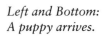

Top:
Hard labor begins. Lift the bitch if she tries to snap the whelp.

Left and Bottom:
A puppy arrives.

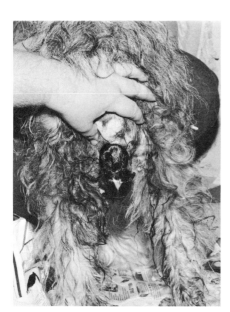

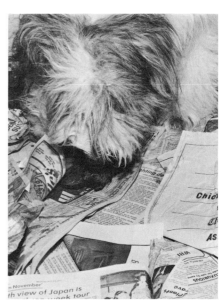

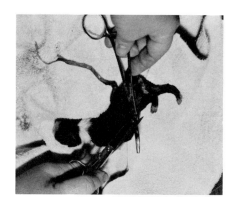

Top: Most bitches whelp unassisted.
Middle Left: The puppy is
attached to the placenta at birth.
Middle Right: If the bitch delays,
clamp and cut the umbilical cord.
Bottom Left: Leave the cord
clamped for a few minutes
to stop bleeding.
Bottom Right: Remove puppies until
the bitch has finished whelping.

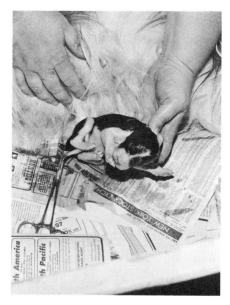

ward, away from the puppy's head. The sack will break easily. Use the cloth to wipe away any fluid from the nostrils and mouth, then give the puppy back to his dam.

The bitch will likely turn her attention to eating the placenta and in the process will sever the attached umbilical cord. The placenta contains hormones that stimulate the uterus to contract after whelping. These hormones also stimulate the production of milk. Bearded Collies are remarkably efficient when whelping and are likely to resent your interference. Observe, but stay out of the way unless the bitch is having trouble or is not taking care of the newborn.

A maiden bitch sometimes does not realize that the expelled mass of fluid and tissue contains a puppy. In this case, remove the puppy from the whelping box so that you can work on him without upsetting the bitch or getting yourself bitten, and proceed to cut and tie the cord. Take the cord between your thumb and forefinger, and milk the blood in the cord toward the puppy. Then, holding the cord firmly near the puppy so that no pressure is on the navel, use the thumb and forefinger of your other hand to pull and tear the cord about one inch from the puppy's body. (If you prefer, you can clamp the cord with a hemostat and sever it with sterilized scissors. This causes more bleeding than does tearing, so leave the hemostat clamped on the cord for several more minutes.) A cord that continues to ooze blood, whether cut or severed by the bitch's teeth, should be tied off with a loop of dental floss about one-half inch from the puppy's stomach. Knot twice, then cut off any excess string so that the bitch cannot pull on it.

Some puppies need to have the fluid cleared from their lungs and trachea. If you hear a puppy "rattling" when he breathes or see one having difficulty breathing, you will need to shake out the fluid. Hold the puppy between the flat palms of your hands, being careful to support his head. Raise your arms straight out in front of you, then bring them sharply downward, stopping abruptly with the puppy's head straight down. Repeat several times if necessary. Take a good hold and, as long as his head is supported firmly, don't be afraid of shaking the puppy too hard. Once the pup gives a good loud cry, you know that his breathing is clear. If a whelp is slow to start breathing, he can often be stimulated by rubbing briskly with a rough towel.

Whelping Difficulties

A call to your veterinarian is warranted when more than two hours pass between puppies, when more than one hour passes since the onset of hard contractions, or if labor ceases completely, yet more puppies are obviously inside the bitch.

Large or Breech Puppies. Sometimes a large puppy, or one that is in the breech presentation, will have difficulty coming through the pelvic opening. A little assistance will generally free the puppy. Have someone hold the bitch so that she cannot snap, and take hold of the puppy with a clean washcloth. Pull him gently and firmly down toward the bitch's stomach. Never pull him straight out. If he still doesn't come loose, pull him gently to one side, then to the other.

You may pull a puppy either by the feet or by the head, depending on which is protruding. However, do not try to pull on only one foot. A gloved finger may be able to find and free the other foot. Never pull a puppy that is presented upside down. Instead, try to turn him over, or seek veterinary assistance.

If you have not succeeded in freeing a puppy, or if the puppy is too far inside the bitch for you to grasp, take your bitch immediately to a veterinarian. You will probably have to muzzle her and load her in a traveling crate. The other puppies may be safely left in their heated box.

Uterine Inertia. The most common problem that a bitch encounters when whelping a large litter is uterine inertia. The bitch simply wears out and stops having contractions in the midst of delivery. Sometimes a short rest and a couple teaspoons of brandy in a bowl of milk will revive the bitch, and she will resume having contractions. An injection of oxytocin (pituitary hormone), one cubic centimeter (cc) intramuscularly, will often revive the contractions. The bitch should start contractions within fifteen minutes of receiving the injection. If a puppy has not arrived within forty-five minutes, it is best to seek veterinary assistance.

Impossible Delivery. If a bitch, for whatever reason, cannot whelp a puppy or a litter naturally, your vet will perform a cesarean section. He can usually remove all of the puppies while they are still alive if you have taken reasonable care and have not waited too long. While the bitch will be groggy for twelve to eighteen hours afterward due to the anesthesia, the puppies will be able to nurse as usual. You may need to remove them from the bitch to prevent her falling on them at first. You should also rub the puppies' stomachs after they eat to stimulate defecation. Within a day, the bitch will be caring for them normally.

POSTWHELPING CARE OF THE BITCH

The bitch will probably be thirsty after whelping and will appreciate a drink of water or warm

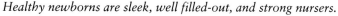

Healthy newborns are sleek, well filled-out, and strong nursers.

milk. She will not want to eat for several hours, and after all of the puppies are cleaned and dry, she will probably fall asleep.

For the first two or three days, fee your bitch lightly and often, gradually building up to her regular ration by the third or fourth day. Broth, cottage cheese, and a little raw liver are good in the interim. Mix her food into a soft gruel and feed only small portions at a time, even though her appetite may become voracious. After about the fourth day, you can give her as much food as she wants. Provide plenty of water at all times.

The bitch's temperature will rise to 101.5 or 102 after whelping. If everything is normal, it will not exceed 102.5. A high temperature or a greenish, pus-filled discharge probably indicates an infection that will require immediate treatment. Some discharge and bleeding are to be expected, but excessive blood loss is cause for concern. Immediately after whelping, as well as while the bitch is in heat, are prime periods for the occurrence of uterine infections, so watch your Beardie carefully.

Some bitches seem to give all of their nourishment to their puppies and are therefore prone to "nursing fits" or eclampsia, caused by having all of the calcium drained from their system. The bitch will appear to stare wildly, she may wobble, or she may go into convulsions, walk stiff-legged, or limp. An injection of calcium, if given immediately, will correct this condition. If left untreated, your bitch could die.

Most Beardie bitches whelp and raise their puppies without complications, so you can relax and enjoy the experience of watching a litter thrive and grow.

Ch. Britannia Sweet Lady, CD, with puppies from the "Spot/Sarah III" litter.

15 *All Beardies Great and Small*

Watching your newborn Beardie puppies can be awe-inspiring. They are so strong and sleek, with a color intensity that makes them resemble little seals. The blacks and browns look like they have been polished to a fine sheen; the blues and fawns are flatter in color but have an iridescent look dusted on the tip of each hair.

If you have not already done so, clip the long hair from directly around each of the bitch's nipples. If this hair is left, the pups have a more difficult time nursing. The long hairs can wrap around the nipple, shutting off the milk supply. If the problem goes undetected for a few days, the nipple can actually be severed from the body. A couple of minutes spent clipping these hairs (preferably prior to whelping) will avoid any problem.

The puppies will search out their first meal as if directed by radar. A healthy pup will fight his way through the other pups until he finds a nipple and latches on. The tongue will wrap around the nipple, and, after the first few frantic tugs, the puppy will lie almost still with his tail held stiffly straight out behind him. He will cause little commotion unless a littermate tries to nose him out. If a puppy cries while nursing or frantically crawls from one nipple to the next, the bitch may not have enough milk. A shot of oxytocin during the first twenty-four hours following whelping may help to bring down the milk, but stimulation from the pups' nursing may be all that is needed.

It is extremely important that all pups nurse well during their first twenty-four hours of life. The milk produced immediately

*One-week-old puppies
at Chriscaro.*

after whelping is called colostrum and contains the antibodies that give the puppies immunity against various diseases during their first few weeks. This immunity is more complete if the bitch has had recent vaccinations. Be sure that the litter has enough functional nipples. The number of nipples can vary from dog to dog, and some Beardies have very large litters. If there are too many pups, you may have to supplement the feeding for some or split them into two groups and alternate the bitch's time between them.

The second immediate concern is that the bitch licks the puppies, because the puppies' urination and defecation are controlled strictly by outside stimulation. Most Beardies are good about this. The first bowel movement, called meconium, is very dark brown in color and should occur during the first hour after whelping. Constipation at this age can result in death. As long as the bitch licks the puppies and checks them periodically, everything should be fine.

If any umbilical cord begins bleeding, remove the puppy to a separate box and apply a hemostat to close off the cord. Bleeding should stop and the clamp may be removed after a few minutes. You can tie the cord with a piece of

dental floss if bleeding persists. If cords are cut to roughly one-inch lengths, the danger is less than if the bitch chews them very close to the body. If the cord is too long the bitch may keep pulling at it, which stimulates bleeding and can also cause an umbilical hernia. A small amount of lost blood is not significant; a large volume can substantially weaken a puppy.

Most Beardie mothers are possessive and efficient with their puppies. These traits are admirable and should be encouraged. If a bitch is not a good mother, especially after her first litter, do not consider her a prime brood bitch, and be aware that these traits will probably be passed on to some of her daughters. Beardies will remain a strong breed only as long as breeders do not perpetuate weaknesses.

EXAMINING THE PUPPIES

Check each puppy for abnormalities and overall condition. Start with the head. Are markings satisfactory? They need not be symmetrical, but a puppy with a predominately white head looks more like an Old English Sheepdog than a Beardie. Be aware that blazes will narrow to about half their width by maturity. Open the mouth and check for a cleft palate, a condition in which an opening in the roof of the mouth allows air and milk directly into the nasal passage. A puppy with this deformity will have trouble sucking, and often milk will bubble from the nostrils. The cleft can vary from a wide gap to a narrow hole near the back of the palate, which is difficult to see. There is no cure, and any defective puppy should be "put down" immediately.

Look at the way the jaws meet. If the puppy had teeth, would they meet in a level or scissors bite? If a puppy is undershot or badly overshot (one-fourth inch or more), he may later have difficulty eating. Therefore, you may want to consider disposing of this puppy now. Bites that are abnormal at birth are much less likely to correct than ones that become problematic during development.

Check nose, lip, and gum pigment (most will be pink at birth). Are the gums very white, or do you notice any other deviation? Anemic puppies or ones that show a bluish cast may have a heart defect or severe parasitic infection (especially hookworm). Watch these puppies very closely for a day or two to see if the color

corrects. If so, the color was probably due to oxygen deficiency during birth and no treatment is necessary. If the condition persists, consult your vet. Parasites can usually be treated, but defective puppies should be diagnosed and euthanized immediately.

Next look at the body for mismarks, club feet, kinked or bobbed tails, or any obvious deformity. Club feet are usually caused by a cramped position in the uterus and may correct themselves by the time the puppy is old enough to walk. Most other problems will not correct.

If some puppies need to be destroyed, do so immediately by having your vet administer an overdose of anesthetic. This is painless and quick. Very few Beardies are defective, but problems will increase if breeders perpetuate the "weakies." It is selfish and foolish to try to raise puppies that are not healthy, normal, typical Beardies. You do not need them yourself, and they should not be sold to someone else. It is much easier to dispose of a puppy immediately before you form an attachment to it. Neither you nor the bitch will miss it after a few hours, and your conscience will be clearer if you are firm about this responsibility from the start.

Lincalder Wild Thyme at Chriscaro nursing her first litter to Ch. Orora's Frand.

EARLY ENVIRONMENT

The puppies should now be placed on a surface that provides proper footing. Most Beardie mothers will not tolerate newspapers (which are unsuitable anyway) or loose towels for bedding and will root them into a corner of their box, leaving the puppies on a hard, bare surface. If you use the previously described whelping box, the canvas provides excellent footing. If you use a flat-bottomed box, the best liner is a piece of indoor-outdoor carpet cut to fit the exact size. This is washable and should certainly be washed before being used for the first time. It is best to have two pieces to alternate while one is being cleaned. Proper footing allows the puppies to have traction while nursing.

Beardies are notorious for whelping early and for having puppies that grow at a tremendous rate. While early pups usually look as strong and healthy as full-term pups, their ribs are softer and more easily crushed by their body weight. If a pup is forced to remain on a hard, slick surface, his rib cage will become flat on the bottom, restricting his lung capacity and

Above:
Two-week-old puppies need lots of sleep.

Below:
Three weeks old and starting to explore.

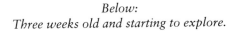

forcing his legs to flail helplessly to the sides. In most cases, this condition corrects itself when the puppy is placed on proper footing.

In extreme cases, a pup may become a "swimmer," a condition in which the puppy's front legs are unable to reach under his body and he is supported solely by his chest. Lung capacity is decreased and heart failure may occur. A swimmer can sometimes be helped by suspending his body inside a cardboard tube. Tape the puppy's body to the top of the tube so that his chest can eventually drop to a normal position, and control his weight by limiting feedings. Fat puppies are more susceptible to swimmer's syndrome.

Be sure to keep the puppies' toenails clipped short. They are very sharp and can scratch the bitch terribly while the puppies nurse. If she gets too sore, the bitch may not feed the puppies as long or as often as she should. Nails should be clipped every third or fourth day. Human-type nail clippers are the easiest to use while the puppies are small.

The puppies must be kept in a draft-free environment. They can catch pneumonia easily in a drafty place even though the temperature is warm enough. The sides of the box should be at least twelve inches high. If a wire crate is used, tie cardboard along the bottom of each side.

Supplemental heat is not needed with Beardie pups unless the litter must be separated from the dam (if puppies are orphaned or if a large litter is split into two boxes). A house temperature of about seventy degrees is adequate for healthy pups. If you have a sick or weak puppy, a heating pad or heat lamp may be used to bring the temperature in the box to eighty-five or ninety degrees. Do not overheat the puppies so that they dehydrate. For this reason, a heating pad that covers only part of the box is safest. Puppies kept on carpet need less additional heat than those kept on paper.

WEAK PUPPIES

Some puppies get off to a bad start. Either they are smaller and get pushed away from the food, or they are thin and weak and just can't seem to snap out of it quickly. If a weak puppy is getting pushed away from the dam, hold the larger puppies back so that the small one can nurse unobstructed every few hours.

Occasionally, a weak puppy will not have the strength to hold onto a teat but can still nurse if held to the dam. Hold this puppy to the bitch and keep him awake and nursing at least fifteen minutes every two hours until he becomes stronger. Making a cupped bed out of a bath towel and propping the puppy against the bitch may suffice if the other puppies are removed. Never deprive the healthy pups for a sick one that will probably die anyway. The weak puppy that doesn't show drastic improvement during the first two days is a very poor risk.

Do not employ extraordinary means to keep puppies alive. Puppies that are this weak rarely make suitable adults, even in a pet capacity. Heat, food, and fluids are all that should be offered, and these only for a limited time.

Tube-Feeding the Weak Puppy

A puppy can be fed with an eyedropper or premature-baby bottle, but neither method is very efficient. If you must hand-feed an entire litter or a sick puppy, learn to tube-feed. At first this is a bit unnerving, but done properly, it is better for the puppy and is far easier and quicker for you.

You will need a ten-cubic-centimeter plastic or glass syringe and a "number five" rubber catheter. You can obtain these from a vet-supply house or from your local hospital. These tubes are used on premature human babies.

Hold the puppy with his head stretched forward. Put the tip of the tube at the puppy's last (rear) rib and, following the curve of the neck, measure to the end of his nose. Mark this point on the tube with a piece of adhesive tape or a bit of nail polish. Boil the tube and syringe to sterilize them.

To feed, attach the tube to the syringe and draw up about one cubic centimeter more milk than the puppy will need. Place the pup on his tummy on a flat surface. Open his mouth and

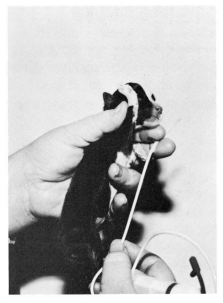

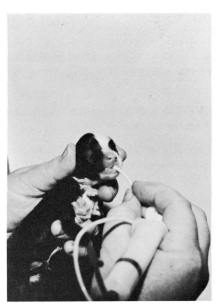

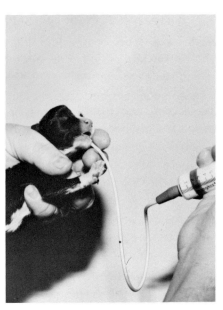

Measure the catheter before feeding.    *Insert the tube gently.*   *Inject the formula slowly.*

insert the tube. Because it is probably still dripping with milk, most puppies will start to swallow the tube on their own. It is important to keep the puppy's head straight and forward while you are inserting the tube so that the tube will slide easily down the esophagus. If the tube hits an obstruction, do not force it. Instead, withdraw it slowly and start over. The tube should slide easily to the mark that you made earlier. If it doesn't, it may be in the lungs.

You may check this in two ways if you are not sure. Draw the milk back into the syringe, remove the syringe from the tube, and listen. If the tube is in the lungs rather than in the stomach, the pup's breathing should be quite audible when the tube is held to your ear. You may also place the end of the tube in a glass of water. If bubbles appear, the tube is in the lungs. With a little experience, you will be able to insert the tube into the stomach easily every time. Care is always necessary, however, for if you inject the liquid into the lungs by accident, the puppy will catch pneumonia and probably die. Luckily, it is very rare that the tube does not enter the stomach as desired, and if it inserts to the mark, you are safe.

When you are sure that the tube is all the way into the stomach, press the plunger of the syringe very slowly until about half of the desired feeding has been given. Check the stomach. It will begin to fill out. If it looks full and stretched, the puppy has had enough. If not, rest a second, then continue forcing the liquid into the stomach until the full amount has been given. Wait a few seconds, then withdraw the tube quickly.

With practice, you will be able to feed an entire litter in a few minutes. The puppy expends no energy in getting his food, and strong puppies will soon be able to go six hours between meals. Start orphaned puppies eating from a dish by three weeks of age, and wean them from milk to solid food as soon as possible.

Feeding Particulars

The easiest and best formula to feed is a bitch's milk supplement, such as Esbilac. This is readily obtainable in either dry or liquid form from any pet-supply store or through veterinarians. If you use the dry form, mix only enough for one feeding at a time. Follow instructions on the can for mixing and storing. The liquid form is much more satisfactory for young puppies. If you absolutely cannot obtain bitch's milk replacer, mix one egg yolk with one-half cup of whole homogenized milk. Heat all formula to about

100 degrees and test it on your wrist to make sure that it feels neither hot nor cold.

Newborn puppies and very small, weak, or sick puppies should be fed every two hours. Larger, stronger puppies can manage with feedings every four hours, and by the time they are one week old, every six hours. It is important to establish a schedule and stay with it. Irregular feedings cause colic. If the puppies cry between feedings, they are probably hungry, and either you are not feeding enough or you need to feed more often. No matter how hungry a puppy is, he should be fed slowly. A puppy that guzzles milk will almost surely get colic.

Each puppy needs an individual amount of food, and this amount depends on the weight and health of the pup. Do not overfeed sick pups; in fact, it is always better to underfeed than to overfeed. As a general rule, a twelve-ounce Beardie puppy should get about one and one-half ounces of formula a day. Divide this by the number of feedings per day to arrive at the amount per feeding. Vary this to suit the puppy. Six feedings, one every four hours, would mean that this puppy would receive one-fourth ounce at each feeding. If the puppy is small or ill, feed at two-hour intervals and do not allow more than two cubic centimeters each time at first. The amount and the interval between feeding can be gradually increased over the next few days.

While a puppy on supplemental formula will not gain as fast as a pup raised on bitch's milk, he should gain at least an ounce every couple of days. If he is getting enough formula, the puppy will sleep contentedly between feedings and his stomach will look full and round. A puppy that is being overfed will look bloated, and his stools will become curdled and yellowish. Cut the strength of the formula in half at the first sign of diarrhea, and cut back on the amount. If diarrhea continues, you may want to switch to liquid glucose in water for a few feedings. It might also be wise to have your vet check a stool sample for coccidia.

Do not forget to rub the tummy of a puppy to stimulate defecation and urination if the puppy is not being placed with his dam between feedings. (See the following section for method.)

Danger Signs in Young Puppies

If you pick up a puppy and he feels limp, cold, clammy, or lifeless, you must act quickly to find and treat the condition. Common causes are starvation, constipation (causing toxemia), overheating, or chilling.

Chilling. First check the temperature of the box and adjust it accordingly. Warm a chilled puppy gradually by rubbing him briskly to stimulate circulation, then carrying him around under your shirt or coat. You can also place him under a heat lamp or on a heating pad, but be careful not to cause shock by raising the temperature too quickly. Heating pads should be set on low heat. Do not feed a chilled puppy until he has been thoroughly warmed, becauses he will be unable to properly digest the formula.

Constipation. If the pup's tummy is full and if the pup appears normal in color and healthy to outward appearances but does not rouse and nurse, then he may be toxic from constipation. Stimulate him by rubbing his tummy with damp cotton balls. If this does not bring relief, and if the puppy strains or whimpers and cries, give one cubic centimeter of warm water as an enema. You must inject the solution slowly to keep from causing too much pressure. If this does not give relief, get the puppy to a veterinarian right away, because the bowel or rectum may be blocked, twisted, or ruptured, and further stimulation could cause complications.

Overheating. An overheated puppy will cry and scream and may pant or hyperventilate. Remove him from the heat immediately and keep him quiet until his body has returned to a normal temperature. He will usually be red, limp, and exhausted, and he may be dehydrated.

Sore Eyes. Occasionally, a puppy's eye becomes puffy and pus accumulates under the lids. This must be removed by gently pressing around the eye socket to force the matter out of the lids. Clean the eye area with a cotton ball dipped in warm water. If the eyes are not yet

*Three puppies by
Ch. Moonhill's
Classic Plus Sign.
Courtesy of Ann Lord.*

open, the eyelid may have to be slit. Use a sterile scalpel and just score the surface, or else have your vet administer treatment.

Diarrhea. This is common in puppies and may be caused by defective milk from the bitch, colic, overeating, incorrect formula mixtures, parasites, or any number of infections. Curdled, extremely foul-smelling or bright yellow feces are serious indications signaling a call to your veterinarian.

Ordinary diarrhea may be treated first with four drops of Kaopectate every four hours. If the puppy is being hand-fed, dilute the formula to half strength, or feed only weak glucose water (Karo syrup dissolved in water) for twelve hours. If the diarrhea has not been curtailed in twelve to sixteen hours, it is time to call your veterinarian. The puppy may require antibiotics, which should be employed only if a specific outside cause for the infection is known.

Check for dehydration (which is recognized by loose skin), and treat if necessary. Pinch the skin together. If it stays together when you release it instead of returning to the way it was, then the puppy is dehydrated. Again, this condition is very serious in a tiny puppy. If the pup is

only mildly dehydrated and is nursing well, just watch him and make sure that the condition corrects within a couple of days. If he is in bad shape, your veterinarian can provide you with sterile fluid to inject under the skin in several places. Repeat two or three times a day until the dehydration is no longer evident. It will take a lot of fluid to correct the condition, so don't be afraid to inject several cubic centimeters. Severe dehydration can kill a puppy within twenty-four hours.

PUPPY DISEASES

Colic and Enteritis

A puppy that cries when touched and that doubles up is probably colicky. This is common in puppies, as it is in babies, and generally is not cause for alarm. Usually, colic is caused by gas in the stomach and intestines, which is precipitated by the puppy swallowing air, either while bottle-feeding, tube-feeding, or nursing. Colic can also be caused by overeating or by bad milk. Give the puppy eight drops of Kaopectate and rub his tummy with cotton to stimulate release of the gas. If the puppy develops diarrhea, treat it accordingly. If the entire litter becomes colicky, the cause is probably in the bitch's milk or is due to parasites. Alkaline milk is quite common and necessitates hand-feeding the litter. You can check this by using Testape, available at any drugstore.

Enteritis is a more serious stomach and intestinal inflammation. The puppy will scream and show obvious signs of intense abdominal pain that occurs rather suddenly. Get the puppy to a veterinarian fast.

Pneumonia

Pneumonia is caused by a puppy becoming chilled, getting milk or other fluid into his lungs, or by a virus. Mechanical pneumonia, caused from fluid going down the windpipe, is probably most common. You will at first notice labored breathing followed by a rattling noise in the chest. The puppy will cry at first, then become limp and pale, later turning blue. Your vet can put the puppy on antibiotics, but the death rate is very high. Usually, the best treatment is simply to keep the puppy warm and tube-feed him until he regains his strength.

Other Diseases

Septicemia is a term used to describe a puppy that has a system full of various forms of bacteria. The feet, nose, and pads of the feet will turn a fiery red color, and the pup will "mew" like a kitten. Prognosis is poor, and a bitch that regularly produces septicemic puppies should be cultured while in season for the presence of *E. Coli* or other bacteria. If the bitch requires antibiotics every time she is bred, she is a questionable brood animal.

Herpes virus is usually contracted from the bitch. The puppy will develop profuse yellowish-green diarrhea. A fat, healthy, week-old puppy will just stop eating and begin to scream endlessly, followed eventually by dehydration, labored breathing, painful whining, and death. Autopsy will reveal liver damage, and the virus can generally be isolated.

Although the cure for these symptoms is unknown, some breeders believe that adding vitamin K or feeding raw-liver blood several times a day can benefit both bitch and puppies. Prognosis is usually poor, and again, it may be best to simply weed out sick puppies and continue with the healthy ones.

EVALUATION OF YOUNG PUPPIES

It is difficult to keep your hands off of the newborn pups. Some bitches become frantic if you pick up their babies, while others proudly display them for your approval. Either way, do not fuss with the puppies to the point that it deprives them of sleep or food. They need all of their strength at this age for survival and growth. Nevertheless, besides checking for defects and health, you will want to note your first impressions and evaluations of the puppies.

A good procedure is to evaluate for structure at birth; at about three days (to verify the initial look); at four weeks, eight weeks, six months, one year, and two years; and at maturity. This progression will help you recognize the growth patterns and normal development for puppies of your line. All lines develop slightly differently, and with experience, you will learn to recognize characteristics peculiar to your line. Most puppies develop uniformly and are consistent in comparison to their littermates throughout development. It is beneficial to watch all puppies from a litter to see how they mature.

The head is the most obvious part to evaluate in a tiny puppy. The head should be broad, rectangular, and relatively flat in the skull and on the sides and have a broad, blunt muzzle. The muzzle should merge smoothly into the skull on the sides with no dip below the eyes. The skull and top of the muzzle should be parallel (viewed from the side) and separated by a

Hold a puppy in this manner to assess his structure.

The same dog, Ch. Parcana Silverleaf Vandyke, Parcana, showing similar traits as an adult.

distinct "stop" or break between the eyes. The underjaw should be full and rounded at the chin by birth, with the same scissors bite preferred in an adult. If the head looks rounded, pinched in muzzle, or Roman-nosed, recheck at three days to see if it has filled out, because some heads are rather compressed at birth. Sharp ridges from the eye back along the sides of the skull generally indicate that the skull will broaden and probably flatten with age.

Next, check overall proportions. The head should fit the body. If the head is too large, the puppy will probably grow into it. If it is too

small, it will probably remain too narrow or "snipey" for the dog. The neck should be moderately long and should be held proudly when the puppy nurses. The body should be long in the rib cage with ribs slanted toward the tail, and the loin should be strong, well-muscled, and not overly long.

Angulation can be evaluated by holding the puppy as illustrated and measuring angles between the shoulder and the upper arm and between the pelvis and the stifle. The ridge to measure along the shoulder blade is obvious, because the layer of fat has not yet formed under the skin of the puppy. Front and rear angulation should be as close to a right angle as possible. The upper arm and shoulder blade should be the same length (be sure that you are measuring the actual length of each of these bones). The stifle should be quite long and the hocks noticeably low set. Tail set and croup cannot be evaluated until sixteen weeks of age when the pelvis drops to the adult position.

Depth of chest can be checked, however, with the best chests reaching the point of the elbow. Many are shallow at birth but improve by eight weeks of age. Rear legs should hang straight and parallel (viewed from the rear) when the puppy is relaxed. Fronts may be a bit crooked at birth, but straight front legs are a real bonus. Bone should be moderately heavy and can be best evaluated by examining the diameter of the legs in proportion to the body.

Coats will be flat and preferably harsh, the more profuse ones being thicker on the back of the neck and on the back of the front legs.

At three days of age, the puppies should present a more perfect picture of this description. By this time, the layer of body fat will be filling out the outline and the heads will be looking stronger.

DEWCLAWS

At three days of age, right after the evaluation is made, the dewclaws should be removed. A dewclaw is the fifth toe located like a useless "thumb" on the inside of the front legs. Although not required to be removed by the breed Standard, dewclaws invite injury to the dog later in life if left intact. They catch easily

Right: A three-week-old puppy showing a weak head. Note snipey muzzle with dip under eyes and sliding stop.

Bottom: A good, blocky head on a three-week-old puppy.

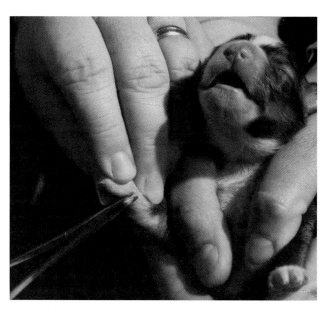

Remove dewclaws when pups are three days old.

in underbrush and can be painfully ripped off, and the nail will grow into the leg if neglected. Beardies almost never have hind dewclaws, but these *must* be removed if they are present.

Dewclaws can be snipped off at the skin line with large sewing shears, or they can be removed with a small, sharp hemostat. The hemostat does a cleaner job of removing bone and causes less bleeding.

Have someone hold the puppy on his back in a spread-eagle position. With the hemostat as close to his leg as possible, close it over the dewclaw and crush the toe. Remove the clamp and reapply it in the same manner at ninety degrees. This prevents most bleeding and removes a minimum of skin. With the hemostat clamped shut, twist it sideways as if you were rolling it along the leg. Apply enough pressure to lift off the dewclaw. It is best to go back and grasp any remaining bone fragments with the tip of the hemostat and pull them loose. It is almost impossible to go too deep, and anything that can be grasped is safe to remove. This prevents lumps in the legs or the possibility of the nail growing back. Sometimes the dewclaw breaks off cleanly with the first operation.

Apply silver nitrate to the wound to seal it and stop any bleeding. You will find that pup-

pies complain because they are being restrained, but once they are back in their box, they show little evidence of pain. Neurologists assure us that pain does not consciously register in a puppy until five days of age, and by then the area is nearly healed. No further treatment of the area is required.

THE TODDLER

At any time after three weeks of age, move the puppies to a larger pen, but make sure that they still have a draft-free bed, especially at night. Use either a four-by-four-foot or a four-by-four-by-eight-foot portable exercise pen, depending on the number of puppies and whether the pen will be set up inside or outdoors. If possible, keep your puppies near a traffic area in your home where they will be exposed to all kinds of attention and new sounds and sights. Be sure that the puppies can see out of their enclosure. Those confined to a solid-walled box never develop as desirably in a mental and emotional capacity. Start putting puppies on the table to be brushed at this age, and begin early leash-breaking. Just be sure to keep it fun.

Expose your puppies to all possible noise and confusion—vacuum cleaners, television, children, washing machines, doorbells—but don't deliberately frighten them. Normally, Beardie puppies accept all of these distractions in stride and adapt easily to any situation. For a puppy that shows a tendency toward shyness at this age, a little extra patience and attention can do wonders. Do not snatch him up every time he comes to you or he will begin ducking away. Puppies want to play on their own level and feel insecure if they do not have their feet on the ground. This is hard to do, but make a conscious effort to keep your hands off of the pups some of the time.

The Four-Week-Old Puppy

At four weeks of age the puppies should be up on their feet, making it easier for you to evaluate their bodies. Front legs should be straight by now, and stance should be square all around. The body may appear shorter because the puppy has grown rapidly in height and is not yet balanced. The muzzle should be square, but the head may be a bit longer and leaner overall because it is now lengthening. Watch for the puppy that falls into a trot most of the time when moving. He will probably become your best mover. As eye color changes from baby blue to the adult color, the first eyes to change will probably be the darkest color.

Temperament Testing

Several sophisticated tests can evaluate basic temperament traits in your puppies, but here are a few very simple tests that can easily be done at home and that, if conducted when the puppy is six weeks old, will be fairly accurate. Most Beardies have good temperaments, and testing usually is not necessary, but it can help to match specific puppies to the right homes and help avoid problems caused by the litter "pecking order."

Take the pups individually to a place where they have never been, preferably a closed room, and have a stranger to the puppies do the testing. The person should not speak to the puppy throughout the tests.

Set the pup down, leave him, and observe his reaction. Does he sit huddled up? Does he check out his surroundings? Is he suspicious, curious, or observant? This test tells a lot about self-assurance and how the pup will react to a new environment.

Set the puppy at one end of the room and have the tester walk to the other side, kneel down, and clap his hands. Does the puppy come? Does he ignore him or run the other way? Responsiveness is the key this time.

Hold the puppy on his back on the floor for a minute, still not speaking to him. The dominant puppy will struggle and fight the entire time. The submissive pup will lie quietly. The pup that is sensible and has a nice combination

of both traits (making him easier to live with) will fight until he realizes that he is overpowered. He will then become quiet and will accept the tester as his boss.

Next, cradle the puppy in your hands, keeping his legs dangling just a couple of inches off of the floor. Hold him this way for thirty seconds and see if he struggles. Most pups will lie quietly for a few seconds and then struggle. A very aggressive puppy will throw a tantrum and will perhaps try to bite, while a very timid one will remain passive. A puppy that trembles when placed on a table is also likely to be timid.

With the puppy several feet away, bang on a pan with a spoon. Does he come to investigate the source of the noise? Does he look toward the sound and then ignore it? Does he panic and run away?

If one puppy is aggressive in all tests and another is submissive, you may want to separate pups into two groups, or put the leader in with older dogs that will "knock him down a peg." These tests are more accurate than just playing with puppies, because pups react differently when they are on familiar ground with their own people.

Weaning

Puppies should be weaned at five weeks of age if they are normal and healthy. If the dam has been on self-feeding with growth or lactation formula, the puppies probably have been mouthing and eating some of her food and may be weaned directly onto the dry food. If the puppies will not eat dry food, some additional moisture is needed. A good way to do this is to put some food in a bowl and add just barely enough water to cover it. Let this sit until all the water is absorbed. The food will be softened but will still hold its shape and will not be sloppily wet. Gradually add less and less water until the puppies are eating the food dry.

The reason for weaning the puppies this early is that Beardies are unusually precocious and have such a rapid growth rate. If pups

Ch. Orora's Impetuosity at six weeks of age.

remain on the dam past the age of five weeks, the dam's condition weakens to the point where it takes several months for her to regain her weight and coat. If the pups are removed at five weeks, the bitch will bounce back in very short order. Take the bitch away for a few days, then let her return to play with the pups and help with their socialization. Check a fecal sample at this age and worm puppies if necessary. The first vaccination should be given at six or seven weeks. So many different immunization schedules are advocated by various people that it is best to follow your own vet's recommendations.

The Beardie goes through distinct stages of emotional development not unlike those for physical growth. Weaning time is stressful for the puppies, and the eighth week is a critical period in developing response to people.

A puppy should be friendly and quick to respond to your attention. At about three months of age, however, all puppies display what is known as avoidance behavior. This is nature's way of allowing the puppy to learn to discriminate between friend and foe. He will probably act as though he wants to play but will remain just out of reach or run away as you approach. Ignore him, and he will soon be in your lap. Within a few weeks, he will be back to being the friendly, aggressive puppy that he once was. Except for these few weeks, he should be self-assured and eager to please.

EVALUATING THE OLDER PUPPY

At eight weeks of age, the puppy should resemble a miniature adult in structure, head, and proportion. Croup and tail set may still be a bit high, and the coat will be rather wooly and of a more or less uniform length over the body. Beard and feathering will not yet be pronounced. The puppy should have broadened again in skull, and the flatter the skull, the better. Ear set can now be evaluated, and the very small, fly-away ears can be detected if they exist. The bite may be starting to go slightly overshot, or it may still be a scissors bite. Movement can begin to be assessed accurately,

Eight-week-old puppy.

and stance and angulation should again reflect the small image of an adult. By this time, eyes begin to show their adult color, and nose pigment should be nearly, if not completely, filled in. Most males have both testicles descended by eight weeks, and this is most preferable. Males that do not have both testicles descended should be held back until this condition corrects if they are to be sold as show or breeding prospects. The rest of the puppies may go to new homes if they are healthy and vaccinated.

During the next few months, the puppy will go through a tremendous growth period and at times will appear to go off in quality and balance. He should eventually return to the picture that he presented at eight weeks. Sometimes a puppy will go quite overshot. This may improve by six or seven months of age but can take until about eleven months to correct completely. Most bites improve if they were correct at birth. At about three months of age, the puppy loses his baby teeth. The baby canines must be pulled if they do not loosen as the adult canines appear. Otherwise, the bite may develop improperly.

Puppies tend to grow taller hind end first, making them high in the rear. They then catch up in the front in a seesaw pattern. After a rapid growth spurt, bone will appear more fine and angulation more straight until balance returns.

Pasterns may become a bit weak at three months, but the feet should point forward.

At six months, the puppy will probably be solid and sound moving and starting to develop a heavy puppy coat. His head should be broad and squared off, his tail carriage more like that of an adult, and his front legs straight. Males without both testicles descended at this age should be sold for pets. Bitches may appear small at this age. Males should be nearly twenty inches at the withers by now unless they have experienced a setback or are from a slow-growing line. Bites may be correct or overshot.

Between six and eighteen months of age, a Beardie will enter adolescence. This period of confusion and uncertainty usually occurs from seven to eleven months of age. His instincts are becoming stronger and puberty has arrived, yet the dog is still a baby in many ways. The conflict is evident in his behavior, and he may become submissive or wary of strangers. It is best not to stress a dog during this age, and training should be delayed until he outgrows his unsureness. By one year of age, most Beardies have regained their former composure in any situation with no special help from their owners. Some dogs remain in adolescence throughout their second year.

Beardies experience no major changes after two years of age and once again become charm-

An excellent head for an eight-week-old pup. Davealex His n' Hers, Davealex.

Hair on a puppy's face is often too wooly.

miraculously, and the dog, although of full height, will look more immature and less impressive than he did a few months before. Bite should be correct by now, and longer, harsher hair should be evident over the withers. During the next few months, the dog will look very "intermediate" in development and may shed coat from the front half of his body, leaving the impression that he looks like two dogs sewn together in the middle. Don't despair. Most Beardies go through this stage and you cannot hurry it.

By two years of age, many dogs will have filled out, and the coat length should be improving. Color, which probably went very light at one year (except in the ones that remained nearly black), will be noticeably darker, and the puppy texture should be less evident. Hair will not be growing over the eyes so badly, and the beard and feathering should be lengthening. Your Beardie should be over any adolescent quirks by now, and he will be looking more and more like a glamorous adult. Body may be a bit thin, but bone should be ample.

Beardies mature between three and four years of age, depending on their line and condition and on whether they have been bred. Although your two-year-old probably looked great at home, the mature dog will look ever so much more impressive. The long, harsh, mature coat has changed his overall appearance, and his body is now very solid and well muscled. Coat color may still change slightly from year to year, always growing in from the roots and breaking off at the tips in a constant rainbow of shades. The mature Beardie will hold this quality and look into old age, making the long wait well worth the time and tears shed along the way.

ing extroverts. Formal obedience training is best started after the dog has become an adult emotionally. He can perform the exercises at a younger age but will not be as steady or as happy about doing so. Males have more trouble with adolescence as a rule, and breeding a dog often speeds up his transition to adulthood.

At one year of age, the puppy coat may be starting to shed, substance will have vanished

Opposite Page: Britannia How Sweet It is, "Zooey," as she grows up.

Zooey is the puppy with the spot on her neck.

At four weeks of age.

Above: At six months of age.

Right: At sixteen months of age.

As an adult winning Best of Breed.

Am./Can. Ch. Britannia Ticket To Ride, "Spot," at seven weeks of age.

Right: Spot at four months of age.

Below, Left: Stonehaven's My Boy Troy at age three months.

Below, Right: Who says Beardies don't like water? Ch. Highlander Wildest Dreams.

16 *Bye Bye, Beardie*

Selling your Beardie puppies will generally be a rewarding experience as the new owners discover the unique, loving personalities of their new pets. Selling puppies can also be frustrating and sometimes time-consuming. It is not always easy. Some breeders cannot keep up with the demand, while others find themselves with half-grown Beardies for which they have no market. The key to Beardie sales is twofold: 1) having a reputation for top-quality dogs and 2) advertising properly and educating potential buyers.

The very best publicity is simply to let your Beardies be seen. Take your dogs everywhere—to dog show, matches, obedience and conformation classes, to the shopping center, to outdoor sports events where dogs are allowed, to the park, or wherever the public will be exposed to your Beardies. Then be prepared to spend a little time answering questions.

Beardies will sell themselves if given the opportunity. Most successful breeders have found that their best market comes from people who have met and become enchanted with a Beardie and who will reserve a puppy from the next litter even before the bitch is bred. Here, too, lies a key to selling all of your puppies: breed only the number of pups for which you feel sure there is a market. Some of your puppies should always be spoken for, or at least the demand should be evident before you breed, and you should never breed unless you want a puppy yourself. This not only prevents overpopulation of the breed but helps to maintain the overall quality of Beardies. Pets should be the lesser-quality puppies from top-quality parents, not puppies from mediocre parents bred just for sales.

It is helpful to have printed information that you can give or mail to persons wanting to know more about the breed. The Bearded Collie Club of America (BCCA) publishes a leaflet explaining the history and characteristics of Beardies, but you may also want to prepare your own flyer that describes your particular line of dogs. That will save you a great deal of time in writing letters. You can follow up with more detail once you know that the person is seriously interested in buying a Beardie. Never lower your prices to make a sale. People who are genuinely interested in the breed and who will care for the dog will not barter. If they cannot afford the price, they may not be able to care for and promote the dog properly. You can accept payments if you like, but keep prices comparable to those of other breeders. Otherwise, everyone, as well as the breed, suffers.

ADVERTISING

Advertising on a national level is a necessity if you are establishing a kennel and hope to make a name for yourself in the show world. Advertising of this type does not mean advertising a litter of puppies—it means image building and keeping your name before the public over a period of time. Reputations are not made in a day, and the new breeder should not expect instant acceptance. It takes time—often several years.

Your first ads may simply introduce your kennel name and your foundation Beardies. If you accumulate show wins of any consequence, keep your public informed with follow-up ads. Also, you may "blow your own horn" about exciting additions to your kennel or about your Beardies' producing a winner, finishing a championship, or winning an obedience or herding trial. Simply advertising puppies will not generate much interest until you have proof of the quality, intelligence, or ability of the parents and the reliability and experience of your breeding program.

The time that it takes to become nationally recognized is directly correlated to the amount of advertising done on a national level, the number of times your Beardies win, and, of course, the fact that your dogs are really top-notch. You will want to experiment with various magazines to see which ones give you the best results. Several all-breed magazines have large readership, some are devoted to obedience or herding, and the BCCA's *Bulletin* is exclusively for Beardies. Your first ads might include a series of three or four running in consecutive issues, followed by smaller ads every second or third issue over a year's time. It cannot be stressed enough that you should not expect instant results from the first one or two ads. It takes time, patience, and skillful promotion to build a reputation as a breeder. Once you have achieved this, sales will not be lacking.

Preparing the Ad

Anyone seriously interested in writing good advertisements should read a book on the subject. Your local library probably has several. Some of the basics are:

1. Be concise. Keep your copy short and to the point.
2. Don't try to cover too much in one ad. Limit your ad to one subject: a win, an introduction, a stud, or a litter.
3. Develop an identity through a logo, slogan, unique typeface, etc.
4. A headline is 60 percent of your ad's effectiveness. Put a lot of effort into a good headline.
5. A photo, if it is a good, honest one, is worth 1,000 words. Use photos whenever possible. If you aren't a good photographer, hire a professional. It will pay off. A poor photo is worse than none at all.
6. Keep ad layouts simple. You can have a layout designed by a professional for a reasonable

Baby puppy, Britannia Steel Wheels, at eight weeks of age, and Britannia Stars and Stripes at four months of age.

sum, and it may be worthwhile. If the magazine staff does your layout, tell them what you want to emphasize, how large to make the photo, etc.

7. Because most magazines use offset reproduction, you can have your logo from letterhead or cards reproduced for no extra cost. Just furnish a clean black-and-white copy.

8. Use repetition. Repeat your logo. Repeat the qualities that you emphasize in breeding. You may even repeat ads occasionally. Keep your name before your public.

9. Besides the large national magazines, you may want to try farm publications for your working Beardies or the local newspaper for your pets. Experiment with various media.

Stud Promotion

Promotion of a stud dog can take many forms. Some of the most standard methods include general advertising in breed publications, distributing stud cards or kennel brochures, handing out printed business cards, and showing your dog. Be sure to always present a stud dog well

groomed and in attractive, healthy condition. You may wish to consider hiring a professional handler to gain exposure for your dog in the show ring over a wider geographical area. Much of your dog's impressiveness can come from your own enthusiasm for him, but keep your presentation honest and within proper limits.

When advertising your dog, again remember that repetition is important. People need to know that you'll be around for more than a year, and your ad has to be current when they start looking for a stud. Repeat the same two or three points that you wish to stress in each ad, and use a good photo. Vary the photo every few ads, but never run a poor shot of the dog. If you do, it is the only thing that people will remember.

As with general ads, do not clutter your copy with too many words or ideas. Choose a simple theme and leave plenty of white space. Feature the dog's name prominently, and stress a few of his special assets. New wins or titles can be listed, along with your name, address, and telephone number, plus the stud fee, if you wish. Tell just enough to make the people contact you for more information. Pride in your dog will show without gushy superlatives.

Keep in Touch with Other Breeders

Most breeders find that many of their puppy sales come from referrals from customers or from other breeders. You can do your fellow breeders a favor by keeping in touch with them and referring buyers to them when you don't have a Beardie for sale. They will do the same for you. Pet buyers often buy spontaneously and may not wait for your next litter. Find them a good puppy while they are looking, or they may end up with another breed or with a Beardie from an undesirable source.

The best and easiest sales come when acquaintances or friends of a previous customer come to visit. Each satisfied customer who has purchased a healthy, correctly dispositioned, honestly represented Beardie from you has the potential of bringing you many more sales. Each dissatisfied buyer who feels that his dog was misrepresented, overpriced, or impossible to live with because of a bad disposition can do you irreparable harm. Always keep this in mind when you are selling your puppies.

PREPARING YOUR PUPPIES FOR SALE

Proper preparation can make or break a sale and may play a large role in the satisfaction of the buyer. Most puppies go through a developmental stage known as the "fear period" between their seventh and eighth weeks of age. Beardie puppies are ready to go to new homes at the age of eight weeks unless they are going to be shipped (in which case it is best to wait until they are nine weeks old). Before they leave, they should have had their first vaccinations, should be eating solid food well, and should have been weaned for at least two, preferably three, weeks. The immunity will not be as effective if the puppy has not been weaned for this length of time before receiving his vaccination.

To help the new owners get off to a good start, most breeders like to send them home with a packet of helpful aids. This packet should, of course, contain the puppy's registration form, his pedigree, and the sales contract stating terms of the purchase and guarantee. But you will also want to include worming and vaccination records and instructions for the puppy's care and training. (It is highly recommended that you include a copy of this book or other source of breed information. You can increase the price of your puppy enough to cover the cost and do the buyer a big favor.) Perhaps you can also include a small bag of the food that the puppy is used to eating and some rawhide chips to keep him occupied the first night in his new home.

The puppy should be bathed and groomed and have his nails trimmed. Each may have a small collar and should have had a lesson or two in leash training. Check each puppy to make sure that he is healthy and eating properly. If any problem exists, wait until it is solved before you let the puppy go.

MAKING THE SALE

Your first contact with a buyer is usually by telephone. Do not try to sell a dog immediately; instead, sell the buyer on coming to look. Sales are generally not made until the buyer walks through your door.

Always get the potential buyer's name and phone number so that you can follow up if necessary. Ask for specific information about the buyer's wants and needs, and determine whether you have a dog that might be suitable. If not, refer him elsewhere.

Every responsible breeder screens his buyers. There are some people to whom you simply would not sell a dog. Certain people are not suited to a Beardie's temperament, while others do not have appropriate quarters in which to keep a large, active dog. Try to determine these factors in that initial conversation. Sometimes your common sense and intuition have to be your guide, but you can learn much by asking questions about the person's experience with dogs, his facilities, his awareness of the expense of keeping a dog, and his attitude toward neutering a pet. If you are dealing by long distance, your insight may not be as clear, but be sure to talk long enough to establish as many answers as possible. Be absolutely certain that the person has a fenced yard, and refuse to sell a puppy to anyone who does not. That dog could easily end up lost or dead in a few weeks, and your conscience would always be troubled by it.

If you have a Beardie that might be suitable, and you have screened the caller to your satisfaction, move the conversation toward when the buyer can come and look. Tell him just enough to entice him, but explain that seeing the puppy is the only way to make an intelligent choice. Offer to show him your adult dogs and tell him more about the breed. Let him know that you have plenty to offer besides the puppy.

If the inquiry comes by mail, you will need to approach the situation a little differently. If you have several puppies available, your first letter should give a little information about each one to test the buyer's interest. You may send a pedigree and photos of the puppies, the parents, or both. Later letters, narrowing down the sale to one possible individual, should be as detailed, explicit, and honest as you can make them. Point out the pup's virtues, and quickly, but thoroughly, go over his faults. Do be honest about the Beardie. Shipping is both costly and risky, and your reputation depends upon your reliability. Again, make sure that you are satisfied with the potential owner's qualifications before you finalize any sale.

Presenting the Dog

You have made an appointment for the potential buyer to visit, and the puppy is ready. Much now depends on the quality of your stock and on your ability as a salesperson.

If you have an office or other room where trophies, ribbons, and photos are displayed, take the buyer there. Let him relax a bit as you get acquainted and find out in more detail what he wants. No dogs are allowed to be present at

Left, Tamevalley Manhattan Mist; right, Tamevalley Milwaukee Storm, at four months of age.

this point except for one friendly, attractive, well-mannered adult.

When the discussion ends, bring in one puppy at a time. Do not take a buyer into the kennel unless he is a breeder or has some particular reason that makes it necessary. It is a good health precaution to limit visitors, especially to your puppy room, because these people probably have been shopping at other kennels and may be spreading disease. Also, pet buyers can be quite turned off by seeing too many dogs at once, particularly in a kennel situation.

If the buyer wants to see the mother or father, bring the dogs in one at a time, if they are available. Several adult Beardies competing for attention can overpower a visitor. It is sometimes helpful to show the buyer an adult Beardie of the same color and type that the puppy is expected to be as an adult. Give the buyer all the time that he needs in looking over the pup, playing with it, and getting acquainted. Sales cannot be rushed. Beardies will sell themselves to the right people, so there's no need for high pressure. Sometimes it will be evident that a particular puppy and person are just not

Chriscaro's Calico

suited for one another. If this happens, remove the puppy quickly and bring in another if you have one. If you feel that the people are not suited for your dogs, tactfully explain that a personality conflict would make neither the buyer nor the puppy happy. Recommend a different breed or kennel that you feel would be suitable for their consideration.

Closing the Sale

Once you see the buyer starting to make up his mind, reassure him that he has made a good choice. Point out all the positive aspects of this Beardie, but also briefly mention his faults. Ask for a commitment from the buyer. "Shall I brush him up for you?" "Do you want to take him now or pick him up later?"

Never reserve or hold a puppy without a nonrefundable deposit—usually about one-fourth the purchase price. You may find yourself missing other sales while the first buyer fails to pay for and pick up the dog.

Make out the papers, explaining the registration form and how to fill it out. Cover the contract in detail, making sure that every aspect is clearly understood (see samples). Adjust the contract to each individual sale. Terms for time payments, if used, should be spelled out in writing,

and the contract should be signed by the buyer, the seller, and a witness. Whenever the contract calls for time payments, puppies back, or neutering of a pet when it is old enough, the registration papers are commonly held by the seller until all terms of the contract have been fulfilled. The buyer gets the original contract; the seller keeps a copy. Receipts should be issued for all payments. If there is any doubt about the validity of a check, the seller may ask for identification and may hold the papers and contract until the check has cleared. Many breeders have found it safest to ask for cash or certified checks.

The new AKC registration applications have a box that can be checked by the seller, specifying that the dog is not to be bred. No offspring of the dog can be registered, and the dog cannot be shown in AKC conformation classes. He can, however, be shown in obedience or other AKC events.

Excellent front movement on an eight-week-old Ch. Brigadoon Heart Breaker. Photo by Blair.

Rules for Writing Contracts

1. Remember that the contract is just a piece of paper representing an agreement between buyer and seller. It is doubtful that it would hold up legally in court.
2. EVERY dog that leaves your house should go with a contract, even if you're giving the dog to your best friend or mother-in-law (particularly in those two instances).
3. Read through the contract with potential buyers. Discuss its contents BEFORE you write the final draft.
4. There are no hard-and-fast rules. Tailor each contract to the situation.
5. Use deposit contracts. They will save you a lot of grief.
6. Register all pet puppies in your name. Transfer ownership upon proof of neutering.
7. If you do not receive full payment for a puppy before he leaves your house, register him in your name. You may not ever get paid, but you will retain ownership.
8. If the dog is to be shown, be sure the following are clear:
   a. When is the dog to be shown?
   b. How often and over how long of a period of time will he be shown?
   c. How will you groom him?
   d. Who will pay the expenses (entries and travel)?
9. If the dog is to be co-owned, be sure that the following are clear:
   a. The duration of the co-ownership and how it will be terminated.
   b. Who pays the expenses (both show and maintenance).
   c. Be sure that the dog will revert to you if the co-owner cannot keep him.
10. If the dog is likely to be used for breeding:
   a. Retain stud rights on all males.
   b. Include a plea for responsible stud ownership.
   c. Stipulate that a bitch be finished and of proper age for breeding.

Write the contract as strictly as possible. You can always bend your rules in unusual circumstances.

From The Soft Coated Wheaten Terrier Club of America, 1984 Breeders' Symposium

SAMPLE CONTRACT OF PURCHASE AGREEMENT (FEMALE)

This agreement will set forth the terms and conditions of the sale of a female puppy between _____(Buyer) and _____ (Seller). The effective date of the sale is:

1. The purchase price for the ____ month-old _____ is:_____ . Buyer and Seller have agreed that the payment shall be as follows:

2. The initial arrangement is understood as a **co-ownership**. This **co-ownership** shall expire upon the receipt of pick puppy from this female's first litter. It is further understood that the Seller will select the stud dog for the purposes of this breeding. Additionally, the Buyer shall be responsible for all expenses associated with ownership of this puppy, including but not limited to veterinary fees, food, AKC show entry fees, advertising, and the stud service.
3. The Buyer and Seller agree that this breeding should take place on her third heat or at age 18 months, whichever comes first. The Buyer will keep good records of her seasons, detailing the start and stop dates of her season and any notations on discharges or reactions by nearby males that might help document her probably breeding time.
4. At the age of 8 to 10 weeks, the Seller shall visit the Buyer's kennel to evaluate the puppies in this first litter and shall select their pick. In return for this pick puppy, the Seller shall immediately forward to AKC the appropriate transfer documentation to make the Buyer the **full owner** of this female puppy.
5. In the unlikely event that the Buyer cannot keep this bitch for any reason including but not limited to illness, divorce, transfer, or relocation, the bitch shall be offered first to the Seller. This would then be followed by transfer of ownership when specified.

This purchase agreement is signed below by the Buyer and Seller to signify mutual acceptance.

BUYER

Name: _____

Address: _____

Telephone: _____ Date: _____

SELLER

Name: _____

Address:_____

Telephone: _____ Date: _____

SAMPLE CONTRACT OF BREEDING RIGHTS/OWNERSHIP AGREEMENT

This agreement will set forth the terms and conditions of the ownership of a puppy between _____ (Buyer) and _____ (Breeder). The most recent Seller was _____ and this transfer was made with the proper registration form being submitted to AKC. The effective date of this transfer is:

1. The Buyer acknowledges that the Breeder may use this dog at stud at no charge on a bitch or bitches for which the Breeder is a registered owner. The Breeder will, however, provide any necessary transportation to the Buyer's location or mutually agreed upon place (i.e., a show site or friend's kennel).
2. The Buyer shall be responsible for all expenses associated with ownership of this dog, including but not limited to veterinary fees, food, AKC show entry fees, advertising and/or any charges associated with transporting the dog to the Buyer, unless some other arrangement is agreed to by both parties in advance.
3. In the unlikely event the Buyer cannot keep this dog for any reason including but not limited to illness, divorce, transfer, or relocation, the dog shall be offered **first** to the Seller. This would then be followed by transfer of ownership when specified.

This Breeding Rights/Ownership Agreement is signed below by the Buyer and Breeder to signify mutual acceptance of this Agreement.

BUYER

Name:_____

Address:_____

Telephone:_____ Date:_____

SELLER

Name:_____

Address:_____

Telephone:_____ Date:_____

SAMPLE CONTRACT FOR SHOW OR BREEDING-QUALITY DOGS

This Agreement will set forth the terms and conditions of the sale of a show or breeding quality dog between _____ (Buyer) and _____ (Seller). The effective date of the sale is:.

Name of Dog: _____   Litter Reg. #: _____   Tatoo #: _____
Color: _____   Sire: _____   Dam:_____
Sex: _____   Reg.#:_____   Whelped: _____
Date of Birth:_____   Place of Birth: _____

1. This animal is guaranteed to be fertile, to be free from all hereditary defects affecting its suitability for breeding, and to be free of disqualifying and serious faults except those due to injur or neglect after sale. Health and temperament are guaranteed for 48 hours and it is recommended that the Buyer have the animal examined by a reputable veterinarian during that period. A full refund will be given for any dog returned in good condition during the first two days. The Buyer will be responsible only for shipping charges.
2. Credit for the amount of purchase less $ _____ will be given toward a replacement for any dog that matures at less than the represented quality at 12 months of age, as determined by the Seller, provided that the original dog has not produced a litter and is neutered. A free replacement will be given for any dog which for hereditary reasons is unsuitable as a pet as determined by the Sellers.
3. The Buyer agrees to use the word _____ (name of kennel) as the first word in the registered name of the dog if it has not been individually registered at the time of sale.
4. In the unlikely event that the Buyer cannot keep this dog for any reason including but not limited to illness, divorce, transfer, or relocation, the dog shall be offered for sale first to the Seller. This would then be followed by transfer of ownership when specified.
5. The Buyer agrees that this dog will be show trained and conditioned and will be shown consistently and competently either by the owner(s) or a qualified handler.
6. Ownership will be transferred when the dog is paid for in full.
7. Special Provisions:

This Purchase Agreement is signed below by the Buyer and Seller to signify mutual acceptance:

BUYER   SELLER

Name: _____   Name: _____

Address: _____   Address: _____

Telephone: _____ Date: _____   Telephone: _____ Date: _____

SAMPLE CONTRACT AND BILL OF SALE FOR COMPANION DOG

This Agreement will set forth the terms and conditions of the sale of a show or breeding quality dog between _____ (Buyer) and _____ (Seller). The effective date of the sale is:.

Name of Dog: _____   Litter Reg. #: _____   Tatoo #: _____
Color: _____   Sire: _____   Dam: _____
Sex: _____   Reg.#: _____   Whelped: _____
Date of Birth: _____   Place of Birth: _____

1. This dog is purebred. The pedigree is correct and given at the time of sale. This dog is registerable with AKC unless the form is withheld for reasons listed here: _____ . Pedigree is attached.
2. At the option and expense of the Buyer, this dog will be taken to a veterinarian for a thorough health exam within 48 hours from time of purchase. Provided this dog is returned to the Seller with a signed statement from a veterinarian, the Seller agrees to a full cash refund or replacement puppy. This dog is to be free from hereditary crippling defects to 24 months of age. Provided Seller is furnished a signed statement from a veterinarian, a full cash refund or replacement puppy will be given.
3. Should the Buyer at any time by unable to keep the dog, Buyer will contact and either return the dog to the Seller or transfer the dog to a new owner who has been approved by the Seller. Such approval will not be unreasonably withheld on condition that the new owner agrees in writing to be bound by the provisions of this contract.

This Purchase Agreement is signed below by the Buyer and Seller to signify mutual acceptance:

BUYER   SELLER

Name: _____   Name: _____

Address: _____   Address: _____

Telephone: _____ Date: _____   Telephone: _____ Date: _____

FOLLOW-UP

Follow-up is so important. It lets you know if your dogs are in good homes, if the buyer is satisfied, and if the temperament and quality of the dog turned out as you had predicted. Sometimes follow-up helps you learn from your mistakes— you thought that a puppy was better than he was, a pet turned into a lovely show animal that will never be shown, or a hereditary or temperament defect crept in where you least expected. You owe it to yourself and to your buyer to discover these things. It will be invaluable in planning future breedings and evaluating related puppies.

Your buyer may need assistance from time to time, and it is part of your responsibility as a breeder to provide this or guide him to another source. Many friendships, protégés, and new breeders develop from continued relationships between breeder and purchaser. Respect your buyer's right to his own opinions, however. A most rewarding experience in the dog game is seeing a rank beginner buy a promising puppy, learn from your advice and from his own initiative, and take the dog to show or obedience victories. He may even establish a successful breeding program based on the stock that you bred and sold.

Beardie trio. Painting by Chet Jezierski.

17 *Showing Off*

The elite of their breeds, groomed to perfection, trot through crowded aisles. A flurry of brushes, dryers, and people's voices all blend into one continuous rumble, topped occasionally by the roar of the crowd cheering on a favorite competitor. The air is filled with excitement and anticipation. There's no doubt about it—the atmosphere of a dog show is contagious! Many new owners purchase a purebred dog with no intention of showing until, out of curiosity, they enter their first show. From that point on, the competition, fun, and excitement continue to grow.

Dog showing originated many years ago in England, probably for the same reasons that we continue this pastime today. It gives the breeder a chance to prove the quality of his breeding stock, it provides social advantages by bringing together breeders from many areas of the country to discuss and compare, and, for the novice, it presents the ideal opportunity to learn about the breeds. Today, almost every major country in the world has a national kennel club responsible for the registration and record keeping of all recognized purebred dogs. The kennel club approves shows, licenses judges, and offers obedience degrees and championship certificates to outstanding canines. Each country has a different system for tabulating these awards. The prizes are based on a point system determined by the scores in various obedience exercises or by the number of dogs over which an individual wins in conformation.

Dog shows in the United States are held under the rules of the American Kennel Club, which has responsibility for licensing judges and superintendents and for keeping records of the points awarded at each show. The show is sponsored by a local all-breed club or by a specialty club whose members are fanciers of a particular breed. The management of the show may be handled by the members of the club or by professional show superintendents who supply the necessary equipment and are responsible for all arrangements.

HOW DOG SHOWS ARE ORGANIZED

Shows may be all-breed conformation only, all-breed obedience only, all-breed conformation and obedience combined, or specialty shows limited to one or a few related breeds. Most American shows are unbenched, meaning that the dogs may be brought to the show grounds just before their class and may leave immediately after showing. A few big American shows and most European shows are benched. All dogs must remain on assigned benches (stalls) for all or for a specified part of the day on which they show, except, of course, for the time that they are in the ring. Benched shows provide spectators a chance to view the dogs up close before and after the judging.

Each breed is judged against the Standard of perfection for that breed. There are six regular classes: Puppy, Twelve-to-Eighteen Months, Novice, Bred-By-Exhibitor, American-Bred, and Open. All of the males compete first in the six classes, after which a Winners Dog and a Reserve Winners Dog are chosen. These are the best of all of the males entered that day. Then all bitches compete in the same way, and the top two bitches are selected. The Winners Dog and Winners Bitch must then compete with both male and female champions for the Best of Breed award. This is the win that everyone hopes for! A Best of Opposite Sex is then chosen, as well as a Best of Winners. If a male receives the Best of Breed award, a female must be chosen for Best of Opposite Sex. She may be a champion, or she may be the Winners Bitch. If one of the Winners is appointed Best of Breed, that dog automatically takes Best of Winners as well.

Championship points are awarded to both Winners Dog and Winners Bitch, but only the Best of Breed goes on to compete for Best in Group and then possibly Best in Show (see chart).

The Classes

Classes are divided by sex and are judged in sequence from puppy to open.

Puppy. Puppies must be at least six months of age to be entered in a point show. At large shows, the puppy class may be split into two groups—six to nine months and nine to twelve months. Puppies may also be entered in any of the adult classes, but only a particularly mature Beardie will be able to compete successfully with adults.

Twelve to Eighteen Months. This class is for dogs that are no longer puppies but that are not yet mature enough to compete with adults.

Novice. Novice is a class for dogs that have won less than three blue ribbons and that have won no points at licensed shows. This is a good class for a beginning handler or an unproven dog.

American-Bred. This class is open to any Beardie of any age bred in the United States. Amateur handlers may prefer this class because it generally is smaller. A dog that is not in peak condition will look better here.

Bred-By-Exhibitor. Any dog owned or co-owned and handled by his breeder can be entered in this class. Competition may be stiff, but numbers may be small. It is a class for which any breeder should be proud to qualify.

Open. Open is a class for mature dogs and bitches in peak condition.

Best of Breed. This is a class in which only champions may be entered. These dogs compete

Owner Irene Carson leaping with joy as her bitch, Ch. Mistiburn Happy Memories, HC, ROM, ROMI, is picked Best of Breed by Judge Suzanne Moorhouse at the 1987 Bearded Collie Club of America National Specialty.

with the best male and best female chosen from the regular classes.

Non-Regular Classes. These are separately listed classes offered primarily at specialty shows. Included are brace, team, veterans, brood bitch, and stud dog.

Sweepstakes. The rules for sweepstakes classes are made by the show-giving club, and the entry fees are generally divided into cash prizes for the winners.

Futurities. Futurities are similar to sweepstakes except that the puppies are nominated before birth and kept eligible at intervals until the time of the show. This is a real test of a breeder's ability to predict the results of his matings and to evaluate puppies as they grow. Cash prizes are usually substantially higher than for sweepstakes.

The Groups

The dog chosen Best of Breed in each breed in a particular group go into the ring at the end of the breed judging to compete for group placements one through four. There are seven groups: Sporting, Hound, Working, Terrier, Toy, Non-Sporting, and Herding. The Bearded Collie is a member of the Herding group, which also contains Australian Cattle Dogs, Australian Shepherds, Belgian Malinois, Belgian Sheepdogs, Belgian Tervuren, Bouviers Des Flandres, Briards, Collies, German Shepherd Dogs, Old English Sheepdogs, Pulik, Shetland Sheepdogs, and Cardigan and Pembroke Welsh Corgis.

New breeds are added as they are accepted by the AKC. There is also a Miscellaneous Class at AKC shows, but these dogs do not compete for points, Group, or Best in Show. It is for exhibition of rare breeds, some of which have applied for AKC recognition but have not yet been granted full AKC status.

Best In Show

The first-place winners of each of the seven groups compete at the end of the day for the coveted Best in Show award. Beardies have proven that they are contenders for this award.

Acquiring a Championship

Only two Bearded Collies will take points toward a championship at any one show. They are the Winners Dog and Winners Bitch. The number of points awarded can range from zero to five and is determined by the number of Beardies of each sex that are entered in that show. The country is divided into several regions, and the number of dogs needed to make a given number of points in any one breed is tabulated on the basis of the number of that breed shown in each region. These numbers are revised yearly by the AKC.

In order for a dog of any breed to become a champion, he must win a total of fifteen points. Two of these wins must be majors (three to five points awarded at a single show), and the majors must be won under two different judges. A dog that wins fifteen points without both majors will not be awarded a championship, and continuing to show at non-major shows if points are not needed is generally considered unsportsmanlike.

As a general rule, it takes more bitches entered to make, for instance, a three-point win than it does males because more females are being exhibited. If a show offers two points in males and three points in bitches and the male takes Best of Winners, he will take three points instead of two. In other words, the Best of Winners always takes the higher number of points.

Obedience Trials

In conformation classes, the dogs are judged on looks and personality, and the judging is somewhat subjective due to personal opinion and individual interpretation of the Standard. In obedience trials, however, the dogs are judged solely on performance. Showing is more relaxed and fun for some people, and there is a definite sense of accomplishment from having trained a winner.

Any dog registered with the AKC or possessing an ILP number (a number assigned to dogs that are obviously purebred but cannot be registered) may compete. Each class has specified exercises that are assigned points totaling a possible 200. To qualify, a dog must score a minimum of 170 points and at least 50 percent in each exercise. Each "qualifying" score is called a "leg," and when a dog has three legs won under three different judges, he is awarded an obedience degree for that level.

There are three levels, varying in degree of difficulty. The companion Dog (CD) degree is awarded to dogs competing in the Novice Class. A Companion Dog Excellent (CDX) is awarded for completion of the Open Class legs, and a

Mary Billman judging the first Beardie Spectacular in Malvern, England, May 1993.

Utility Dog (UD) degree is given for three legs in Utility classes. Matches often offer two additional classes: Sub-Novice for dogs not ready to work off-leash as in Novice, and Graduate Novice for dogs training for the Open Class.

Novice Class. This class is divided into section "A" for dogs with owners who have never handled a dog at an obedience trial, and "B" for professional handlers or anyone who has previously shown in obedience. The Novice exercises and scores awarded for correct completion are:

Heel on Leash	40 points
Stand for Examination	30 points
Heel Free	40 points
Recall	30 points
Long Sit	30 points
Long Down	30 points
	200 points

When a dog has received confirmation of his CD degree, he can no longer compete in Novice obedience classes.

Open Class. This class is also divided into sections "A" and "B," but this time "A" division is for all dogs that are owner handled and that have a CD but not a CDX degree. Dogs that have three qualifying scores in the class may continue to compete in section "B" along with dogs shown by professional trainers or handlers. Exercises are as follows:

Heel Free (off leash)	40 points
Drop on Recall	30 points
Retrieve on Flat	20 points
Retrieve over High Jump	30 points
Broad Jump	20 points
Long Sit	30 points
Long Down	39 points
	200 points

Utility. This most advanced class is open to any dog that has a CDX degree. Exercises include a signal exercise in which the dog performs a series of heeling maneuvers and other movements in response to hand signals with no verbal commands; a scent discrimination exercise in which the dog selects his handler's article from among many identical articles by scent alone; a directed retrieve in which the dog is signaled to pick up one of three gloves; a directed jumping exercise; and a group stand for examination. Utility dogs may continue to

Ch. Arcadia's Bentley of Walkoway, UD, ROM, HC, clears a broad jump.

compete in both Open and Utility classes after they have qualified for the UD degree.

For more complete information on rules and regulations, write to the AKC for the free pamphlet, "Rules Applying to Obedience Trials."

Advanced Titles

In addition to the three basic degrees, the AKC offers a Tracking Dog degree (TD), Tracking Dog Excellent (TDX), and an Obedience Trial Championship (OTCh).

While a dog must earn the CD, CDX, and UD titles in sequence, he may compete for the Tracking Dog title at any stage of training. A dog trained in tracking may be useful in locating lost or missing people, lost objects, or strayed livestock. He may also compete in AKC-approved tracking tests.

The ultimate achievement for the obedience dog is the OTCh, which is acquired by earning 100 points in obedience competition as deter-

mined by Table 17-1. The dog must already have his Utility degree. The dog must win at least three first places, one in Utility, one in Open B, and the third in either class. A dog may continue to compete in Open or Utility even after he has earned his Obedience Championship, but no further titles are available.

OBEDIENCE CHAMPIONSHIP POINTS

No. Dogs Competing	Open B Class Points for 1st Place	Points for 2nd Place
6-10	2	0
11-15	4	1
16-20	6	2
21-25	10	3
26-30	14	4
31-35	18	5
36-40	22	7
41-45	26	9
46-50	30	11
51-56	34	13

Utility Class

3-5	2	0
6-9	4	1
10-14	6	2
15-19	10	3
20-24	14	4
25-29	18	5
30-34	22	7
35-39	26	9
40-44	30	11
45-48	34	13

Junior Showmanship Competition

Junior showmanship classes are judged according to the handler's presentation, rather that the quality of the dog. Classes are: Novice Junior for boys and girls at least ten and under thirteen years of age who, at the time entries close, have not won three first places in a Novice class at a licensed show; Novice Senior for youths thirteen to seventeen years of age who have not won three first places in a Novice class; Open Junior for youths ten to thirteen years of age who have won three or more first places in

Left and Above:
Ch. Daybreak Storm at Candelaria U.D., H.C.,
owned by Laura Price.

Left: Heel off lead

Above: Retrieve over high jump.

Photos © Callea

Novice; and Open Senior for youths thirteen to seventeen years of age who have won three first places in a Novice class.

MATCH COMPETITION

Before a club is licensed to hold a point show, it must earn the privilege by holding several matches. These matches are strictly for fun. They give the exhibitors and the show committee a chance to practice. There are several types. "Fun" matches do not meet AKC requirements and may be held by any club, including those not recognized by the AKC (such as small new clubs, 4-H groups, or humane societies). These matches often include classes such as best-dressed dog, team obedience events, and classes for puppies as young as eight weeks of age.

"B" matches are the beginning level contests approved by the AKC. Pre-entry is not always required, but the show is organized in the same manner as a licensed show. A three- to six-month-old puppy class may be allowed. An "A" match is run in the same way as a regular show, complete with pre-entry and even a catalog listing all competitors. Only standard regular and nonregular classes are allowed.

No championship points are awarded at any match, and champions may not compete.

ENTERING A SHOW

You can learn about shows in your area by contacting a local kennel club or professional handler or trainer. You may also consult the list of upcoming shows in *AKC Gazette* (see "Other

Junior Showmanship: Glen Eire's Charlie Brown with junior handler Jennifer Babineaux.

Sources"). In order to enter an AKC-licensed show, you must fill out an official entry form. Copies are not acceptable unless they also have the rules copied on the back of the form. Entry forms are obtainable from the show superintendent, or blank forms may be obtained by writing the AKC office. After you have entered a few shows, you will be placed on that superintendent's mailing list. Addresses of some of the more popular superintendents include:

- Jack Bradshaw, P.O. Box 7303, Los Angeles CA 90022
- Norman E Brown, P.O. Box 2566, Spokane WA 99220
- Thomas Crowe, P.O. Box 22107, Greensboro NC 27420

- Ace Mathews. P.O. Box 86130, Portland OR 97286-0130
- Jack Onofrio, P.O. Box 25764, Oklahoma City OK 73125

Show entries generally close two and one-half to three weeks prior to the show date, so send your entry in early. Entry forms must be completely and accurately filled out and accompanied by the entry fee.

SHOWS IN ENGLAND

English shows are very much like those in the United States, but the terminology and the point system are quite different. "Exemption" shows are practice events similar to matches in the United States except that entries are small and dogs of different breeds compete together. One international judge must be among the judging staff.

"Limit" shows are those especially for the young and unproven dogs that have a limited number of wins to their credit. Wins do not count toward a championship. "Open" shows are for all breeds and are similar to championship shows except that no challenge certificates are awarded. However, these shows are considered prestigious because top-notch competition is judged by respected, knowledgeable judges.

"Championship" shows are the equivalent of our "licensed" or "point" shows. However, not every breed will be awarded a challenge certificate at every show. The Kennel Club allots only a specified number of challenge certificates to each breed each year, and these are parceled out among the various shows. As a breed becomes more popular, more challenge certificates are issued.

In order to win a championship in England, a dog must earn three challenge certificates, or "tickets," under three different judges. In a country as small as England, this is a difficult task; therefore, a championship means a great deal. Once a dog is "made up," or "finished"—the term used to describe when a dog becomes a champion—the dog can still continue to enter in the Open Dog or Open Bitch classes at championship shows and must be defeated before another Beardie can earn a CC. There is no separate class for champions or Best of Breed.

SHOWING YOUR BEARDIE

You and your Beardie will have plenty to do in preparing for your first show. Winning may be fun, but it also requires hard work and discipline. Become familiar with the ring patterns and methods of handling, and work, work, work. Your Beardie should be well trained (see Chapter 18) and working smoothly on leash before you even consider entering a show.

Edmar Solo Flight being groomed before a show.

But that day will come, and you will find yourself packing up for your first show-bound trip. You will need a kit of basic grooming tools (see Chapter 6), show leads, and a crate or exercise pen in which to confine your dog while you are waiting to enter the ring. A folding grooming table will make preshow preparations easier, but it is not a necessity. You will need, however, a grooming smock or coat to protect your clothing from dog hair, a supply of towels, and a damp washcloth. If it is to be an all-day affair, include some newspapers for the exercise pen, a bottle of drinking water, and a water bowl for your dog.

Your own apparel is always a consideration. Most shows today are reasonably casual, but you will want to look neat. Select clothing that will not interfere with your own or your Beardie's movement and that will not show hair easily. Men usually choose slacks and either a sport shirt or sport jacket with tie, while women wear culottes, dresses, or pantsuits.

The show superintendent will mail confirmation of your entry several days prior to the show. Included in this form, which allows you admittance to the show grounds, will be a schedule telling the time and the ring number at which each breed will be judged. Following the breed listing will be three numbers representing, in this order, the number of dogs, bitches, and champions entered at this show.

Most exhibitors like to arrive at the show grounds at least an hour before their breed is scheduled for judging. This allows the dogs and their handlers to become familiar with the surroundings and to relax. After your last-minute grooming is finished, take advantage of any waiting time by going to your ring to watch the judge in action. Each judge works a little differently, so it helps to familiarize yourself with his or her favorite patterns, hand signals, and commands. You will be less confused and less likely to make a mistake when your turn to show arrives.

Get to the ringside as early as possible when your class is scheduled. No matter how well trained a Beardie may be at home, he will probably go absolutely bananas the first time he sees another Beardie. The love and excitement that these animals have for one another is totally amazing, so let them get their greeting capers over with outside of the show ring.

The dogs will enter the ring circling counterclockwise at a trot. Usually, they will be asked to continue around the ring until the judge signals for all handlers to halt, but some judges will prefer that you walk into the ring and stand in a lineup before moving. If you are a novice, try to allow a few experienced handlers in front of you and follow their lead. However, at some shows you will not have a choice, as you will be asked to enter the ring in the order of your armband numbers. The handler at the front of the lineup must be especially alert to the judge's commands.

All of the dogs may first be gaited simultaneously and then examined or gaited individually, or the individual examinations may be performed first, followed by group gaiting. Watch your dog as much as possible, not the judge, but always be aware of the judge's location and be attentive to his or her commands. Some judges, having large numbers of dogs to see in a day's time, get impatient if they have to repeat or explain instructions.

Good sportsmanship in the ring is the only other thing required of you. Show common courtesy to the judge and to the other exhibitors. Don't crowd or distract another handler's dog; treat co-exhibitors, as well as the judge, with respect; and don't make excuses if your dog is not up to par.

Handling in the Ring

Most judges prefer that any working breed, Beardies included, be shown on a loose lead and walked into a natural stance without stacking (placing the feet and holding the head). If you are handling a young or unsteady dog, you may want to place his feet and hold him a little more firmly than you would a more experienced Beardie. In England, it seems to be common practice to stack a Beardie and hold him in position, but we much prefer the more natural method that is commonly used in the United States. Temperament is more easily evaluated this way.

It is difficult for a judge to evaluate a dog that is moving in a jerky manner or that is weaving rather than moving at a steady tempo in a straight line. Be aware of your dog's best trotting speed and try to move him accordingly. If your dog breaks stride or begins to play in the ring, it is acceptable to stop him and repeat the part of the pattern that he performed badly. When coming back to the judge, be sure that your Beardie, not you, is directly in front of the judge. Slow your dog gradually to a halt about six feet away from the judge. He will want to see front stance and expression at this point. If mats are narrow, make certain that the dog is the one gaiting on them.

Handlers set up their dogs for the judge to view.

Left: Bobbie Brie, "Sutter," gaiting individually.

Right: Individual examination by the judge.

Bottom: Group gaiting at the Windsor show, England.

Four standard patterns are used for individual gaiting, and you should learn and practice all of them. The judge may call for you to move straight down and back (Figure a), in an "L" pattern (Figure b), in a triangle (Figure c), or in a "T" pattern (Figure d).

Your Beardie may be a perfect angel in the ring, but please don't count on it. Most Beardies love shows, and they like to have more fun by making a game of the situation. Don't be surprised if your "super dog" decides to eat the judge's carnation, pretends that he has never worn a leash, or rolls over to "play dead." Derek Stopforth, Davealex Beardies, recently wrote of a typical experience that he had with his first Beardie, Eng. Ch. Davealex Blaze Away at Osmart, "Charlie."

At his second show at just over six months, he (Charlie) decided to act up a

Most judges will use one of these standard gaiting patterns when evaluating individual dogs.

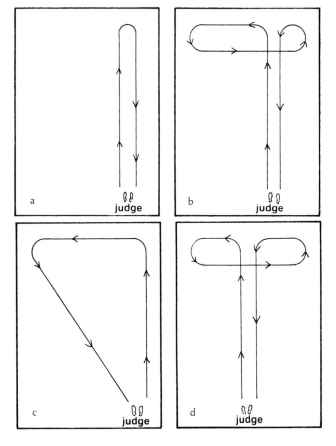

Am./Can. Ch. Edmar Solo Flight awaits his turn in the ring. Owners: Christy and Tom Williams.

bit, as puppies do. He wasn't too bad whilst the judge was examining the other dogs, but when it came to his turn, he decided he liked the judge so instead of standing, he rolled over on his back and put four paws in the air and invited the judge to tickle his tummy.

Nevertheless, Charlie (according to his owner) was one of the greatest showmen seen in the Beardie ring, and he enjoyed every minute of it.

Jenny Osborne also tells of moments when she would have liked to simply disappear into the ground. Her bitch, Eng. Ch. Blue Bonnie of Bothkennar, pulled some famous ring pranks. So, hold your head up and simply be proud that you own a breed with "character." You'll both enjoy the experience of showing much more than if you expect perfection!

Judges

Most judges are volunteers who may give up an entire weekend for nothing more than their transportation and lodging and the chance to be of service. They are generally on their feet all day, often in very uncomfortable environments. A considerate exhibitor, therefore, does everything

Adult Bearded Collies are usually stacked with the handler standing in front.

Right: You may get better results if you hold a puppy.

Below: Steady your Beardie as he is being examined.

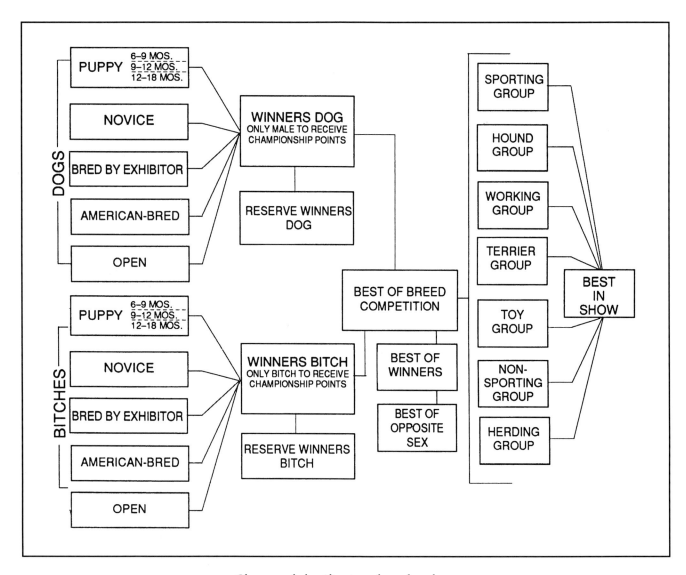

Classes and classifications for a dog show.

that he can to make the judge's work as easy and as smooth as possible.

Some judges are "all-rounders," licensed to judge all of the registered breeds, while other are licensed for only a few breeds. Some judges are themselves Beardie breeders. On the whole, they are knowledgeable, honest, and objective; but, being human, they may also at times put undue emphasis on one particularly favored trait or pet peeve, play politics, or behave discourteously. A sharp exhibitor observes as many Beardie judges as possible to determine their preferences and styles of judging. But even

with a wide knowledge of individual preferences, it is trite to believe that you must win every time. There will be days when the competition is much different from the previous day, and the dog that has had a long winning streak may not even place. Other times, either you or your Beardie may simply not be mentally or physically "up."

Before you make rash judgements about the way in which a class was placed, remember that there are many small details that only the judge can know—bite, testicles, structural defects, and expression may not be visible to another exhibitor, much less from ringside. Also consider that while as a breeder you may see problems with the way in which a dog will develop, or potentials that *will* exist but are not there today, the judge cannot consider these. He must judge the dogs as he sees them at this time.

Finishing a Champion

Finishing a champion often requires three elements: patience, perseverance, and money. While some Beardies finish speedily with three five-point majors, others will need to be shown twenty times or more. This varies depending on the quality of the individual, the competition, the preferences and experience of the judges, and the number of points offered at each show. Entry fees at the time of this writing average about twenty dollars per show, but like everything else, costs of showing continue to rise. Add these fees to the travel, lodging, and equipment required, and you will rapidly see the costs mount. If you prefer to have someone else show your dog, you can hire a professional handler.

In order to finish your dog, you must first believe in him. Secondly, you must show wisely. Whenever possible, select judges who are known to like what your Beardie has to offer. Try to show your dog in his prime. Puppies can rarely compete successfully with quality adults, and one- to two-year-old Beardies are usually in an awkward teenage period.

Thirdly, you must keep trying. Never give up without giving your dog a really fair chance. You will know that it is time to stop showing if the money that you are spending begins to outweigh the dog's value, or if your Beardie is aging and is continually being defeated by younger dogs of lesser quality. Most Beardies have their peak winning period between three and six years of age, and it is during this time that your dog is most likely to capture that elusive Best in Show or simply Best of Breed.

Ch. OTCh. Windcache A Briery Bess H.C., owned by Barbara Prescott, shows off her high jump skills.
Photo © Ray Hoyt.

18 *The Happy Herder*

The Bearded Collie is a highly versatile herding dog capable of working a variety of livestock in diverse situations. In its native Scotland, the breed is used in many ways, the most common being:

- As a "huntaway," casting out over vast hilly, brushy areas, barking as the dog runs, to flush out hiding or lost sheep (the barking moves sheep that cannot see the dog but can hear him), and then gathering them into a large flock

- As a "drover's dog," driving stock down lanes or from pasture to pasture

- As a "hill" dog, casting out and gathering up sheep from the moors and bringing them to their shepherd.

Because a variety of talents were needed for these many uses, some Beardies (perhaps the majority) are naturally gathering (fetching) dogs, while a few will naturally drive. Some will show varying degrees of "eye," while some will be loose-eyed and use barking.

While many styles of work are to be tolerated in the breed, owing to its many uses, a Beardie with good herding instinct should show a desire to keep the stock well grouped and moving, exhibiting a clearly defined technique as well as a desire to conform to the wishes of his owner.

WORKING STANDARD

In March, 1993, the BCCA adopted a working Standard for the breed, outlining what to expect of Beardies. It may be used by trial judges in evaluating performances:

Introduction

The Bearded Collie is an ancient Scottish breed of herding dog. It is a long, lean, medium-sized shaggy dog ideally suited to the terrain and climate of its native land. The smaller, lighter-boned brown Beardie of the Highlands was used for rough work, often independent of commands, in gathering sheep from the rugged hill and mountain pastures.

Beardies were also used as "huntaways," where both the dog and shepherd are behind the sheep with the Beardie working back and forth down the hill keeping up an incessant barking to flush out hidden or lost stock. The larger, black Beardie of the Lowlands was most often used as a drover's dog in driving sheep and cattle to market. Today's Bearded Collie is a blend of these two strains.

Trainability

The Bearded Collie has a strong desire to please, exhibits good stock sense, is biddable, and should show typical herding behavior in gathering and wearing stock. It is a versatile, highly intelligent herder, capable of thinking for itself and working accordingly. The Beardie is a powerful, confident dog that should readily adjust to free-moving or stubborn stock.

Working Style

Due to its heritage, the Bearded Collie can exhibit *either* fetching or driving styles, and has the innate ability to handle all types of stock.

Most, but not all, Beardies are loose-eyed. They tend to work closer to the stock and in a more upright position than a dog with more eye. *Untrained*, loose-eyed dogs will typically run a straight course toward stock, casting out wider as they approach.

The Bearded Collie can be quite vocal and *must not be penalized for barking.* Expect Beardies to respond to a challenge from the stock with force, bark, and bounce, using grip when warranted.

Beardies are an extremely agile, fast-moving dog. Often, during initial exposures to stock, they will work the stock too fast and require time to settle.

Undesirable Traits

Predatory or aggressive behavior toward stock. Body biting, wool pulling, or unwarranted gripping. Chasing stock with no purpose. Inattention or refusal to respond to commands. Excessive fear of handler, judge, or stock.

HERDING INSTINCT

The herding instinct is merely a divergence from the wild dog's instinct to hunt. Wild dogs lived and hunted in packs. The faster dogs ran ahead of the prey and turned it back toward the pack, while the slower ones completed the kill. The forerunners of the pack were developed by man into herding dogs through careful selection and adaptation. The slower types evolved into hunting and trailing (particularly hound) breeds.

The strong "eye" exhibited by some breeds, notably Border Collies, is also an adaptation from the wild dog's instinct. Foxes and coyotes will "eye" (stare intently at) their prey before pouncing on it. Pointers and setters exhibit the same instinct in a more controlled way. Beardies sometimes show a tendency to eye, but this is of less importance than an attitude of intense concentration on the stock. In fact, a dog with too much eye may frighten the sheep with his fixed stare, or he may be so concentrated on staring that he "sticks" and does not move.

While it is possible to train almost any Beardie to herd, a good stock dog must possess strong herding *instinct.* It is this urge to herd that makes a dog a willing and eager worker. Forcing a dog to work stock is never really successful. When a young dog "starts to run," he does it instinctively. He is like a youth who suddenly develops an interest in the opposite sex—the time has come when nature's influence takes over.

In addition to the herding instinct, Beardies have a dominant/submissive nature. The instincts to herd and to submit must be balanced. The stronger the herding instinct, the stronger the willingness to submit must be. Otherwise the dog becomes uncontrollable.

Am./Can. Ch. Silverleaf Gifted Artisan HT, ROM, age fifteen years. Owned by Harry and Ann Witte.

In their wild state, only a few dogs were pack leaders, while the majority followed them. The modern "pack-leader type" is usually too independent to become a good herder. The submissive "follower" will accept his human master as a substitute pack leader. This submissive instinct is what makes the dog trainable. It is apparent in the young puppy that follows you around and licks your hand for attention. As the dog matures, the submissive instinct should diminish unless it is developed and directed by training. The *overly* submissive Beardie may never want to leave his handler to work independently.

The herding and the submissive instincts must be encouraged to become useful. Normal herding instinct can be discouraged or killed by harshly disciplining a puppy for showing interest in stock, chasing, or trying to herd pets or children. Such behavior must be encouraged if possible. The submissive instinct, on the other hand, is developed through basic training and by praising the pup's responsiveness to commands. A dog that is to be trained for herding should learn to accept discipline in the form of leash training and the teaching of basic household manners, and he should never be reprimanded for chasing or showing interest in livestock.

TEMPERAMENT IN A HERDING DOG

Most Beardies are fairly "hard" with stock and will tend to rush in boldly and work too fast. A few dogs, however, may be "soft" or hesitant with the stock and generally also more sensitive to their trainer. The "hard" dog is perhaps easier to start because he will always act boldly and aggressively, but he needs a tougher, knowledgeable trainer to control him. The "soft" dog is generally more tractable and may make the better pet, but he may try to run away rather than deal with a frightening situation. It takes considerably more patience to train this dog.

Moderation is preferred so that the dog is neither too hard nor too soft, In addition, the dog's temperament must be compatible with his trainer's disposition. Some people can obtain marvelous results with a hard dog and accomplish nothing with a soft one, or vice versa.

Common sense is another important attribute of the herding dog. This is primarily apparent in the older puppy or dog and is developed with experience and exposure to various situations. A good stock dog is capable of thinking for himself and adapting to problem situations.

CHOOSING A HERDING DOG

The herding instinct is not always evident in a young puppy. It develops as the dog matures and usually become apparent somewhere between his sixth and eighteenth month of age. Occasionally, you will notice a puppy herding or eyeing his littermates almost as soon as they start playing. Just as common is the dog that refuses to look at sheep until well over a year of age. Either Beardie can become a superior herder if he develops an interest in stock.

It is usually advisable to choose a young puppy that you can raise to suit yourself. A partially trained adult may be spoiled or have formed bad habits, and the professionally trained dog may perform admirably for his expert handler but not at all for a novice owner.

Choosing a puppy for herding is largely a matter of chance, but the odds may be improved slightly if you select a puppy from working parents, or if the puppy himself shows interest in herding. He may exhibit a tendency to circle or bunch other animals, or even a rubber ball. At three months of age, a few Beardies will actively approach stock. They are too young to understand basic commands and, except to demonstrate this interest, should be prevented from working stock. Pick the puppy up or confine him. Puppies that are allowed to work livestock

Ch. Parcana Lord Cerwin, CD HC earning his HC at the age of six months, six days .

COMMONLY USED HERDING TERMS

APPROACH: The manner in which the dog comes in to the stock, a "smooth" approach being highly desirable.

BALANCE: The correct position of the dog, stock, and handler, relative to each other.

GATHERING: A style of bringing animals toward the handler; also, collecting scattered stock in a field.

DRIVING: Moving stock from behind and away from the handler, either naturally or on command.

FETCH: Bringing the stock to the handler from some distance away, preferably in a straight line.

STRONG-EYED DOG: A dog that works by staring at the stock, working silently and from a crouching position.

LOOSE-EYED DOG: A dog that does not show an intense gaze at all times, works upright, and usually barks to move stock.

OUTRUN: When the dog is sent out some distance to gather the sheep.

LIFT: Starting the stock in motion after the outrun.

SIDES: The direction in which the dog is to go—either clockwise or counterclockwise.

WEARING: The pendulum motion, in a short arc, that the dog makes to keep the stock grouped while he is moving them.

FORCE BARK: The bark used by a quiet-working dog if he is challenged or the stock refuses to move.

GRIP: A nip or bite used as needed or on command to move stubborn stock.

of any kind too early will only learn bad habits or become frightened. Such puppies are not good risks as herding prospects. However, familiarity with livestock so that the dog is not frightened is beneficial.

Do not choose a shy Beardie or an overly excitable or aggressive pup. Look for soundness and for the puppy that is quick on his feet. Poor angulation, crooked legs, weak pasterns, or other structural faults will inhibit free movement and cause the dog's structure to be too weak for the demands of hard work.

INTRODUCING THE BEARDIE TO STOCK

The dog's first reaction to stock is very important. As long as he does no real damage, encourage any positive interest or action that your dog makes. The most favorable response is when your Beardie tries to circle or move the sheep. He may "grip" or bite them as well. This is normal in a young, inexperienced dog and should not be discouraged at this time.

Puppies tend to be overenthusiastic and want to charge the stock, while an older dog that has never seen stock may show no initial interest in herding. If this dog watches the sheep with an intense fascination, it is sufficient. After several introductions to livestock, this dog's herding instinct will probably be awakened.

It is best to cultivate the herding instinct and start your dog herding *before* initiating formal obedience training. It is imperative, however, that your Beardie be leash trained and that he understand the meaning of the basic commands, "Come" and "Down." An obedience-trained dog can become a good herder, but it may take longer because he will probably watch his handler rather than the stock. The handler must have established dominance over the Beardie before stock-dog training is attempted, and he must maintain this dominance in direct proportion to the dog's increasing aggressiveness with the sheep.

Never introduce a puppy to aggressive or mean livestock, or to ewes with young lambs. One kick or butt at this time may turn your Beardie off herding forever. The young pup that shows interest in herding will probably chase chickens, ducks, sheep, or anything else that he can find to run. In the process, he is not only liable to be hurt, but he also will develop many bad habits. The best way to prevent this is to pick up the puppy or snap a leash onto his collar whenever he is around livestock. *Do not scold him for showing interest or chasing.*

The Beardie is ready to work when he is full grown and fast enough to outrun the stock— usually eight or nine months of age. Younger puppies may be started on lambs or ducks.

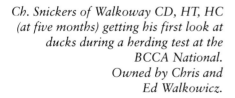

Ch. Snickers of Walkoway CD, HT, HC (at five months) getting his first look at ducks during a herding test at the BCCA National. Owned by Chris and Ed Walkowicz.

TRAINING POINTERS

Once your Beardie is "turned on," you can begin serious training. There are as many ways to train a herding dog as there are trainers. If you can possibly do so, start out with a trainer, preferably one who is experienced with Beardies, instead of trying to do it on your own. If you have to do it yourself, the following tips might help you.

The equipment that you will need includes: a collar, preferably a wide, nylon one, loosely fitted so that you can easily get your hand under it to position your dog and release him quickly; a line twenty to thirty feet long to snap onto his collar; a shepherd's crook or a five-foot-length of one-half-inch PVC pipe that is light, that will not hurt dogs or stock, and that is cheap to replace if broken.

Commands That Your Dog Must Learn

Stop: Any number of words may be used, and the stop does not need to be in any specific body position. Among the stop commands are "There," "Down," "Sit," "Stop," "Halt," or "Haw." The intention of the stop is to have the dog cease moving. He does not need to do any-thing but stop; he may remain on his feet. But if you use "Sit" or "Down," the dog must do that specific action. Often the most intense dogs will be easier to control if they have to lie down or sit.

Come: or "Come here" or "Here." This command does not need to be as precise as an obedience command, but your dog should come to you when he is called.

Get Back: or "Back off" or "Back." This command is used to remind your dog to keep a proper distance from the stock.

Sides: Each change of direction has a specific command. For the dog to run counter-clockwise, the command is "Away to me." The clockwise direction command is "Go bye" or "Come bye." The intent of these commands is to turn the dog, not to keep him going that way. Once he has changed directions, he should still stay behind the sheep.

Speed: Most Beardies are moving at top speed anyway, so you need a command word to indicate that your dog should slow down. Such words as "Easy," "Steady on," or "Slow down" may be used, particularly in a sing-song fashion in a slower cadence than the dog's speed.

Walk Up: This is the command to approach the sheep straight on and move them in a straight line.

Wyncliff Unicorn Sterling herding at ten years of age. Courtesy Ruth Colavecchio

*Ch. Gaelyn Copper Artisan PT,
age 11½ years.*

Look Back: If the sheep have split and the dog has not gathered all of them, he has probably lost count. Although he may well spot the escapist eventually, he should learn to look for his lost lamb on command.

Out or Get Out: This command is used if the dog is either cutting in very close to the stock to split the flock or is diving to pull wool or bite without need or command.

That'll Do: This is the last command, which means that the dog is finished working. It should be an absolute call off.

Basic Training in the Commands

If you and your Beardie are inexperienced, start your training only on "dog-broke" sheep. These are sheep that are accustomed to being worked by dogs, and they will tend to stay flocked around the handler, moving freely away from the dog toward the handler. In the beginning, work in an arena or corral so that you won't have too far to run and can keep better control.

The first step is to let your dog get control of the sheep and then for you to take control of your dog. Snap the long line on his collar and let him drag it. If you need to stop him, you can step on the line and stop him without scolding

or discouraging him. He will probably take off at full tilt, circling the sheep. Keep moving, walking backward with the sheep following you. Use the pipe or crook to move him back if he circles too close to the sheep. Do not scold him even if he rushes in and snatches a bit of wool or splits the stock. Instead of saying "No," say his name in a warning tone to get his attention. Stop him once or twice and keep him away from the sheep briefly before letting him work again. This way, he learns that he can go back to the sheep. This may be all that you do at the first session. Keep it short—five to ten minutes are ample. Praise him when you quit.

You will use the long line until your dog is reliably stopping on command. He may "down" or stop perfectly at home but will probably ignore your command when he is intent on the stock. Work on this on lead outside the fence and when you are in with the sheep but not attempting to work them. When your dog will consistently obey your "stop" command, you can remove the long line. You can also teach the "come" command while he is on the long line.

The next step is to keep your dog behind the sheep. Again, keep moving backward with the sheep following you. (It might be easier to do this along a fence at first.) As your dog circles the flock, use the pipe to turn him back as he

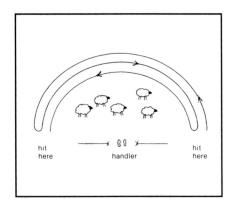

Train the dog to bring the sheep toward you.

The dog circles the flock.

Use the crook to turn him back.

Keep the dog behind the flock.

Now he can move the flock in your direction.

The outrun can be widened with training.

The dog must learn to move the sheep away from the fence.

Left: Keep the dog behind the sheep to teach the "walk on."
Right: As the dog progresses, control him from a greater distance.
Bottom, Left: The dog approaches the sheep in a straight line for the "walk on." He may do an outrun to reach this position.
Bottom, Right: A dog that has learned the "walk on" can drive the sheep as well as herd them. Ch. Parcana Silverleaf Vandyke, "Parcana."

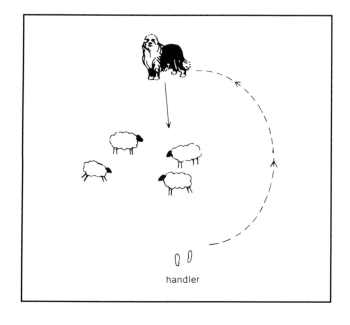

handler

comes around. Tap the pipe on the ground in front of your dog and praise him as he turns back. Give the commands for sides while simultaneously tapping the pipe so that your dog associates the commands with what he and the sheep are doing. Do not try to teach the commands away from the stock.

Keep turning your dog from side to side until he stays on the opposite side of the sheep from you. Do not rush this step. Use as many training sessions as you need. Gradually use the pipe less and less until your dog will turn on voice command alone. At the same time, incorporate the "stop" command by halting him occasionally as you work. Also, you can use the "get back" command while using the pipe to push him off if he gets too close to the stock.

When your Beardie is taking his stop and side commands readily, you can teach the "walk up." This is very easy with "dog-broke" sheep that will follow you. Stop your dog when he is directly opposite you, then walk backwards in a straight line, giving the command, "Walk up." The sheep will follow you, and because the dog will want to follow the sheep, he will be doing what he has been told.

These are all of the basics. Try to always end each training session on a positive note, after your dog has done something right. If you or your dog gets frustrated, tired, or cranky, stop. Give plenty of praise when he does what you ask.

HERDING ORGANIZATIONS

Three organizations offer tests for herding instinct and herding trials at varying levels in which Bearded Collies may participate. They are: The Bearded Collie Club of America (BCCA), the American Kennel Club (AKC), and the American Herding Breed Association (AHBA).

Testing or Certification

All of the organizations sponsor herding tests that allow untrained dogs to be tested for basic herding instinct. To enter, a dog must be six months of age or older, and at least for the BCCA, the entry form must be accompanied by a three-generation pedigree. Testing is on a pass/fail basis, and a dog may be retested several times if he does not pass on the first try. For some, the test is also the first introduction to livestock.

Tests are held in a small, enclosed area, and the only thing the dog is required to do is show interest in driving and gathering. Five ducks or five sheep are used. The handler is allowed to move about with the dog and encourage him.

After successfully passing a test, a dog is awarded a certificate and the initials of the particular test are listed after his registered name. Only one passing score is required to gain certification. The degrees awarded are:

AKC:	HT	Herding Tested
BCCA:	HC	Herding Certified
AHBA:	HCT	Herding Capability Tested

A second pre-trial level is also offered. This test, although also a pass/fail, requires some basic training. It is held in a fenced area at least 100 by 100 feet, and the dog and handler must move the stock between two cones or markers. A dog must pass two tests under two different judges to gain this degree.

AKC:	PT	Pretrial Tested
AHBA:	JHD	Junior Herding Dog

Herding Trials

More and more opportunities for herding competition are opening up and the rules, courses, and titles have been in a constant state of flux. Therefore, check with the various organizations for the most current rules and regulations when you are ready to participate. Currently, three organizations offer herding trials in which Beardies are eligible to compete: the AKC, the AHBA, the Australian Shepherd Club of America (ASCA), and the Canadian Kennel Club (CKC). The basic structure is similar. The first three organizations

HERDING INSTINCT CERTIFICATION TESTING FORM

Breed _____

Registered Name _____

Color _____ Sex_____ Registry and No. _____

Sire _____ Dam _____

Birthdate_____ Breeder_____

Name of Owner _____

Address _____

Phone _____

Sponsor of Test _____

Signature of Representative _____

Test Location _____

On this day of _____ , I, _____

did test this dog for herding instinct using:

ducks_____ sheep_____ goats _____ cattle _____

This dog, on this day: Passed _____

Did Not Pass _____

With regard to working style and characteristics, the following best describes this dog's herding instinct:

STYLE _____ shows gathering (fetching) instinct
_____ shows driving instinct
_____ shows no clear style preference

APPROACH _____ runs wide
_____ runs wide through training
_____ runs close

WEARING _____ shows "wearing" to keep herd grouped
_____ shows a little "wearing"
_____ shows no "wearing"

BARK _____ works silently
_____ force barks
_____ barks a good deal

EYE _____ shows strong eye
_____ medium eye
_____ loose eye

AGGRESSIVENESS _____ forceful without excessive aggression
_____ uses excessive force for the circumstances
_____ shows no force (appears weak)

TEMPERAMENT _____ appears readily adjusted
_____ easily distracted
_____ frightened of situation

TESTER'S COMMENTS: _____

Signature of Tester: _____

1

offer three trial levels (and thus three titles) with a similar progression of training and ability required for each, plus a championship title. All work is done on a course that consists of a series of chutes, panels, and pens that simulates a working ranch situation. All trials are scored events, with a dog required to score at least 70 percent in each exercise in order to qualify.

Basically, in the first level or Started class, the dog and handler work the course together. At the Intermediate level, the dog must show some ability to work independently. Typically a line is drawn which the handler cannot cross. At the Advanced level the dog works independently of the handler, who is required to stay at a fixed point.

TRIAL TITLES

AKC

HS	Herding Started
HI	Herding Intermediate
HX	Herding Advanced
HCh.	Herding Champion (awarded to the dog that acquires 15 points while competing in the advanced division on either cattle or sheep)

ASCA

Initials after the title indicate the type of stock the title was erned on
(s = sheep; d = ducks; c = cattle)

STD	Started Trial Dog
OTD	Open Trial Dog
ATC	Advanced Trial Dog
WTCh.	Working Trial Champion (awarded automatically to dogs that earn advanced titles on all three classes of stock)
RTD	Ranch Trial Dog. This is an additional title offered by ASCA. It requires advanced-level work with large flocks, sorting, penning, and unpenning.

AHBA

Initials following title indicate type of stock it was earned on

HTDI	Herding Started
HTDII	Intermediate
HTDIII	Advanced
HTCh.	Herding Trial Champion (awarded to the dog earning 10 qualifying scores with 80 percent or better on each exercise, after he has completed his Advanced title)

CKC

ISC	Intermediate
ADC	Advanced

Trial Courses

Course "A". Designed as an all-around farm course, the "A" course is based loosely on the Australian Shepherd Club of America courses. Three to five head of stock (sheep, cattle, or ducks) are worked through the course by the handler. There are three levels of difficulty—

Started, Intermediate, and Advanced—and all elements must be completed within ten minutes. To qualify, the dog must earn a minimum of 60 points (of 100 points possible), with a minimum of half the points available in each element of the trial course. The elements are: (1) the outrun, lift, and fetch; (2) the "Y" chute; (3) the "Z" chute; (4) the panel runway (started) or hold-exam pen; (5) the center-line "gate;" and (6) the pen.

Course "B". This is a modified version of the International Sheep Dog Society course, and ducks or sheep are the accepted livestock. Stock numbers, levels of difficulty, and scoring are the same as in the "A" course. Course "B" is triangular, with seven elements: (1) the outrun; (2) the lift; (3) the fetch; (4) the turn around the handler's post; (5) the drive or fetch through gate #1; (6) the fetch or drive through gate #2; and (7) the pen and hold. At the advanced level, the dog must also shed or separate two head of stock from the other stock.

Above, Left: Ch. Artisan Romani Rai HS, age 7½.
Below: Ch. Artisan Bronze Paladin, HS.

Course "C". This is a modified European tending course. Course "C" allows the use of sheep only and requires thirty to forty-five minutes per run. There must be a minimum of twenty head of sheep. The elements include: (1) removing the stock from a pen; (2) crossing a bridge; (3) pauses; (4) negotiating road traffic; (5) letting the sheep graze in marked areas; and (6) penning. Scoring is as before.

Can/Am. Ch. Potterdale Double Image HC.

Ch. Highlander Lorna Doone, HC, CD, ROM, ROMI.

Ch. Daybreak Rising Sun, UD, HC, owned by Barbara Prescott.

19 *Kennels in England, Canada, and the United States*

England was the primary source of both Canadian and American Beardies and is still contributing strongly to these and other countries. Although the breed originated in Scotland, it was in England where the modern-day Beardie got its start through the efforts of Mrs. G.O. Willison. The following are kennelogs on some of the English Beardie kennels that have had a major influence on the breed.

ENGLISH KENNELS

Bothkennar
Mrs. G.O. Willison

The Bearded Collie was actually saved from extinction through the efforts of Mrs. G.O. Willison. Her first bitch, Jeannie, was a brown, about twenty-one inches tall, of working parentage. In 1950, a twenty-three-inch slate male, Bailie of Bothkennar, was acquired. After a judge passed the two for registration as pure-bred Beardies, they were bred and produced a litter from which Mrs. Willison kept a bitch, Buskie, and three dogs, Bogle, Bruce, and Bravado. These became the foundation for Bothkennar.

Above: First registered litter (by Bailie ex Jeannie): left to right: Bravado, Buskie, Bruce, and Bogle.

Left: Three Beardies pose near an old stone bridge in England.

Below, Left: Bailie of Bothkennar and son, Bruce ofBothkennar.

Jeannie ofBothkennar

Another working bitch, Bess, was obtained. Buskie was bred back to her father, Bailie, to produce Bra' Tawny. When Bess was also bred to Bailie, she produced Briary Nan. Another early Beardie that was passed for recognition, Newton Blackie, was mated to Briary Nan, producing a male, Ridgeway Rob, owned by Clifford Owen. Rob mated to Bra' Tawny resulted in Baidh of Bothkennar. Baidh was bred to Bravado, produc-

ing the first Beardie to get a ticket (in 1959) as well as the first Beardie champion, Eng. Ch. Beauty Queen of Bothkennar.

Because Mrs. Willison preferred linebreeding over inbreeding, she used several other Beardies of working parentage in her program. Britt of Bothkennar, a very successful sire, was registered from working-dog parents. Eng. Ch. Bronze Penny of Bothkennar was a pick-of-the-

Jeannie of Bothkennar.

Left: The first Bearded Collie champion, 1959, Eng. Ch. Beauty Queen of Bothkennar, owned by Mrs. G. O. Willison.

litter bitch from a litter sired by Bruce out of a red-brown bitch passed for registration as Jennifer of Multan. A daughter of Bailie and Bess was bred to an outcross Scottish dog to produce Eng. Ch. Bobby of Bothkennar.

Mrs. Willson's stock became the foundation for Willowmead, Wishanger, Osmart, Edenborough, and others.

Eng. Ch. Bravo of Bothkennar.

Bawbee of Bothkennar (left) and grandsire Bailie of Bothkennar.

Willowmead
Suzanne Moorhouse

The oldest Beardie kennel still in existence, Willowmead was founded primarily on Bothkennar dogs. Suzanne purchased Willowmead Barberry of Bothkennar (Ridgeway Rob ex Bra' Tawny) from Mrs. Willison and showed the bitch to her title. Barberry was first bred to Britt, an outcross farm-bred Beardie of lovely type and temperament, producing Wil O'Wisp of Willowmead. Barberry was next bred to Eng.

Braelyn Broadholme Crofter (by Ruairidh of Willowmead ex Bobby's Girl of Bothkenner). Breeder, Mrs. D. Hale. Owner, Suzanne Moorhouse, England.

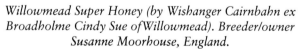

Willowmead Super Honey (by Wishanger Cairnbahn ex Broadholme Cindy Sue of Willowmead). Breeder/owner Susanne Moorhouse, England.

Ch. Bobby of Bothkennar to produce Merry Maker of Willowmead. When Merry Maker was bred to her half-brother, Wil O'Wisp, Suzanne got the lovely Eng. Ch. Willowmead My Honey, dam of many champions. Another bitch from this breeding, bred to a dog of working lineage, produced Sweetheart of Willowmead, dam of Ruairdh of Willowmead (by Wil O'Wisp). Ruairdh is the sire of Eng. Ch. Broadholme Cindy Sue of Willowmead, Eng.

Far Left: Eng. Ch. Willowmead Perfect Lady.

Left: Eng. Ch. Broadholme Cindy-Sue of Willowmead, age ten years.

Ch. Willowmead a Star is Born.

Ch. Willowmead Summer Wine.

Willowmead Wish Upon a Star.

Ch. Broadholme Adorable, and Braelyn Broadholme Crofter, all well-known producers out of Bobby's Girl of Bothkennar.

Ch. Willowmead Perfect Lady was the only Beardie to win Best Bitch and CC for three years in a row. Ch. Willowmead Juno of Tambora, mated to Willowmead Pure Magic, produced the top-winning Ch. Willowmead Star Attraction, whose offspring are also winning. Willowmead Beardies have been exported to nineteen different countries and have covered all aspects of the dog world, including working sheep and cattle, serving as guide dogs for the blind, and as search-and-rescue workers, gaining international and obedience show championships and becoming agility winners.

Wishanger
Mary Partridge

Another influential early kennel that is no longer active is Wishanger, which also was established on Bothkennar lines. Barley (Rob ex Bra' Tawny) was purchased from Mrs. Willison and Eng. Ch. Willowmead My Honey was obtained from Miss Suzanne Moorhouse. The two were mated to produce the famous sire, Eng. Ch. Wishanger Cairnbahn, a lovely brown known for correct temperament, lovely head, and substance. Other English champions bred by Miss Partridge include Ch. Wishanger Waterfall, Ch. Wishanger Craggy Tor, and Ch. Wishanger Crab Tree.

Eng. Ch. Osmart Bonnie Blue Braid, Doubletop.

Eng. Ch. Wishanger Cairnbahn.

Eng. Ch. Osmart Bonnie Blue Braid.

Osmart
Ken and Jenny Osborne

Osmart was founded in 1962 with three Bothkennar Beardies: Eng. Ch. Bravo of Bothkennar, Eng. Ch. Blue Bonnie of Bothkennar, and Bluebell of Bothkennar. Bonnie was a heavy-boned, solid bitch that excelled in the brood box, becoming the dam of five English and one international champion. Bravo was lighter in bone

Eng. Ch. Blue Bonnie of Bothkennar.

Eng. Ch. Osmart Black Pollyanna..

than Bonnie and very attractively marked, almost black in color.

In 1965, Blue Bonnie gave birth to her last litter (by Bravo) and presented the Osbornes with two of their finest representatives: Eng. Ch. Osmart Bonnie Blue Braid and Eng. Ch. Osmart Bonnie Black Pearl. The litter also included Eng. Ch. Osmart Bonnie Blue Ribbon and Swedish and Int. Ch. Osmart Bonnie Black Diamond.

Blue Braid became one of the breed's top sires of his time. He was a magnificent Beardie with almost human personality, very sound and with an exquisite head and expression. He garnered such wins as a 1973 Best of Breed at Crufts and the Any Variety Progeny class at the 1974 Windsor championship show. Braid has produced many champions worldwide.

The first American chamion, 1977, Brambledale Blue Bonnet CD, owned by Mr. and Mrs. Robert Lachman.

Brambledale
Lynne Evans

Also established in 1962 but no longer active, Brambledale had as foundation Eng. Ch. Heathermead Handsome, by Eng. Ch. Benjie of Bothkennar ex Honeybee of Bothkennar; Brambledale Briquette of Bothkennar (Britt of B. ex Biscuit of B.); and Brambledale Heathermead Moonlight (Bausant of Bothkennar ex Beehoney of B.).

Representatives of the Brambledale line include: Eng. Ch. Brambledale Balthazar, Brambledale Bathsheba, Brambledale Bluebell, Ch. Brambledale Blackfriar, Ch. Brambledale Boz and Int. Ch. Brambledale Billet Doux. Lynne also bred the first United States champion, Brambledale Blue Bonnet, who also became the first Beardie to go Best in Show, all breeds, in this country.

Far Left: Eng. Ch. Brambledale Balthazar.

Left: Int. Ch. Brambledale Billet Doux.

Tambora
Jackie Tidmarsh

The Tidmarsh farm is located in true "Beardie country," high in northern England and offering a magnificent view of steep, rugged sheep pastures divided by miles of low stone fences. Jackie's foundation dogs were the bitch Amberford Bracken (Banter of Bothkennar ex Musical Maid of Willowmead) and the male Bausant of Bothkennar.

Probably the most famous Tambora Beardie is Eng. Ch. Edelweiss of Tambora (Eng. Ch. Wishanger Cairnbahn ex Burdock [Bausant ex Bracken]). A lovely brown bitch with beautiful dark eyes, Edelweiss was top-winning Beardie in England in 1969, and she was the dam of six champions. In her first litter by Eng. Ch. Osmart Bonnie Blue Braid, she produced Eng.

Eng. Ch. Edelweiss of Tambora.

Ch. Juno of Tambora, top-winning Beardie in 1971; and Canadian Ch. Bronze Javelin of Tambora, top-winning Beardie in Canada.

Can. Ch. Bronze Javelin of Tambora.

Edenborough
Shirley Holmes

Edenborough began with the purchase of Eng. Ch. Bracken Boy of Bothkennar (Bravo ex Blue Bonnie, a brother to Blue Braid) and Blue Maggie from Osmart, a Braid daughter. Bred to a

Above:
Left to Right: Eng. Ch. Edenborough Blue Bracken,
Bracken Boy of Bothkennar, and Rowdina Grey Fella.

Left:
Eng. Ch. Edenborough Star Turn at Beagold.

Eng. Ch. Edenborough Blue Bracken, top-winning English Beardie.

Cairnbahn daughter, Bracken Boy sired Rowdina Grey Fellow, who, bred to Blue Maggie, produced Edenborough's most famous champion, Edenborough Blue Bracken. He was the first Beardie to win a Best in Show in England and obtained multiple BIS wins at championship shows. He is the sire or grandsire of three of the all-time top-producing North American Beardies. It was a very impressive sight to see Blue Bracken stacked off-lead in the ring, standing like a statue until Shirley released him.

Orora
Bryony Harcourt-Brown Trafford

Established in 1970, Orora has been producing a distinct line of sound, well-balanced Beardies based on Eng. Chs. Wishanger Cairnbahn, Osmart Bonnie Blue Braid, and Edenborough Blue Bracken. Eng. Ch. Mignonette of Willowmead at Orora was top Beardie in England in 1975 and 1976. Bred to Blue Braid, she produced Eng. Ch. Orora's Frank. Frank was Top Beardie in 1984 and 1985, with BOB at Crufts at the age of ten and a half. He is the sire of eleven English champions and several American ones.

Other well-known Orora dogs were Eng. Chs. Orora's Sugar Bush, Orora's Blue Basil, Orora's Huckleberry, Orora's Laughing Water,

Above: Orora's Chal-Cedony.
Below: Ch. Orora's Frank. © M. Trafford.

Ch. Orora's Frank. Note the nice reach and drive and level topline.

Above: Ch. Mignonette of Willowmead at Orora. Top Beardie in England in 1975 and 1976 and BOB Crufts 1976.
Below: Left to Right: Ch. Orora's Sugar Bush, Ch. Orora's Blue Basil, Ch. Orora's Huckleberry,
Ch. Mignonette of Willowmead at Orora.

and Orora's Impetuosity. Bryony's Ch. Chriscaro Chrystal at Orora is the dam of Orora's Chalcedony, whose first son and Frank's last son is Orora's Argyll, destined to be Frank's replacement.

Davealex
Derek and Jean Stopforth

A small kennel that made a big impact on the breed, Davealex started with a male, Eng. Ch. Davealex Blaze Away at Osmart (Bravo ex Bonnie). Their foundation bitch was Eng. Ch. Cala Sona Western Isles Loch Aber, dam of English,

Above: Eng. Ch. Davealex Royale Baron.
Below: Eng. Ch. Davealex Blaze Away at Osmart and Eng. Ch. Cala Sona Westernisles Loch Aber (front).

Canadian, American, and Australian champions. She was either top- or joint top-winning Beardie bitch in England from 1967 to 1971, and top- or joint top-brood bitch from 1971 to 1977. Davealex Beardies are noted for good, steady temperaments, soundness, correct coat texture, and flat, broad skulls. Representative sires were Eng. Chs. Davealex Royle Baron and Davealex Royle Brigadier. Brigadier was the sire of top-winning bitch Eng. Ch. Andrake Persephone.

Sunbree
Barbara Iremonger

Mrs. Iremonger had the opportunity to work for Mrs. Willison at Bothkennar and of course fell in love with the breed. Her charming country cottage built in the 1700s is furnished with antiques, some of which once belonged to Mrs. Willison. Among her influential dogs was Eng. Ch. Sunbree's Magic Moments of Willowmead, sire of Am./Can. Ch. Shiel's Mogador Silverleaf CD, an American Best in Show winner and an all-time top-producing sire.

Charncroft
Jackie James

Charncroft was founded in 1963 with the purchase of Wishanger Spring Harvest for obedience work, at which she was very successful. She went on to become very well known on television and in films when in the ownership of animal trainer John Holmes. Tazzy did much to publicize the breed, and people began to recognize the hairy dog as a Beardie.

From her litter by Alastair of Willowmead, Jackie kept Charncroft Chit Chat, who is behind all of the Charncrofts. She was the dam of Ch. Cassandra, Ch. Corinth, and Ch. Coralline. Seven British champions, three American champions, and one world champion, have been bred at Charncroft.

Int. French, German, Luxembourg Ch., World Chamion FCI 1981, VDH-Ch. Davealex Willy Wumpkins. Willy has sired more than 250 children, including American, English, German, Luxembourg and International champions. He has a son and a daughter who both were junior world champions. Willy is sired by Ch. Legal Aide from Davealex ex Davealex Gold Tang. Breeder, Mr. and Mrs. Stopforth, England. Owners, Jan and Rose DeWit, Holland. Tandewis Photo.

Above: Eng. Ch. Sunbree's Magic Moments of Willowmead.

Below: Charncroft Casique.

Above: Ch. Coalacre Curiosity, top sire in England, 1993.

Below: Ch. Coalacre Crackerjack.

Coalacre
Sally and Lesley Tomlinson

The name "Coalacre" came from the field at the side of the house, the site of a former small coal mine. Their first Beardie, acquired in 1975, was not a great show dog, but she produced Coalacre Beachcomber, who contributed his lovely head and soft expression to all of the

Coalacre dogs of today. His grandson, Ch. Coalacre Curiosity, sired champions in several countries and was top sire in 1988 and leading sire in 1993.

Among Coalacre' champions abroad are Am./Can. Ch. Coalacre Just Johnny, Best of Breed at the 1991 BCCA specialty, and Int./Nor./Swedish Ch. Coalacre Capability, top-winning dog in Norway.

Chriscaro
Olga and Norman Douglas

Chriscaro started in 1980 with Lincalder Wild Thyme at Chriscaro, and she produced their first generation of winning dogs. By Ch.

Orora's Frank came Ch. Chriscaro Chrystal at Orora, Ch. Chriscaro Chianti, Int. Ch. Chriscaro's Norse Conqueror, and Am. Ch. Chriscaro Calico. By Ch. Potterdale Philosopher came Eng. Ch. Chriscaro Chanel.

Many second-generation dogs were exported to Europe, where they are doing well. They have retained Chriscaro Carolina and Chriscaro California (Chanel by Chriscaro Karloff) and Chriscaro Coquelicot (Chianti by Potterdale Maestro at Mybeards), and all three have been consistently successful in the ring.

Tamevalley
Maureen Reader

Twilight Mist Over Tamevalley was bred to Ch. Potterdale Ptolemy, producing three champions. Maureen retained Ch. Tamevalley Light'ning Storm, winner of her Junior Warrant, four Best in Show at all-breed Open shows, and two Best Puppy in Show. A male went to Australia, Aust. Ch. Tamevalley Kindred Spirit, who is a multiple BIS and Best in Group winner. His greatest achievement was Best in Show at the Perth "Royal," the only Beardie to date to do so. Another male is owned by Mary Billman, Am./Can. Tamevalley Limerick. There are also two Res. CC winners from this litter. Storm was recently bred to Potterdale Preclusion.

Ch. Tamevalley Light'ning Storm.

Bendale
Anne Wilding

Anne bought her first Beardie, Bridgrove Black Rory, in 1975, but it was her second, Ch. Willowmead Summer Wine, that brought her success. "Maggie" proved to be the perfect show-girl, quickly gaining her Junior Warrant and title. She is the dam of six American champions, the

Ch. DIotima Secret Love, dam of 3 American Champions.

Aust. Ch. Tamevalley Kindred Spirit, a multiple BIS winner owned by David and Joan Smith.

most notable of these being Am./Can. Ch. Bendale Special Lady UD. Lady had many Best in Show wins as well as Best of Breed at both American and Canadian specialties. Another daughter to make her mark is Ch. Bendale Sweeter than Wine, dam of Am./Can. Ch. Britannia Ticket to Ride, another BIS and BISS winner.

In 1986, Anne bought Ch. Diotima Secret Love, who is the dam of three American champions. One, Ch. Bendale Rave Reviews, went Winners Dog at the 1991 BCCA specialty and Best of Winners at the Michigan specialty, and another, Ch. Bendale Leading Lady, earned her ROM in her first litter.

Sammara
Sue and Willie O'Brien

The foundation for Sammara was Ch. Willowmead Star Attraction, top-winning Beardie in the United Kingdom in 1981 and Best of Breed at Crufts in 1982. His daughter from a breeding to Ch. Willowmead Perfect Lady produced Eng./Am./Can. Ch. Sammara Standing Ovation (Boysie), who was Top Beardie in 1987. Following his show career in the United Kingdom, Boysie went to the United States

Eng./Am./Can. Ch. Sammara Standing Ovation, Top Beardie in England, 1987.

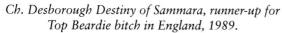

Ch. Desborough Destiny of Sammara, runner-up for Top Beardie bitch in England, 1989.

where he earned his American and Canadian championships and sired a number of champions before returning home. The O'Briens also own Ch. Desborough Destiny of Sammara, who was runner-up Top Bitch in 1989 and who has produced several overseas champions.

Potterdale
Janet and Mike Lewis

The Potterdale kennels have been the top show kennel in the United Kingdom for twelve consecutive years, producing more than fifty United Kingdom and overseas champions. They started with Ch. Pepperland Lyric John at Potterdale, who won thirty CCs and was BIS at a club show. His eighteen United Kingdom champions hold the breed record. He is also the sire of Ch. Potterdale Privilege, the current show record holder with thirty-nine CCs.

Ch. Potterdale Philosopher, winner of 11 CCs, at age 10.

Ch. Blumberg Hadriana of Potterdale. Photo by Garwood.

Ch. Potterdale Persuasion.

Ch. Blumberg Hadriana at Potterdale was one of their foundation bitches, and produced six champions, including Ch. Potterdale Philosopher with eleven CCs and eight champions. Another foundation bitch was Ch. Tamevalley Easter Song of Potterdale with nineteen CCs and the breed record for Top Dam with eight champions, including Ch. Potterdale Classic of Moonhill, the bitch CC record holder with twenty-five and a BIS at Crufts in 1989. Other outstanding producers are Ch. Potterdale Persuasion and Ch. Potterdale Philanderer.

CANADIAN KENNELS

The Bearded Collie Club of Canada was founded in early 1970 by Carol Gold, Barbara Blake, Alice Bixler, Audrey Benbow, and Muriel Ratner. In August 1970, the breed was accepted into the working group by the Canadian Kennel Club.

This was not the first instance of Beardies in Canada, however. In a 1919 issue of a Canadian Kennel Club publication, an article on Scottish breeds zeroed in on the Bearded Collie with the comment, "About 30 or 40 years ago there were no other cattle dogs than bearded collies used about the slaughter houses in the east end of Montreal." The author told how the dogs had been brought over by Scottish immigrants and became popular with French-Canadian drovers of the 1880s.

Nine decades later, Carol Gold brought a pup from England, destined to become Ch, Wishanger Marsh Pimpernel CD ROM (Gael), the first Beardie to be shown in Canada. Gael also was the first Canadian champion and the first to earn a CD and was the dam of the first registered litter of Canadian Beardies. She also was the top-winning Beardie in conformation for 1970 and 1971 and the first group-placing Beardie.

Raggmopp
Carol Gold

In addition to her success with Gael, whose offspring were the foundation for other kennels, Carol imported Banacek Fawn Fabric, who earned both his Canadian and American championships and was the sire of specialty winners and numerous champions in both countries.

Colbara
Barbara and Colin Blake

In addition to their foundation bitch, Tarskavaig Black Maria, and Ch. Raggmopp First Lieutenant CD, they added Can./Am. Ch. Brambledale Boz Am. ROM, the sire of many champions, including Can./Am. Ch. Ha'Penny

Left: Three of Canada's earliest Beardies (left to right): Ch. Wishanger Marsh Pimpernel CD, Osmart Brown Barnaby, and Hermione of Stonehall.

Above:
Am. Can. Ch. Banacek Fawn Fabric ROM, both U.S.
and Canada (by Ch. Osmart Bonnie Blue Braid ex
Banacek Black Bobbin).
Below:
Can. Ch. Raggmopp Jamocha Fudge, ROMI,
Can. ROM.

Am. Can. Ch. Brambledale BOZ, JW, ROM, BOW,
Westminster KC.

Ch. Ha'Penny
Blue Blossom
(by Ch.
Brambledale
Bet ex Ch.
Brambleadale
Blue Bonnet),
dam of 9
champions and
top winning
bitch.

Blue Blossom ROMX. By the time Colbara was dissolved in 1985, the kennel had produced thirty-one champions.

Bedlam
Alice Bixler

A chance meeting with Carol Gold and Gael infected Alice with Beardie fever. She initially imported three British dogs and took a pup from Gael's first litter, Ch. Raggmopp First Impression Can./Am. CD, the first North American-bred Beardie to earn a championship and also the first to earn a dual CD in Canada and the United States (the latter achieved on an ILP number, becauses the breed had not yet been recognized in the United States).

The most successful of the early imports was Ch. Bronze Javelin of Tambora, who became Canada's top-winning Beardie for 1972 and was the first male Beardie to annex group placings.

Can./Am. Ch. Bedlam Go Get'em Garth started his show career by taking Winners Dog, Best of Winners, Best Puppy, and Best Canadian Bred over specials at the 1978 BCCC National Specialty at the tender age of six months. After retiring from the show ring, he appeared in still ads, television commercials, videos, and movies. He is one of thirty-three champions produced to date by Bedlam kennels.

Am. Can. Ch. Bedlam's Go Get'em Garth, Can. Am. CD, appeared on television and in movies.

Penstone
Jean Jagersma

Jean first brought in Lovelace of Tambora and then imported three more that were to write their names in the record book: Can./Am. Ch. Misty Shadow of Willowmead, Ch. Sweet Romance of Willowmead, and Can./Am. Ch. Macmont MacIntosh. All three became BCCC specialty winners, and Shadow ranked as top Canadian Beardie in 1974 and 1977. Mac headed the charts in 1980 and 1982, winning BOB at the national specialty three years in a row.

Algobrae
Jeannette and Lindi Waite

The Waites imported the first English champion, Edenborough Grey Shadow, who earned his Canadian, American, and Bermudan championships as well. He won the 1976 BCCC specialty and four Best in Shows. He was also the sire of two BIS winners: Am./Can. Ch. Tudor Lodge Koala at Crisch and the winning and top-producing Can./Am. Ch. Algobrae Sterling Silver. The Waites produced a number of champions but are no longer active.

Bannochbrae
Sally and Tony Taylor

The Taylors imported another English champion, Eng./Can./Am. Ch. Edenborough Kara Kara of Josanda, a litter sister of Grey Shadow. Kara Kara not only won the 1978 BCCC specialty, but came from the classes to win the first BCCA national.

Dovmar
Diane and Arthur Newman

Dovmar imported Greylen Bonnie From Robdave in whelp to Charncroft Crusader, producing Ch. Blue Gatling of Dovmar. Later she was bred to Macmont MacIntosh, producing Can./Am./Ch. Dovmar New Man About Town, top-winning Beardie of 1984.

Ch. Shaggylane's Beaming Teak has both U.S. and Canadian Best in Show wins on his record.

Shaggylane
Barbara Nidrie

Barbara Nidrie's foundation bitch was Yager Gigue, who was bred to Ch. Raggmopp First Chance, producing Can./Am. Ch. Shaggylane Beaming Teak. This dog was twice Top Beardie, gained thirteen Best in Show wins, and was the first of the breed to go BIS in both Canada and the United States.

Classical
Bea and Kevin Sawka

In 1978, The Sawkas bought Tyler, who became Can./Am. Ch. Algobrae Sterling Silver Can./Am. ROMX ROMI. He became the first owner-handled Beardie to win BIS and was top Canadian Beardie for three years, winning the 1983 BCCC specialty. He sired more than eighty champions in Canada and the United States.

Above: Can. Am. Ch. Potterdale Double Image, winner of 27 BIS and Canada's all-time top producing sire. Below: Kevin Sawka with Can. Am. Bda. Ch. Benbecula's Classical Jazz and Can. Am. Ch. Classical's Star Baby HC.

Can. Am. Ch. Classical Play A Rhapsody, first Beardie bitch to win a BIS in Canada.

A Tyler daughter, Can./Am. Ch. Classical's Silver Cloud, was BCCC Top Brood Bitch for four straight years. Her offspring include: Can./Am. Ch. Classical Paris Original, winner of the BCCC specialty in 1986, 1987, and 1988; Can./Am. Ch. Classical Play a Rhapsody, the first Beardie bitch to win BIS in Canada and also Best of Winners and Select at the 1990 BCCA specialty; and Can./Am. Ch. Classical Guess Who CD, a BIS winner in the United States and BOB at the 1990 BCCC specialty.

Can/ Am. Ch. Classical Paris Original, three-time winner of BCCC Specialty.

Classical's most famous import is Burton, Can./Am. Ch. Potterdale Double Image, who won his first BIS in the United States at twelve months of age. In 1993, he set a new world's record for the most all-breed Best in Shows by a Beardie, with twenty-seven. He won the 1988 BCCA specialty and the 1993 BCCC specialty. He was top Beardie in Canada for four years and number one dog in the herding group for two years. He is the breed's all-time top-producing sire in Canada and ranks as one of the leading sires in the United States.

Sheiling
Cathy and Merv Perry

The foundation bitch for Shieling was Can./Am. Ch. Benbecula's Crystal D'Arque, co-owned with Bea Sawka. She was a multiple group winner and dam of nine champions, including Can./Am. Ch. Shieling's Silver Dollar, a BIS in the United States and an Australian BIS dog. The Perry's later obtained Ch. Algobrae Chelsea Blue, who produced seven champions and earned the BCCC Top Brood Bitch award five times.

Left:
BIS Am. Can Ch. Sheiling's Silver Dollar.

Below:
Can. Am Ch. Benbecula's Crystal D'Arque.

Amberlea
Jean Henderson

Amberlea was begun in 1980 with the purchase of the pup that became Can./Am./Bda. Ch. Birkhill's Ebony Dexter, a multiple group winner. Jean co-owned several Beardies with Bea Sawka and produced more than twenty champions. Other notable dogs were Can./Am. Ch. Amberlea's Sharper Image and Can./Am. Ch. Amberlea's Midnight Special OTCH, who was Winners Dog at the 1990 BCCA specialty. Health reasons forced Jean to discontinue breeding in 1990.

AMERICAN KENNELS

The first Bearded Collie on record to be imported to the United States was Brand X of Bothkennar, imported by Mrs. Ralph Stone in 1962. Others followed, and in November 1967, the first American-bred litter was whelped and registered to Mr. and Mrs. Lawrence Levey. Since that first litter, many American breeders have entered the scene. The following kennels are represented because of the widespread influence that they have had in the past or are having in the present.

Silverleaf
Freedo and Barbara Rieseberg

Silverleaf Beardies started with two puppies from England, later to become Am./Can. Ch. Shiel's Mogador Silverleaf CD ROMX HC ("Kent") and Ch. Shepherd's Help from Shiel CD ROM HC. Later imports were Am./Can. Ch. Osmart Silverleaf Goldmine ROM, Parcana Possibility ROMX, and Ch. Osmart Blueprint of Braid.

With this foundation, Silverleaf produced more than sixty-four champions and, though no longer active, was influential in founding a number of United States and Canadian kennels. Kent was the first male to go Best in Show in the United States.

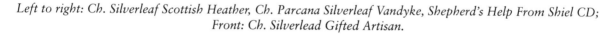

Left to right: Ch. Silverleaf Scottish Heather, Ch. Parcana Silverleaf Vandyke, Shepherd's Help From Shiel CD; Front: Ch. Silverlead Gifted Artisan.

BIS Am. Can. Ch. Shiel's Mogador Silverleaf CD, HC, ROMX, ROMI. *Still one of the top producers of champions with only 25 litters sired. Photo by Ron Wentz.*

Glen Eire
Ann Dolan

Glen Eire's two foundation bitches were Ch. Glen Eire Molly Brown ROM and Ch. Luath Bonnie Blue Bairn ROM. The top stud dog was Ch. Glen Eire Willie Wonderful ROMX, the sire of twenty-five champions. Ann is no longer actively breeding.

Ch. Rich-Lins Molly of Arcadia ROM (by Rich-Lins Rising Son ex Edenborough Full of Life ROM), all-time top dam with 25 champion offspring.

*Above:
Ch. Glen Eire Molly Brown ROM (center) with daughter, Ch. Glen Eire Good Gracious ROM (right), and granddaughter Glen Eire Dendarea Charity.*

*Right:
Ch. Glen Eire Willie Wonderful ROM (by Ch. Misty Shadow of Willowmead ex Ch. Luath Bonnie Blue Bairn ROM). Willie has made his mark in the show ring and is in the top sires list.*

Rich-Lin
Richard and Linda Nootbaar

Rich-Lin's foundation bitch was Edenborough Full O'Life, who made her mark through her daughters, Ch. Rich-Lins Royal Shag ROM and Ch. Rich-Lins Molly of Arcadia ROMX, all-time top-producing bitch with thirty-three champions. Ch. Edenborough Adventure ROM was imported and later bred to Royal Shag to produce Ch. Rich-Lins Mister Magoo ROM, number one Beardie in 1978. The first American-bred Best in Show winner was Ch. Rich-Lins Outlaw. The Nootbaars are no longer actively breeding.

Parcana
Jo Parker

After breeding Shelties for twenty-five years, Jo turned to Beardies in 1974. Her foundation stud was Ch. Parcana Silverleaf Vandyke ROM HC. Foundation bitches included Ch. Edenborough Parcana ROM and Ch. Osmart Smoky Blue Parcana ROMX ROMI.

Above: Am. Can. Ch. Parcana Jake McTavish, ROM.
Left: Ch. Parcana Blue Breeze.

Linebreeding on these and averaging fewer than one litter per year, Jo has bred twenty-nine champions (nearly all owner handled). Of these, there are nine ROMs, five group winners, and a Best in Show winner. Among the outstanding dogs have been BIS Am./Can./Bda. Ch. Parcana Lord Corwin CD HC, Am./Can. Ch. Parcana Jake McTavish ROM, and Ch. Bon Di Parcana the Patriot ROM HC, all multiple group winners, and the group-winning bitches Ch. Parcana Penosa Chelsea ROM HC and Ch. Parcana Penosa Emily.

Parcana dogs were among the first Beardies to be herding certified, as well as some of the first to earn the AKC title of HT.

Jande
Janice and De Arle Masters

The Jande Beardies were founded on imports from Australia, Wales, and England, incorporating bloodlines from Edenborough, Willowmead,

Left to Right: Am. Can. Ch. Jande's Just Dudley, Am. Can. Ch. Jande's Oxford Knight in Blue, Ch. Jande's Lucky Tri, and Ch. Jande's Lucky Mary.

and Brambledale. International Ch. Beardie Bloody Mary ROMX, from Australia, was BOS winner at the 1981 BCCA National Specialty. Outstanding descendents include: Ch. Jande's Just Dudley ROMX, Ch. Jande's Winsome Winnie ROMX, and Ch. Jande's Lucky Tri CD ROM, winner of Best of Breed at the 1983 national specialty.

Gaymardon
Gail Miller

Gail became interested in Beardies while living in England when she met Eng. Ch. Wishanger Cairnbahn. The Millers brought back to the United States Ch. Gaymardon Chesapeake Mist ROMX and her littermate, Ch. Gaymardon Yorktown Yankee ROMX. "Misty" took Best of Breed at Westminster in 1981 and Best of Breed from the veteran's class at the 1982 BCCA specialty. Gaymardon produced many show winners totaling hundreds of BOBs and many group placements. Another top producer was Ch. Gaymardon Crack O'Dawn ROMX. Gail is no longer actively breeding.

Artisan
Ann and Harry Witte

Artisan Beardies was founded in 1976 with the acquisition of Am./Can. Ch. Silverleaf Gifted Artisan HT ROM, whose Herding Tested title

Above, Right: Am. Can. Ch. Silverleaf Gifted Artisan HT, ROM.

Right: World, Int., de las Americas Am. Can. Mex2 Ch. Gaelyn Copper Artisan HC PT ROMX ROMI, the most titled Beardie in America.

was earned at the age of fourteen and one-half years. He was the sire of "Cooper," World/Int./de las Americas/Am./Can./Mex.2 Ch. Gaelyn Copper Artisan HC PT ROMX ROMI, the most titled Beardie in America. He earned more than 187 Bests of Breed as well as multiple group wins. He is the sire of twenty champions, including Am./Can. Ch. Artisan Gypsy Baron ROMX ROMI, who in turn is the sire of two top herding dogs, Ch. Artisan Bronze Paladin HS and Ch. Artisan Romani Rai HS.

The foundation bitches for the kennel were Am./Can. Ch. Artisan's Burnish'd Silverleaf ROMX ROMI and Ch. Thaydom Greysteel Artisan HC ROMX ROMI. Breeding for both conformation and herding ability, Artisan has produced more than fifty champions and thirty herding titles.

Aellen
Ruth Colavecchio

Aellen Bearded Collies was established in 1975 with the co-ownership of Ch. Wyndcliffe Unicorn Sterling HC ROMX. She started her career with Best in Match at the 1976 BCCA match, and her soundness still lives through four generations of Beardies.

In 1981, Ruth acquired Ch. Willowmead Summer Magic ROMX ROMI. "Shane" had outstanding success at BCCA specialties, winning BOS in 1985, BOB in 1986, and Veteran Dog in 1989, 1991, and 1992.

Ruth feels that the work of producing sound Beardies is rewarded by the joy that they bring to her life and to the lives of others.

Arcadia
Jim and Diane Shannon

Arcadia's first Beardie, bought in 1974, was Rich-Lins Rising Son, who was bred to Can./Am.

Above, Right:
Ch. Wyndecliffe Unicorn Sterling HC, ROMX.

Right:
Left to Right:
Aellen's And So It Goes, Aellen's Going Platnum, Ch. Aellen's Dixieland Jazz, and Ch. Unicorn Aellen's Quicksilver ROM.

BIS Ch. Arcadia's Family Tradition ROM and BIS Ch. Arcadia's Cotton-Eyed Joe ROMX.

Above: BIS Ch. Classical's Guess Who CD, Canada's number-one Beardie in 1991. Below: Briarpatch Rambling Rose at eight weeks of age.

Ch. Hootnanny of Bengray ROM. This breeding produced Ch. Rich-Lins Whiskers of Arcadia ROM, who was number one Beardie in 1977. Rising Son was also bred to Blue Bracken's littermate, Edenborough Full O'Life ROM, producing their first foundation bitch, Ch. Rich-Lins Molly of Arcadia ROMX, dam of thirty-three champions—the all-time all-breed record.

In 1977, they imported the male Ch. Edenborough Happy Go Lucky ROMX, who is the number two all-time sire with fifty-four champions, and the bitch Ch. Edenborough Quick Silver ROMX, the number two top dam behind her kennel mate. Both of these have produced Best in Show winners. Based on the bloodlines of these dogs, Arcadia has bred more than 200 AKC champions and many Best in Show and group winners, and they have bred or owned almost forty ROMX or ROM sires and dams.

Briarpatch
Lucy Campbell-Gracie

In 1982, Lucy acquired her first bitch, Am./Can. Ch. Algobrae Liquorice Candy ROM. In 1986, she added Am./Can. Ch. Amberlea's Hope and Glory CD HC, and in 1989, she acquired Ch. Amberlea's Briarpatch Chorline ROM. Her first stud dog was

Am./Can. Ch. Braemar Robbie at Briarpatch CDX Can. CD.

In 1987, Lucy obtained co-ownership of Am./Can. Ch. Classical's Guess Who CD, who has been outstanding as a show dog and sire. He won the Sweepstakes at the 1988 BCCA specialty, received a Select at the 1989 BCCC and the 1990 BCCA specialties, and was BOB at the 1990 BCCC show. He was number one Beardie and number ten Herding dog in Canada in 1991. He won his first Best in Show in 1993. He is the sire of several champions and current winners.

Lucy claims that Briarpatch is really just a group of couch potatoes and bed bunnies who happen to clean up nicely to go to shows on weekends.

Chelsic
Pat McDonald

Pat's first Beardie, bought in 1980, was Ch. Bosque's Pampas Patty CD ROM HC. In 1987, she acquired Am./Can. Ch. Britannia Love Me Do ROM HC. "Colanne" is a multiple group winner and was BOS at the 1991 BCCA specialty. In 1991, Colanne was the top Brood Bitch. A male from England was added in 1988, Am./Can.

Ch. Diotima Fortune Smiles ROM HC. Bred to Colanne, the litter produced two BIS winners (one of whom was also a BISS), a multiple group winner, and two champion bitches.

Since then, Pat has imported Ch. Bendale Leading Lady, ROM HC, and top-winning Ch. Diotima Bear Necessity HC CGC TDI, a multiple BIS and group winner and number ten herding dog, all breeds, for 1994.

Right, Above:
Ch. Chelsic Cape Breton and Mc HC.

Right:
Am. Can. Ch. DIotima Fortune Smile ROM HC.

Ha'Penny
J. Richard Schneider

The first Bearded Collie came to Ha'Penny in 1972 after a long search in England for the ideal specimen. Two littermates were imported, Ch. Brambledale Black Diamond and Ch. Brambledale Blue Bonnet. Bonnet became the first American Bearded Collie Champion and was top-winning Beardie in 1977 and 1978. In 1980, the Schneiders imported English Ch. Chauntelle Limelight.

Ha'Penny Beardies combine Brambledale and Edenborough lines. The kennel has produced a Best of Breed winner at Westminster, plus group and Best in Show winners.

Above:
Ch. Ha'Penny Moon Shadow, a group winning dog.

Left:
Eng. Am. Ch. Chauntelle Limelight, top winning Beardie.

D'Arbonne
Velda and Bob Fitchett

The Fitchetts were living in Alaska in 1986 when they acquired their first Beardie, Am./Can. Ch. Edmar Solo Flight. He won many group placements and was the number one Herding dog and number two All Breed in Alaska. Later they obtained the bitches Ch. Crish Maddie Haira ROM and Am./Can. Ch. Britannia Ride to Blue Heaven ROM. Shortly before moving to Louisiana, they acquired Am./Can. Ch. Chelsic D'Arbonne Brigadier ROM as their foundation sire. At the age of three years, he tied for fourth as top sire in 1992.

Ch. Crish Maddie Haira ROM.

Southampton
Donna and Roger Herzig

Beginning in 1983, the kennel has finished forty-seven champions and is home to four Best in Show winners: Ch. Ha'Penny Blue Max at Braemar, Ch. Ha'Penny Daw Anka Velvet Touch ROMX (number one Brood Bitch All-Breeds in 1989), Ch. Ha'Penny Such Sweet

Above: Ch. Windfiddler Bound to Be A Star ROMX.

Left: BIS Ch. Ha'Penny Daw Anka Velvet Touch ROMX.

Thunder ROM, and Am./Can. Ch. Southampton Chief's Crown who was Canadian Best Puppy in Show. In addition, Ch. Southampton Imagine That, a multiple group winner, was number one Select at the 1992 BCCA specialty.

Ch. Windfiddler Bound to Be A Star ROMX was acquired in 1989, siring thirty-three champions in just two and one-half years.

Melita
Jean Richland

The Richlands saw their first Beardie at the 1965 Cruft show in England. After a concerted effort, they imported Beagold Ben Nevis, Beagold Misty Morn, Glendonald Copper Kate, and Estryd Sam. Their first litter was in 1973, and since then they have produced thirty-five Melita champions, including Ch. Melita Harbiner of Spring ROM and Ch. Melita Poppy's A Poppin' ROM.

A litter at Melita.

Walkoway
Chris Walkowicz

Chris began showing German Shepherds in 1965 and added Beardies in 1977. She is now breeding and showing Beardies exclusively. Her foundation bitches were Ch. Edenborough

Ch. Arcadia's Tiger Paws O' Walkoway ROM. Owned by Chris and Josh Walkowicz. Photo by J. Rich Johnson.

Quick Silver ROMX (all-time number two brood bitch) and Ch. Arcadia's Marcy of Rich-Lin CD ROM. Using a blend of Edenborough, Arcadia, and Willowmead lines, as well as a sprinkle of one or two others, Walkoway has bred more than thirty champions, four ROMs, twenty herding-certified Beardies, and eleven obedience titled Beardies (including two UDs and a BCCA High in Trials). All but three have been owner or breeder handled.

Mental and physical soundness are a priority at Walkoway, and Chris believes in promoting the versatility of the breed, working her dogs in obedience and herding as well as in the breed ring.

Crisch
Chris Schaefer-Blair

Chris was showing Whippets when she saw an AKC article on the soon-to-be-recognized Bearded Collie and thought that she would get just one. He was Ch. Loch-N-Mead Br'er Bear CD, although he was never bred. Then she met Joan Blumire and succeeded in buying a puppy that turned out to be Am./Can. Ch. Tudor Lodge Koala at Crisch ROM (Marci), the first American-bred Best in Show bitch. Every Beardie that Chris owns or has bred goes back to Marci, and most are linebred on her.

Among the favorite dogs are Am./Can. Ch. Crisch Midnight Bracken ROM, Am./Can. Ch. Crisch Midnight Magic ROM HC, Am./Can. Ch. Crisch Sun Dance at Hapif'lds ROM HC, Int. BIS and BISS Ch. Crisch Daybar Wizard, Ch. Crisch Double Impact, and, of course, Marci, without whom there never would have been a Crisch kennel full of top-ten dogs, BIS winners, and specialty winners.

Brigadoon
Virginia (Penny) Hanigan

Brigadoon was founded in 1982 with the purchase of Britannia Will "O" Wisk (Wiskie), who was bred to Ch. Copper Clarence at Beagold, producing Ch. Brigadoon's Tara Terrific. Wiskie was later bred to Ch. Crisch Midnight Magic,

Above:
BIS Am. Can. Ch. Tudor Lodge Koala at Chrish ROM first American-bred BIS Beardie bitch, and BIS Am. Bda. Ch. Crisch Midnight Bracken ROM at six months of age.

Left:
Multiple group winning Am. Can. Ch. Crisch Sundance at Haysif'lds HC ROM.

Multiple group winning Am. Can. Ch. Brigadoon's Magic Lady.

BIS Ch. Brigadoon's Extra Special was BOB at Westminster and BOB at the 1993 BCCA National.

producing the multiple group winning Am./Can. Ch. Brigadoon's Magic Lady and the group winning Am./Can. Ch. Brigadoon Something Special. From the breeding of Tara Terrific to Something Special came Ch. Brigadoon's Extra Special (Rugby) and Ch. Brigadoon's Tuxedo Special.

Rugby was Best of Breed at Westminster at eighteen months of age, is a multiple group and BIS winner, and was Best of Breed at the 1993 BCCA National Specialty. Penny's breeding program has produced eighteen champions.

Windfiddler
Nona Albarano

Nona got her first Beardie, Ch. Mistiburn Promise of Victory CD from Jane Turner in 1977. Her second, Ch. Cricket's Lookin' Good, who was Winners Dog at the 1980 BCCA specialty, came two years later. She bred her first litter in 1981 and after nine litters has twenty-two homebred champions and finished thirty overall.

After Jane Turner's death, Ch. Mistiburn Merrymaid went to Windfiddler, where she

BIS Am. Can. Ch. Potterdale Prosperity ROM HC.

Am. Can. Ch. WIndfiddler's Still Crusin' ROM.

Above: Am. Can. Ch. Tamevalley Limerick.
Below: Ch. Fox Lane's Headliner.

produced seven champions, including Am./Can. Ch. Windfiddler's Walloch CD HC ROM. In 1984, Nona was able to acquire co-ownership of Am./Can. Ch. Classical's Star Baby, who also had seven champions, including Ch. Windfiddler's Bound To Be A Star.

Later, Nona imported from England Am./Can. Potterdale Priority and his sister Am./Can. Ch. Potterdale Prosperity ROM HC, a BIS bitch who has produced six champions to date, including Am./Can. Ch. Windfiddler's Still Cruisin' ROM, a multiple group winner that is owner handled. In 1989, Nona had the opportunity to have Eng. Ch. Sammara Standing Ovation live with her for eighteen months, the first English Beardie to come to America and then return to England. While he was here, he gained his American and Canadian championships and sired several champions.

Fox Lane
Mary Billman

An ad in a Collie magazine led Mary Billman to investigate Beardies, and it was love at first sight when she met Carol Gold's Ch. Wishanger Marsh Pimpernel. The present Fox Lane Beardies are based on the Tamevalley and Potterdale kennels. Am./Can. Ch. Tamevalley Limerick and Ch. Potterdale Kalkulated Risk have formed the foundation, along with Coalacre Innocence, Am./Can. Ch. Achates

Full Carat, and Chs. Binbusy Nocturne, Fox Lane's Proper English, and Dolinbrook's Misty Moonlight.

Britannia
Michele Ritter and Chet Jezierski

Britannia's first Beardie was Am./Can. Ch. Bendale Special Lady UD HC, who became a six-time Best in Show winner and the only Beardie thus far to win both the American and Canadian national specialties in the same year—1985. Lady was the dam of eight champions, including Ch. Britannia Sweet Lady CD HC (Sara), a multiple BIS winner and number one Beardie for 1989 and 1990.

Ch. Bendale Sweeter Than Wine was imported next and has produced seven champions, including Am./Can. Ch. Britannia Ticket To Ride (Spot) and Am./Can. Ch. Britannia Love Me Do HC, BOS at BCCA and BCCC specialties and the dam of two BIS winners. Spot was top Beardie in 1991 and 1992, winner of six specialties, including both the BCCA and BCCC nationals, seven BIS, and more than ninety Group 1s. He was Top Stud Dog in 1991 and has sired twenty-seven champions to date.

In her turn, Sara has produced five champions, including Ch. Britannia How Sweet It Is, who was BOW and sixth Select at the 1993 BCCA specialty, with her younger sister Britannia Sweet Temptation going reserve to her.

Ch. D'Arbonne Connemara Kidol (18 months) and Britannia Sweetest Taboo (12 weeks). Photo by Rayleen

Bearded Collie. Photo by Noel Bosse. Courtesy Mrs. Richard S. Parker.

20 *Judge for Yourself*

PART ONE: OUTLINE
By Cynthia Mahigian Morehead

One of the first observations that a judge makes when the dogs enter the ring is the overall shape and silhouette of the animals. That initial impression is very important and often colors the way in which a judge will later perceive an individual dog in the hands-on portion of the examination. The Beardie possesses a unique individual outline, one that should immediately impress judge and spectator alike with its unmistakable shape. It is too easy to lose sense of the overall and get bogged down in the specifics. How is the head? What about the shoulders, the loin, and the tail? And even, how is the dog groomed? What color is he? It is the *sum* of all of these points, after all, which defines the breed; taken singly, they are essentially out of context. Still, judges and spectators seem to have more of a problem visualizing the whole rather than just the parts.

Eight Beardie outlines are caricatured here. Markings, color, eyes, and most other details have been omitted in order to make the task less confusing. Some aspects have been exaggerated for the sake of clarity. Assume that the dogs are in essentially the same condition, are groomed, and are presented in comparatively

similar manners. Assume that they are all well within the Standard regarding size and that they are approximately the same age. These are all distractions that can be arbitrarily done away with, but don't get bogged down in problems inherent in drawings . . . this is a learning tool.

This, then, is your Open Dog Class. They come in and go around the ring (a nice, large, flat one) and stand, as a class, for your examination. You are doing your first overview. Look carefully at each dog, concentrating on the shape and overall structure. What does it tell you? How do you place them? You be the judge. And remember, a judge should judge each dog against the Standard, not against the other dogs in the ring.

First Place

If you picked Beardie E, you and I are in agreement. However, if you picked Beardie C, you have a very good case, too. Beardie E wins in my mind on three points over C — length and straightness of back, balance, and head. Beardie E's body is longer than it is high — in the approximate five-to-four ratio. His back is level and blends smoothly into the curve of the rump. The tail is set low. The shoulders are well laid back at an approximate forty-five-degree angle. The neck is in proportion to the length of the body. It is strong and slightly arched and blends smoothly into the shoulders. The hind legs have well-bent stifles, and the hocks are low but not excessively so. They are perpendicular to the ground, and the hind feet fall just behind a perpendicular line from the point of the buttocks. The head is in proportion to the size of the dog. The skull is flat, and the stop is moderate but clearly discernible. The muzzle is strong and full, and the foreface is equal in length to the distance between the stop and the occiput. All of these traits can be seen in the drawing, and they all are called for in the Beardie Standard. This Beardie should be able to move freely, supply, and powerfully. His balance should combine good reach in the forequarters with strong drive behind. He should appear to glide effortlessly on the move.

Second Place

I give second place to Beardie C. As they say in England, this dog was "unlucky to meet number one" today. This is another nice, long dog, especially in the well-arched neck and the proper tail set. There is a slight rise over the point of the croup, however, preventing the topline from being completely level. Moreover, Beardie C appears to be slightly straighter, both front and rear, than Beardie E — that is, less angulated, especially in the front. The position of the front legs is slightly less under the dog. This could also be caused by poor handling technique. However, because we agreed that all of the dogs were handled the same, we must conclude here that Beardie C's shoulders are not as well laid back or that the whole forequarter section is less well constructed than that of Beardie E. Because the rear of Beardie C (while less angulated than that of Beardie E) is more angulated than his own front, the balance of the dog is thrown off slightly. This will surely show up in the way in which the dog moves — possibly sidewinding — although a dog this long may not move as badly as a shorter-backed one with the same problem. Finally, the back skull of Beardie C appears to be slightly domey or rounded, with a slope where the well-defined occiput should be. Still, in all, this is a nice overall picture of a slightly different type of Beardie than E.

Third Place

The situation gets a little murkier as you go down the line. My third-place pick is Beardie H. While not as elegant a dog as either E or C, Beardie H has several points to recommend him — but he has even more to keep him out of the first two places. First, he is considerably shorter in body length, although he does appear to have a level topline. Most glaring is the high, poor tail set, which completely spoils the outline of the croup and makes the dog appear even shorter in back than he really is. On the move, this tail will probably be carried very high, possibly beyond the vertical. His very low hocks (excessively low

hocks are as improper and unuseful as high ones) are combined with a short, very angulated stifle — a combination that often means lack of drive and extension in the rear. By contrast, his front doesn't look too bad — but all four legs appear to be a little short, even for his cobbier back. He does have a nice head and adequate neck; the neck appears to blend nicely into the shoulders. This is a finishable dog, but not a special one.

Fourth Place

Beardie F takes fourth place. This dog is very similar in type to Beardie H. He appears, however, to be slightly straighter in front and more angulated in the rear. Moreover, he is longer in the stifle. This type of unbalance results in more drive than reach. You often will see such a Beardie hackneying in his attempt to get his front out of the way of his more dynamic rear. The dog has another high tail set, but this one looks as if it might have even been fixed. (Yes, it does happen in Beardies.) That unnatural "break" point is suspicious looking, although it can happen congenitally as well. In any event, the set-on is too high, and the carriage makes it look even worse. The head is not too bad, but if you were to take off more heavy head coat, you might notice that it is just a little small for a truly pleasing, proper balance. It requires a bit more stop to allow for the bright, inquiring expression that is one of the hallmarks of the breed.

What About the Others?

Beardie A's steep croup, short back, and wide rear keep him out of the ribbons. His foreface is also considerably shorter than his backskull — a construction that makes the cheeks appear to be well-filled beneath the eyes, whether, in fact, they are or not. This is usually the "cutesy" type of Beardie face. His front doesn't look too bad; but again, he has more rear than front.

Beardie B's topline is atrocious; the slope adds to the already short back and makes it appear even shorter. This Beardie will appear to be racing around the ring like an Irish Setter, whether he is going anywhere or not! He is short in foreface and his backskull drops off. He does not appear to have enough neck (probably because his layback is inadequate), making his front too straight.

Beardie D is short in back. Even so, his topline dips. You often find a similar dip when the dog is too long in loin and the length of back comes from there instead of from the proper long, angled-back rib cage. Additionally, his steep croup and/or high tail set add to the general problem. He is tall on leg as well. The whole effect is of a square dog rather than a rectangular one like the Beardie. He is extremely straight both front and rear — especially rear — and high on hock. His foreface and backskull are the right length, but his foreface is downturned too much.

Beardie G's head isn't too bad, but his withers appear to be around his ears. Whether he is truly short on neck or is another case of inadequate layback (making it appear that he has no neck) would be determined by feel. He does seem straighter in the front than in the rear. He, too, is slightly high on hock. Again, a short back and rise over the point of the croup make him unlikely to move with ease or authority.

And What About That Elusive Word, "Type?"

The question of "type" has barely been touched on here for one good reason — these comments are universal and applicable to all Beardies, regardless of type. There simply is no "type" of Bearded Collie that should have a short back, a high hock, or a domey head. Where type comes into play is when everything else is equal in quality. Then, and only then, should the judge allow himself the luxury of choosing the type that he finds personally the most pleasing. To choose a particular type over a better-constructed and better-moving dog type that is not similar to what you have in your own kennel is irresponsible judging. Breed the type that you like, but look for the best overall dog in the ring when you judge.

PART TWO: SIDE GAIT
By Jo Parker

Movement is not, in itself, soundness. Rather, it is a measure of soundness. Correct movement covers the maximum amount of ground with a minimum amount of effort — essential to a working dog that is expected to perform for long hours.

Learning to analyze gait takes practice, because it necessitates training the eye to "stop" motion. The eight drawings of a Beardie's side gait have all "stopped" the action at approximately the same point in the stride. In judging them, remember that a correct trot is a two-beat gait with diagonal feet hitting the ground at the same time; i.e., right front/left rear; then, left front/right rear.

In this exercise, only side gait is being considered. In actual judging, side gait would be balanced with gait coming and going as well as with all other aspects of a Beardie.

First Place

Hopefully, you picked Beardie C as the dog with the best side gait. He has a lovely, long stride with excellent reach in front and extension in the rear, indicating very good angulation both front and rear. He is reaching well under his body with his hind leg. His left front and right rear feet are hitting the ground at the same time, and he is lifting the other feet just enough to clear the ground. His back is level, and his tail carriage is correct.

Notice that the lines of each diagonal pair of legs are approximately parallel, and the distances between the two front legs and the two hind legs are approximately equal. The right front foot is lifted just enough to clear the right hind foot without crabbing or overreaching. The length of body enables this to occur even with this length of stride.

This dog would float around the ring with a perfectly balanced trot and a minimum number of steps, a level topline, and little or no up-and-down motion at the withers.

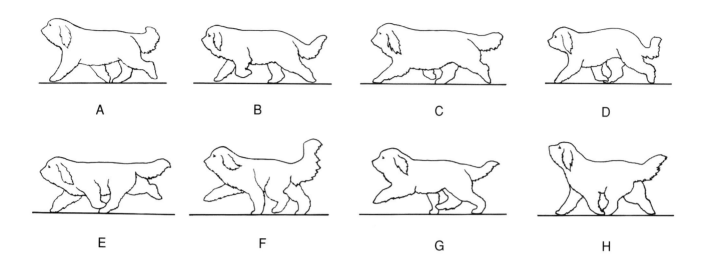

A   B   C   D

E   F   G   H

Second Place

My choice is Beardie E. The positives are reasonably good reach, parallel lines of right front and left rear legs, the hind leg reaching well under the body, level topline, and good tail carriage. The negatives are a kick-up of the right rear leg, the imbalance of lines of the left front and right rear legs, and possibly a bit of an overreach because the left front foot is outside the left rear *foot*

I would expect this dog to move with drive and determination but, because of the kick-up, not quite as smoothly as Beardie C.

Third Place

Beardie A would get the nod here. He has fairly good reach in front, and his diagonal legs are nearly parallel. His topline is level, and his right front foot will clear the right hind foot. However, this dog has much more reach in front than drive from the rear. His hind foot does not reach very far forward under his body, and he has no extension of the left rear hock joint. A slight kick-up possibly indicates sickle-hocks.

In motion, this dog would give the impression that his front is going somewhere but his rear is just trailing along for the ride.

Fourth Place

I would give fourth place to Beardie H. Although his stride seems to be quite short, it is partially due to his high head carriage. His stride is balanced front and rear, he is reaching well under his body with his hind leg, and he has adequate follow-through with the right hind leg. On the negative side, his short body is causing him to overreach, and his topline is not level.

This dog would take more steps to cover the same ground. He would move reasonably smoothly, but not with a great deal of energy.

Fifth Place

My choice would be Beardie B, even though he is pacing. A pace is also a two-beat gait, with the legs on the same side moving together rather than the diagonal legs moving together. It should also be balanced. In Beardie B, the gait is not balanced. There is little reach in front and no follow-through with the left front leg. There is more length of stride in the rear than in the front, indicating more rear angulation than front angulation. He drops off a bit in croup.

This dog, going around the ring, would probably give the impression of plodding rather heavily. Hopefully, a quick jerk on the lead would bring him out of the pace into a trot.

Sixth Place

Beardie D's gait is more balanced than that of Beardie B, but he lacks follow-through with his left hind leg. He is also showing some overreach. The biggest problem is with his topline. He is wheel-backed and drops off badly in croup.

Seventh Place

Both Beardie G and Beardie F show a fault that is sometimes mistaken for reach. The front leg is extended well out in front, but it is much too far above the ground. The maximum reach should be achieved at the moment the front foot touches the ground (*see* Beardie C). By the time the front foot on both dogs touches the ground, the body will have moved forward, making the stride very short. When the foot comes down, it will hit with a jar (pounding).

I give seventh place to Beardie G, because his gait is more balanced than that of Beardie F. He will exhibit a lot of up-and-down motion, which wastes energy and lacks smoothness. His right front foot is not coming off of the ground in time to avoid the hind foot moving to the inside.

Ch. Candelaria Glengarry O'Riley CD HC. Owned by Laura Price and Judith M. Leroy.

Eighth Place

Beardie F is totally unbalanced, is pounding, is short-strided and short-bodied, and his topline is poor. He will go around the ring in a very jerky manner, as his front and hind legs are completely out of synchronization. There is a huge amount of wasted energy here.

If you do not agree with all of these placings, that's alright. People have different opinions on the relative importance of various traits. As long as you give Beardie C first place, you can argue for the exchange of second and third placements, fourth, fifth, and even sixth. F and G should definitely be at the bottom.

21 *Bearded Collie Club of America*

The Bearded Collie Club of America was founded in 1969 and gained AKC recognition in the Miscellaneous Class in 1975. The breed was granted full AKC status in 1977.

Among other activities, the club drafts the Breed Standard, hosts the Bearded Collie National Specialty each year, and issues awards for various achievements.

BCCA SPECIALTY WINNERS

1979

BOB & BW & WB	Eng./Can. Ch. Edenborough Kara Kara of Josanda Mr. and Mrs. A.D. Taylor
BOS	Ch. Glen Eire Willie Wonderful Carol Dean and Ann Dolan
WD	Gaymardon's Baron of Braemel John and Kaye Webb
Futurity Only	Tudor Lodge Anne Boleyn Roy and Joan Blumire

1980

BOB:	Ch. Mistiburn Merrymaker	Jane W. Turner
BOS:	Ch. Brambledale Blue Bonnet	Mr. and Mrs. Robert Lachman
BW & WB:	Glen Eire Good Gracious	Carol Dean and Ann V. Dolan
WD:	Cricket's Lookin Good	Nona Albarano
Obedience (first time held):	Ch. Cauldbrae's Mardi Gras	Karl and Sheryle Nussbaum
Futurity:	Aellen's Dawn of Blu Fantasia	Arlene Byers Rutherford andRuth Colavecchi
Sweeps: Best:	Ch. Rich-Lin's RC	Sondra Franc
OP:	Cricket's Pennyroyal	Mr. and Mrs. Robert Lachman

1981

BOB:	Ch. Brambledale Blue Bonnet CD	Mr. and Mrs. Robert Lachman
BOS:	Ch. Chauntelle Limelight	Ha'Penny Kennels, Judith Goldworm and Dr. Thomas Davies
WD	Ha'Penny Moonshadow	Robert W. Greeitzer and J. Richard Schneider
BW & WB:	Ha'Penny Sweetwater Agility	Mr. and Mrs. Thomas Garrett
OBED:	Sno-Berry Black Blazer	Lynn Giewartowski
Futurity:	Ch. Jande Just Dudley	Janice and DeArle Masters
Sweeps:	Ch. Jande Just Dudley	Janice and DeArle Masters
Junior Handler (first time held):		Gail Elizabeth Miller

1982

BOB:	Ch. Gaymardon Chesapeake Mist	Donnell and Gail J. Miller
BOS:	Ch. Arcadia Blue Grass Music	David and Marilyn Lowe
BW & WD:	Wyndcliuff Foolery O' The Picts	Helen O'Bryan and Cathi Cline
WB:	Glen Eire Hope at Dendarra	Sherry and Doug Fisher
OBED:	Windcache A Blustery Day UD	Barbara Wilson
Sweeps: Best:	Arcadia's Tennessee Rose	David and Marilyn Lowe
OP:	Arcadia Perrier	Margie and Dennis Haarsager
Junior Handler:		Gail Elizabeth Miller

1983

BOB:	Ch. Jande Lucky Tri CD	Bruce and Janet Buehrig, Donnell Miller
BOS:	Am./Can. Ch. Benbecula's Classical Jazz	Kevin and Bea Sawka
BW & WD:	Britannia Just Jeffery	Michele Ritter
WB:	Cauldbraes Corrie Doon	Moira Morrison
OBED:	Raggmopp Leading Lady	Antonia Tuck and Carol Gold
Sweeps: Best:	Mistiburn Hey Mickey	Nona Albarano
OP:	Parcana Kylie	Mrs. Richard S. Parker
Junior Handler:		Gail Elizabeth Miller

1984

BOB:	Ch. Littlefalls Rose Ellen	Carole Foster and Kathy Hossack
BOS:	Am./Can. Ch. Potterdale Paris	Bea and Kevin Sawka
BW & WD:	Bearanson Blue Peter	Cynthia and Robert Yeakle
WB:	Shiloh's Breezy Blue Angel	Sandi Ellington and Kim Lindemoen
OBED:	Ch. Arcadia Bentley O'Walkoway CD	Carleton J. Bates
Sweeps: Best:	Classical Star Baby	Bea and Kevin Sawka
OP:	Briary Knob Winter Harvest	David and Mary Jean Rudd
Junior Handler:		Nancy Groh

1985

BOB:	Am./Can. Ch. Bendale Special Lady CDX	Michele Ritter and Stonybrook Kennels
BOS:	Ch. Willowmead Summer Magic	Ruth Colavecchio and Pamela Gaffney
WD:	Lord Barclay of Loetree	Donald Aron
BW & WB:	Harmony Show Biz	Kathy Berry
OBED:	Ch. Arcadia Bentley O'Walkoway CD	Carleton J. Bates
Sweeps: Best:	O'Kelidon's Inverness Diplomat	Melissa Knapp
OP:	Lochingar Kyloe Having It All	Jill Rankin and J. & L. Conro
Junior Handler:		Kirsten Haarsager

1986

BOB:	Ch. Willowmead Summer Magic	Ruth Colavecchio
BOS & WB:	Shadowmist Promise of Spring	Ken and Chris Hays
BW & WD:	Crisch Midnight Braid	Antonia Tuck
OBED:	Britannia Master Thinker CDX	Sandy Weiss
Sweeps: Best:	Crisch Autumn of Tudor Lodge	Beverly Barton and Chris Schaefer
OP:	Torwynd Ilus	Susan Smart
Junior Handler:		Jennifer Thomas

1987

BOB:	Ch. Mistiburn Happy Memories	Irene Carson and Ted Turner
BOS:	Am./Can. Ch. Briery Know Winter Harvest	David and Mary Jean Rudd
BW & WD:	Revel Manor's Magnum Force	Sandra and Daniel Harzell
WB:	Linmar-Aellen Star Attraction	Linda Weeks and Ruth Colavecchio
OBED:	Britannia Master Thinker CDX	Sandy Weiss
Sweeps: Best:	Sugar Bear Pinch of Arcadia	Lisa Dean Goodman
OP:	Potterdale Double Image	Bea and Kevin Sawka
Junior Handler:		Elise Van Fleet

1988

BOB:	Am./Can. Ch. Potterdale Double Image	Bea and Kevin Sawka
BOS:	Am./Can. Ch. Classical Star Baby	Nona Albarano and Bea Sawka
BW & WD:	Artisan Caribou O'Hollybush	Sherry and Greg Meininghaus
WB:	Ruffhouse Raggedy Ann	Harry and Mary Ellen Siemen
OBED:	Britannia Master Thinker UD	Sandy Weiss
Sweeps: Best:	Classical Guess Who	Bea and Kevin Sawka
OP:	Potterdale Prosperity	Nona Albarano
Junior Handler:		Daniel Herzig

1989

BOB:	Ch. Shilstone Charlie Charcoal	Sheila Green
BOS:	Ch. Chriscaro's Calico	Katherine B. Widell
BW & WD:	Aellen's Eye Of The Tiger	Carol and Ruth Colavecchio
WB:	Crisch Black Eyed Susan	Chris Schaefer
OBED:	Ch. Daybreak Storm at Candelaria UD	Laura Price
Sweeps: Best:	Coalacre Just Johnny	Ann and Bruce Lewis
OP:	Ch. Southampton Homestead Kiska	Valerie, John, and Delores Williams
Junior Handler:		Daniel Herzig

1990

BOB:	Ch. Ha'Penny Moonshadow	Robert W. Greitzer and J. Richard Schneider
BOS:	Am./Can. Ch. Bendale Special Lady UD	Michele Ritter, Cheryl Folendorf, and Christina Marley
WD:	Can. Ch. Amberlea Midnight Special	Sharon Dunsmore and J. Henderson
BW & WB:	Classical Play a Rhapsody	Bea Sawka and Sandy Corey
OBED:	Llwynogyn's Chelsea Morning	Deborah B. Ritchie
Sweeps: Best:	Britannia Bubblicious	Michele Ritter
OP:	Scotsdales Tonka of Walkoway	Linda Kelly
Junior Handler:		Christina Marley

1991

BOB:	Ch. Coalacre Just Johnny	Diane Clark and Bruce and Ann Lewis
BOS	Ch. Britannia Love Me Do	Patricia MacDonald
WD:	Bendale Rave Reviews	Cheryl Folendorf, Michele Ritter, Colavecchio, and Carter
BW & WB:	Classical Dreamfinder	Bea and Kevin Sawka
OBED:	Invernesas Alakazam	Kikki Ryan
Sweeps: Best:	Windfiddler Still Cruisin'	Lynn Zagarella and Nono Albarano
OP:	Classical's One And Only	Bea Sawka and Julie Smith
Junior Handler:		Christina Marley

1992

BOB:	Ch. Britannia Ticket To Ride	Michele Ritter
BOS & WB:	Ha'Penny Mirimar Leontyne	Mr. and Mrs. J. Richard Schneider
WD & BW:	Dupton Double Scotch	Nina Brusin
OBED:	Ch. Walkoway's Frosted Flakes CDX	James G. Leek and Linda Leek
Sweeps: Best:	Ch. Hyatt's Formal Attire	Rosemary Shroeder
OP:	Simi Memories of Summer	Carrol Newkirk and
		Connie Wentling
Junior Handler:		Alexandra Feldman

1993

BOB:	Ch. Brigadoon Extra Special	Virginia and Michale Hannigan
BOS:	Ch. Pipadene Hosanna	Rosemary Shroeder
WB & BW:	Britannia How Sweet It Is	Michele Ritter
WD:	Edmar Lil Dickens At Tiffany	Audrey Barnes
OBED:	Sunshine's Risky Business	Cynthia Nellipowitz
Sweeps: Best:	Aellen's Going Platinum	Linda J. Weeks
OP:	Ch. Glengarry Dreams That Last	Debbie K. Doty and Carolee DeWitt
Junior Handler:		Kathleen Ferguson

1994

BB:	Ch. Britannia How Sweet It Is CD	Michele Ritter
BOS:	Ch. Brigadoon Top Hat And Tails	Kathy and Gary Wildson
WD & BW	Meadows' Entertainer	Angela and Robert Wright and
		Claudia McNulty
WB:	Edmar Freedom Fawn Fabric	Marilyn Dockstader
OBED:	Ch. Otch. Walkoway's Frosted Flakes UD	James G. and Linda Leek
Sweeps: Best:	Shanaspree's Double Delight	Betty Jo Walker
OP:	Sheiling Nonesuch Spirit	I. Noseworthy, G.M. Perry, and
		C.G. Perry
Junior Handler:		Amy Alspaugh

1995

BOB	Ch. Windfiddler's Still Crusin	Lynn Zagarella and Nona Albarano
BOS:	Ch. Britannia Sweet Temptation	Robert Stuart and Michele Ritter
BOW & WD:	Ch. Sheiling Nighttime Secret	G. M. and C. G. Perry
WB:	Can. Ch. Classical American Woman	Bea Sawka and Julie Smith
OBED:	Can. Ch. Ms. Murphy Brown	Mary Rashel
HERD:	Holm Mike L. Doglas, NA	Charles and Susan Gibson and
		Susan Holm

1995 (continued)

Sweeps:	Best:	Hermosa Mtn. Castle Storm	Nancy Shock
	OP:	Arlin My Cousin Vinnie	Arlene Fenney
Veteran:	Best:	Ch. Southampton's Imagine That CD	Donna Herzig and Gail E. Miller
	OP:	Ch. Windfiddler's Walloch C.D.	Mary Ann Pflum
Junior Handler:			Laura Ellen Faris

1996

BOB:		Ch. Britannia How Sweet It Is	Michele Ritter
BOS:		Ch. Potterdale Huck Finn	Dr. Judith Leroy
BOW & WB:		Rallentando Razzle Dazzle 'Em	Ian and Rebecca Copus
WD:		Diotima Take A Look	Brenda Wantlaand and Karen Kaye
OBED:		Ch. OTCh. Walkoway's Frosted Flakes UDX	James and Linda Leek
HERD:		Ch. Balgrae's Sean Mackay CD PT	Joanne Williamson
Sweeps:	Best:	Ch. Tartan's Stewart O'Dundee	Carole Griffith and Teddi Harsch
	OP:	Meadow's Just the One	Claudie McNulty and Suzanne McCrate
Veteran:	Best:	Ch. Britannia Love Me Do	Pat McDonald and Susan Lybrand
	OP:	Ch. Shilstone Charlie Charcoal	Sheila Greens
Agility:		Buaidh Mithandril Xerox O'Jen	
Junior Handler:			Amy Alspaugh

Left Photo: Ch. Daybreak's Rising Sun, UD, HC
Right Photo: Daughter and Father: Left: Ch. Highlander Lorna Doone, HC, CD, ROM, ROMI;
Right: Ch. Parchment Farm's Mr. Kite, HC CD, ROM. Owned by Beth Tilson.

TOP WINNERS

All-time top-winning records are based on Best of Breed, Group, and Best in Show wins. At the end of 1996, the all-time top-winning Bearded Collie was:

Ch. Diotima Bear Necessity
(Eng. Ch. Potterdale Just William ex Eng. Ch. Diotima Gabriella)
Bred by: Mr. and Mrs. S. C. Appleby of the U.K.
Owners: Pat McDonald, Susan Lybrand, Karen Kaye, Linda Swain, and Pat Hyde

The all-time top-winning Beardie bitch was:

Ch. Ha'Penny Hoyden at Edmar
(Eng. Am. Ch. Chauntelle Limelight ex Am. Can. Ch. Ha'Penny Blue Blossom)
Bred by: J. Richard Schneider and Barbara J. Schneider
Owners: Marie and Edward Moe

A few of the other all-time top winners, in alphabetical order, are:

Ch. Brigadoon's Extra Special
Ch. Britannia Ticket To Ride
Ch. Chauntelle Limelight
Ch. Crisch Midnight Bracken
Ch. Ha'Penny Moonshadow
Ch. Bendale Special Lady
Ch. Britannia Sweet Lady
Ch. Ha'Penny Blue Blossom
Ch. Ha'Penny Such Sweet Thunder
Ch. Ha'Penny Daw Anka Velvet Touch

TOP PRODUCERS

The BCCA awards a Register of Merit (ROM) to dogs that have sired five champions and to bitches that have produced three champion offspring. A Register of Merit Excellent (ROMX) is awarded to sires of fifteen or more champions and dams of ten or more champions. In addition, the club tracks all-time top producers in the breed based on the total number of champion offspring.

Am. Can. Ch. Britannia Ticket To Ride, HC ROMX, with breeder/owner/handler Michele Ritter.

As of late 1996, the All-Time Top Sire was:

Ch. Britannia Ticket To Ride, sire of 62 champions
(Am. Can. Ch. Potterdale Double Image ex Ch. Bendale Sweeter Than Wine)
Breeder/owner: Michele Ritter

Other ROMX sires, in numerical order:

Ch. Chauntelle Limelight	59
Ch. Edenborough Happy Go Lucky	56
Ch. Windfiddlers Bound to Be A Star	54
Ch. Potterdale Double Image	50
Ch. Algobrae Sterling Silver	46
Ch. Ha'Penny Moon Shadow	42
Ch. Shiel's Mogador's Silverleaf CD	41
Ch. Windfiddler's Still Cruisin'	29
Ch. Willowmead Mid-Winter Boy	28
Ch. Glen Eire Willie Wonderful	25
Ch. Arcadias Cotton-Eyed Joe	24
Ch. Arcadias Steel Dust	24

Ch. Sammara Standing Ovation	24
Ch. Britannia Just Jeffrey	23
Ch. Chelsic D'Arbonne Brigadier	23
Ch. Gaymardon Yorktown Yankee	22
Ch. Briery Knob Winter Harvest	21
Ch. Gaelyn Cooper Artisan	20
Ch. Brambledale Boz	19
Ch. Tamevalley Highland Ballad	19
Ch. Cauldbrae's Brigadoon	18
Ch. Classical's Guess Who	18
Ch. Jande's Just Dudley	18
Ch. Orora's Humphrey	18
Ch. Willowmead Summer Magic	18
Ch. Arcadias Family Tradition	16
Ch. Diotima Fortune Smiles	16
Ch. Ha'Penny Blueprint Of Arcadia	16
Ch. Osmart Smokey's Silver Starter Chan	15

The All-Time Top-Producing Beardie dam was:

Ch. Rich-Lin's Molly of Arcadia, dam of 33 champions
(Rich-Lin's Rising Star ex Edenborough Full O'Life)
Breeder: Richard Nootbaar
Owners: James and Diann Shannon

Other top-producing dams, in order of number of offspring, were:

Ch. Edenborough Quick Silver	24
Ch. Ha'Penny Blue Blossom	20
Ch. Ha'Penny Daw-Anka Velvet Touch	17
Ch. Artisan Burnish'D Silverleaf	16
Ch. Beardie Bloody Mary	16
Ch. Britannia Sweet Lady CD	16
Parcana Possibility	16
Ch. Rodoando Culloden At Chaniam	16
Ch. Arcadias Bita Amber O'Hemlock	12
Ch. Crisch Maddle Haira	12
Ch. Crisch Midnight Summer Sun	12
Ch. Wild Silk Of Willowmead	12
Ch. Windfiddler's Walloch CD	12
Ch. Arcadias Midnight Munday	11
Ch. Ha'Penny Lucy Locket	11
Ch. Ha'Penny Mercedes O'Stonehill	11
Ch. Wyndcliff Unicorn Sterling	11
Ch. Chriscaro's Calico	10
Ch. Crisch Black-Eyed Susan	10
Ch. Gaymardon Chesapeake Mist	10
Ch. Gaymardon Crack O Dawn	10
Ch. Jande's Winsome Winnie	10
Ch. Osmart Smoky Blue Parcana	10
Ch. Thaydom Greysteel Artisan	10

PERFORMANCE AWARDS

Obedience

Through 1996, only two Bearded Collies earned Obedience Trial Champion titles. They were:

Ch. OTCh. Windcache A Briery Bess UD
    Owned by Barbara Prescott
Ch. OTCh. Walkoways Frosted Flakes UDX
    Owned by Jim and Linda Leek

Utility Dog Titlists

Two Beardies have been awarded Utility Dog Excellent (UDX) titles:

H B Thimbleberry UDX
    Owners: Bob and Carol Spector
Ch. OTCh. Walkoways Frosted Flakes UDX
    Owners: Jim and Linda Leek

A number of Bearded Collies have earned Utility Dog (UD) titles, including:

Windcache A Blustery Day
    Owner: Barbara Wilson
Sno'berry's Black Blazer
    Owner: Lynn Giewartowski
Ch. Glen Eire's Bedazlin Beethoven
    Owners: Kiann and Kandy Robinson
Am. Can. Ch. Beagold's Black Tiffany
    Owners: Roy and Joan Blumire
Pandora
    Owner: Mary Jayne Frantz
Ch. Tudor Lodge's Anne Bolyn
    Owner: Joan Blumire
Britannia Master Thinker
    Owner: Sandra Weiss
Am. Can. Ch. Bendale Special Lady
    Owner: Michele Ritter
Ch. Daybreak's Rising Sun
    Owner: Barbara Prescott
Ch. Daybreak Storm At Candelaria
    Owner: Laura Price
Ch. Windy Hill Rerun
    Owner: Barbara Wilson
Ch. Monet's Sunrise of Lonetree
    Owners: Pamela and Mark Harns
Ch. Arcadia'a Bently O'Walkoway
    Owner: Carleton J. Bates

Am. Can. Ch. Sir Dworkin of Arrochar
  Owner: Joanne Williamson
Ch. Greysteel Joan of Bark
  Owner: Diane Conroy
Ch. Raggmopp Leading Lady
  Owner: Antonia H. Tuck
HB Thimbleberry
  Owners: Bob and Carol Spector
Ch. Kiku Coffee and Cream
  Owner: Ann Rambaud
Ch. Walkoway's Frosted Flakes
  Owners: Linda and James Leek
Ch. Kinloch's Willow Signature
  Owners: Elsa Sell and William Farr
Briardale Wizard of Oz
  Owner: James E. Heeter
Golden Blondie
  Owner: Karen Allen
Ch. Greystone's Jessica James
  Owner: Carolyn House
Ch. Sunshine's Risky Business
  Owner: Cindy Nellipowitz
Ch. Kinloch's Willow Signature
  Owner: Dr. William Farr

Tracking

Tracking Dog Excellent (TDX) degrees have been awarded to three talented Bearded Collies:

Ch. Cannamoor Hones Rose, Am. Can. CD
  Owner: Virginia Parsons
Ch. Birdsong O'Braemoor
  Owner: Virginia Parsons
Ch. Raggmopp Leading Lady UD
  Owners: Antonia Tuck and Carol Gold

Agility

The BCCA has recently implemented an Agility Committee and an annual Agility Award.

The first Bearded Collie to earn *any* agility title was Ch. Jande Hellava Knight CD, HC, AgI, PUP, owned by Beth and Richard Canner. He paved the way for Beardies competing in all forms of agility.

The first Beardie to earn an AKC Agility Novice title was Am. Can. Ch. Melville's Poetry in Motion TT, HC, NAD CGC, ADC, FbCH, owned Glen Hamilton and Emily Venator.

The first Bearded Collie to achieve the Master Agility Dog (MX) was Ch. Arcadia's Caliburn Smokey Topaz CDX, MX. To earn this title he had to have three novice qualifying scores, three legs each in Open and Excellent, and then ten more excellent legs for the MX.

Versatility

The club offers this award to Bearded Collies that have titles in any combination of three performance areas: conformation, obedience, tracking, herding, and agility.

Herding

The BCCA offers a Herding Certification program for untrained dogs to be tested for basic herding instinct. The dog must be at least six months of age. Testing is done on a pass/fail basis, and retesting is encouraged if the dog does not pass the first time out. A dog that qualifies, or passes, one test is awarded a certificate and the designation HC (Herding Certified) may be used following his registered name.

Advanced titles at trial level are also awarded to Bearded Collies by the BCCA, AKC, ASCA (Australian Shepherd Club of America), AHBA (American Herding Breed Association), and the CKC (Canadian Kennel Club). The following are currently the top herding titled Beardies:

Britannia Master Thinker UD HX OTD-s STD-d HTD-Is
  Owner: Sandy Weiss
Ch. Glen Elder Silver Artisan HX ATD-ds OTD-c RTDs HTD-1s ISC
  Owner: Ann Witte
Crisch Phantom Intruder HX ATD-s STD-d HRD-1c,s HTD-1d
  Owners: Robert C. and Leslie K. Ewing
Murphy's Lawbreaker CGC HI OTD-s HTD-1s, CGC
  Owner: Joel Levinson
Silverhammer's Maxwell HI OTD-s RTDs HTD-1s
  Owner: Jim New

Ch. Artisan Bronze Paladin HI STD-s HTD-1s
   Owner: Ann Witte
Ch. Artisan Romani Rai HI
   Owner: Ann Witte
Ch. Artisan Starbuck HI, OTD-d, STD-c,s
   Owner: Ann Witte

REGISTER OF MERIT INSTINCT

The Bearded Collie Club of America also honors top producers of Herding Certified Beardies with a Register of Merit Instinct (ROMI) award. This designation is given to dogs that sire 10 or more Herding Certified offspring, and to bitches that produce 5 or more HC offspring. The following have earned this award through the 1996 National Specialty. ROMIX awards are for sires of 20 or dams of 10 or more Herding Certified offspring.

ROMI Bitches:
Aellen's Castle in the Sky
Arcadia's Dixieland Delight
Aellen's Dixieland Jazz
Artisan Burnish'd Silverleaf
Artisan Copper Sileen
Beaconview Ebony At Colbara
Bendale Special Lady
Bon Di Chasing Rainbows
Cauldbrae's Paisley Promise
Chelsic Limerick O'Duinnin
Chriscaro's Calico
Crisch Maddie Haira
Edenborough Quick Silver
Gaymardon Crack O'Dawn
Greysteel Molly Brown
Haute Ecole's Callender Girl
Hermosa Mtn. Frosty Blue Echo
Highlander Lorna Doone
Kiltie's Katie-Beirdie

Lavontz's Daisy Glow
Mistiburn Happy Memories
Mistiburn's Mistletoe
Mistymor Megan of Willowmead
O'Kelidon's Afternoon Delight
Oakengates' Gillyflower
Osmart Smoky Blue Parcana
Parcana Kylie
Parcana Peppermint Patti
Rodoando Culloden At Chaniam
Shenedene Miss Crispen
Silverleaf A Cameo Of Chelsea
Skye's First Twinkle
Thaydom Greysteel Artisan
Umilik Genii Of Dandenong
Windfiddlers' Walloch
Wyndham Wildwood Irish Creme

ROMI Dogs:
Artisan Gypsy Baron
Briery Knob Winter Harvest
Chelsic D'arbonne Brigadier
Chauntelle Lime Light
Gaelyn Copper Artisan
Gaymardon Yorktown Yankee
Parcana Jake McTavish
Potterdale Double Image
Willowmead Mid Winter Boy
Willowmead Summer Magic
Wildfiddler's Still Crusin
Wyndcliff Foolery O' the Picts
Caulbrae's Six Gun O'Bannon

ROMIX Bitches:
Britannia Sweet Lady

ROMIX Dogs:
Algobrae Sterling Silver
Britannia Just Jeffrey
Britannia Ticket To Ride

OTHER SOURCES OF INFORMATION

ORGANIZATIONS

For the address of clubs or breeders in your area or for registration information, contact your national club. Regional club addresses are subject to change annually.

The American Kennel Club (AKC), Customer Service
5580 Centerview Dr., Suite 200, Raleigh, NC 27606

The Canadian Kennel Club (CKC)
Commerce Park, 100-89 Skyway Ave.
Etobicoke, Ontario M9W 6R4

American Herding Breed Association
Bearded Collie Coordinator, Carl Widell
3055 218th Ave. S.E., Issaquah, WA 98027

Canine Eye Registration Foundation (CERF)
Veterinary Medical Data Program, Purdue University
West Lafayette, IN 47907

National Dog Registry
31 Albany Ave.
Woodstock, NY 12401

North American Dog Agility Council (NADAC)
HCR 2, Box 277, St. Maries, ID 83861

North American Flyball Association
1 Gooch Park Drive, Barrie, Ontario, Canada L4M 4S6

Orthopedic Foundation for Animals (OFA)
University of Missouri, Columbia, MO 65211

Therapy Dogs International
260 Fox Chase Road, Chester, NJ 07930

U.S. Dog Agility Association
P.O. Box 850955, Richardson, TX 75085

BEARDED COLLIE CLUBS

The Bearded Collie Club of America (BCCA)
c/o Diana Siebert
1116 Carpenter's Trace, Villa Hills, KY 41017

The Bearded Collie Club of Canada (BCCC)
Yvonne Poole, Secretary
22 Juniper Crescent, Unionville, ON L3R 3Z7, Canada

Southern Counties Bearded Collie Club
129 Green Lane, Clanfield, Hampshire, P08 01G
England

Bearded Collie Club of Victoria
1860 Ballan Rd.
Anakie, Victoria, Australia
Bearded Collie Club of Sweden, Eva Sederholm
Rabykorset 1, S-724 69 Vasteras, Sweden

REGIONAL BREED CLUBS
(For addresses, contact the BCCA secretary, or the AKC.)

Garden State BCC (New Jersey area)
National Capitol BCC (Washington, D.C.)
Dixie BCC of Southeast Florida
BCC of Greater New York
Northern California BC Fanciers
Northwest BCC of Puget Sound
Rocky Mountain BC Connection
Chicagoland Bearded Collie Club
BCC of Southeastern Michigan
Great Plains BCC of Omaha
Minuteman BCC

BEARDED COLLIE RESCUE
c/o Paul Glatzer
10 Eden Drive, Smithtown, NY 11787

INTERNET LOCATIONS

http: / / www.akc.com
http: / / www.hoflin.com / B BeardedCollie.html
http: / / www.info2000.net / ~grant / dnagrant.html
    (DNA testing)
http: / / www.dogpatch.org / agility.html (agility)
http: / / www.cofc.edu:80 /~huntc / dogpage.html
http: / / www.dogbooks.com
http: / / www.onofrio.com (Onofrio Show Supt.)
http: / / www.dog-play.com

TELEPHONE HOTLINES

Behavior Problems: (503) 476-5775
National Animal Poison Information: (217) 337-5030

BEARDED COLLIE PERIODICALS

Beardie Bulletin (BCCA member publication)
Cynthia Mahigian Moorhead, Editor
8150 Fleener Road, Bloomington, IN 47408

OTHER PERIODICALS

TRAINING
Off Lead
100 Bouck Street, Rome, NY 13440

Front and Finish
P.O. Box 333
Galesburg, IL 61402

GENERAL
AKC Gazette
51 Madison Avenue, New York, NY 10010

Dog World
29 N. Wacker Dr., Chicago, IL 60606

Dog Fancy
P.O. Box 6050, Mission Viejo, CA 92690

Dogs in Canada
89 Skyway Ave., Suite 200, Entobicoke, ON M9W 6R4

HERDING
The Herdsman
Lori Herbel, Editor
Route 2, Box 52A, Putnam, OK 73659

National Stockdog
P.O. Box 402, Butler, IN 46721

Ranch Dog Trainer
HRC3, Box 500, Del Rio, TX 78840

BOOKS

All About the Bearded Collie, Joyce Collis, Pelham Books, London.
The Bearded Collie, Chris Walkowicz, Alpine, 1995.
Talking About Beardies, Moorhouse, 1990.
Bearded Collie Champions, 1977-1987.
Bearded Collies, Gold, TFH, 1990.
All Breed Sheepdog Training, Taggart, Alpine, 1991.

Herding Dogs, Progressive Training, Holland, Howell, 1994.
Huntaway Herding, Witte, Artisan Beardies, 1991.
Sheepdog Training, A Way of Life, Jones, 1983.
Working Sheep Dogs: Management and Training, Templeton and Mundell, Howell, 1988.

GENERAL TOPICS
Beyond Basic Dog Training, Bauman, Howell, 1991.
Beyond Basic Dog Training Workbook, Bauman, Alpine, 1994.
Canine Reproduction: A Breeder's Guide, Holst, Alpine, 1990.
Dogsteps: Illustrated Gait at a Glance, Elliott, Howell, 1983.
Dynamics of Canine Gait, Hollenbeck, Denlinger Publishers Ltd., 1981.
Flyball Training from Start to Finish, Parkin, Alpine, 1996.
Guide to Skin and Haircoat Problems in Dogs, Ackerman DVM, Alpine, 1995.
The Health of Your Dog, Bower and Youngs, Alpine, 1989.
How to Raise a Puppy You Can Live With, Rutherford and Neil, Alpine, 1991.
Love on a Leash, Giving Joy to Others through Pet Therapy, Palika, Alpine, 1996.
Medical and Genetic Aspects of Purebred Dogs, Forum, 1994.
Owner's Guide to Better Behavior in Dogs, Campbell, Alpine, 1995.
Peak Performance, M. Christine Zink DVM, Ph.D., Howell, 1992.
Practical Scent Dog Training, Button, Alpine, 1990.
Preparation and Presentation of Show Dogs, Brucker, Alpine, 1982.
Successful Obedience Handling, The New Best Foot Forward, Handler, Alpine, 1991.
Techniques of Breeding Better Dogs, Fleig, Howell, 1992.

VIDEOS

Best Foot Forward (VIDEO), Handler, 1992.
Gait: Observing Dogs in Motion, AKC.
Herding Series, Las Rocosa Aussies, 1695 Upland, Boulder, CO 80304
How to Raise a Puppy, 2 to 5 Months, Rutherford and Neil, Alpine, 1996.
The Bearded Collie, AKC.
Your Athletic Dog (VIDEO), Clothier, 1995.

INDEX

abortion, 136-138
Addison's disease, 105
adolescence, 168, 173
advertising, 172-173
Aellen, 240
AKC, 6, 7, 181, 188, 206, 267
Algobrae, 231
Amberlea, 235
American kennels, 235-250
anal glands, 58
angulation, 12, 13, 18, 162, 167, 252, 253
Arcadia, 240-241
arthritis, 74
artificial respiration, 79
Artisan, 239-240
autoimmune, 105

backpacking, 93
Bannochbrae, 231
bathing, 53
BCCA, 6, 257-267
    performance awards, 264-265
    publications, 267
    rescue, 33, 267
    Register of Merit Instinct, 266
    specialty winners, 257-262
    top producers, 263
    top winning Beardies, 263
Bedlam, 230
bee stings, 79
Bendale, 225-226
bites, 80
bleeding, 80
body, 8-9, 10, 15
Bothkennar, 211-213
Brambledale, 217
breeders, locating, 32
breeding,
    cost of, 127-128
    planning a, 120, 123, 126, 127
    responsibilities of, 97, 119
    (see also mating)
breeding quality, 31-32
Briarpatch, 241-242
Brigadoon, 246-247
Britannia, 251
brood bitch, 128, 132-133
    care of, 132, 151-152
brucellosis, 138
buying, 33-36
    age to buy, 31
    contracts, 34
    guarantees, 35
    sex, choosing, 30
    terms, 35

Caesarian section, 151
Canadian kennels, 228-235
Canine Good Citizen Test, 92

Charncroft, 222
cells and cell division, 98
Chelsic, 242
championship, 184
    finishing a champion, 195
Chriscaro, 224-225
Classical, 232-233
cleft palate, 155
Coalacre, 224
coat, 9, 14, 48, 65, 111-117
    adolescent coat, 114-115, 116, 168
    smooth, 108
coccidia, 72
Colbara, 228-229
collars, 85-86
color, 9, 11, 15, 111-118
    breeding for color, 82
    greying, 114
    tan markings, 114
    white body markings, 113
color section (photos), follows page 16
colostrum, 154
conception, 131
conditioning, 61, 65-66
constipation, 74
contracts, 34
conversion table for measurements, 74
crates, 40
Crisch, 246
cryptochidism, 106
cuts, 80

D'Arbonne, 243
Davealex, 222
dehydration, 75, 160
dermatitis, 74
dewclaws, 163
diarrhea, 74, 160
diseases, 74-78
    of puppies, 162-163
distemper, 75
dog shows (see shows)
dominant genes, 100
Dovmar, 231

ear mites, 75
ear set, 10
ears, 8, 11,
    care of, 54-56
    inflammation of, 75
Edenborough, 218-220
English kennels, 211-228
enteritis, 75, 160
epilepsy, 107
estrous cycle, 128-129
evaluation, 7, 17
euthanasia, 67, 155
exercise, 65

eyes, 9, 11, 101-103
    color, 9, 11, 115
    defects, 101-103
    inflammation of, 75
    plucking hair around, 51

faults, 9, 19-27
feeding, 62-65
    puppies, 154, 157-159, 165
feet, 9, 13, 15
    care of, 57
food, 62-65
    supplements, 64
    types of, 62
first aid, 77-81
flyball, 94
forequarters, 8, 11, 25-27
Fox Lane, 248-249
Frisbee, 94

gait, 9, 17-27
Gaymardon, 239
genetics, 98-100, 111-118
    color genetics, 112
    dominants and recessives, 100
    genetic defects, 109
Glen Eire, 237
grooming, 47-59
    for shows, 153-154
    tools, 47-48

Ha'Penny, 243
head, 8
heart defects, 106
heart disease, 75
heat stroke, 80
hepatitis, 76
hereditary defects, 101-109
    congenital vs. inherited, 101
    controlling, 109
herding, 197-212
    choosing dog for, 200
    herding instinct, 4, 197, 198
    organizations, 206
    terms, 200
    testing, 206-207
    titles, 208
    training for, 201-206
    trials, 206-212
hip dysplasia, 103-105
hindquarters, 9, 11, 23-24
history, of breed, 4, 6, 211-249
hocks, 12, 13, 15, 23
housebreaking, 39

immunizations, 69
importing, 36
inbreeding, 123-124

Jande, 238-239
judging, 192, 251-256
junior showmanship, 86-87

kennel cough, 75
kennel facilities, 40-42
    sanitation of, 41
kidney and bladder problems, 76

leash breaking, 88
leashes, 85
leasing, 36
leptospirosis, 76
linebreeding, 123, 124
lost dogs, finding, 44
Lowland Polish Sheepdogs, 5

match shows, 187
mating, 130-136
    handling a, 135-136
    selecting a mate, 132
    when to breed, 130
medication
    conversion table for, 74
    how to give, 73
Melita, 245
monorchidism, 106
muzzle, applying a, 78

nails,
    broken, 80
    trimming, 56, 157
National Dog Registry, 44, 267
neck, 8, 13
neutering, 30

obedience trials, 185-187
occiput, 12
old age, 66-67
Orora, 220-222
Osmart, 216-217
outcrossing, 124-125

parasites, 70-72
    external parasites, 72
    internal parasites, 70
Parcana, 238
parts of the Beardie, 12
pasterns, 12, 13, 20, 22
pedigreees, explanation of, 123-125
Penstone, 231
personality, 2
pet quality, 31-32
pigmentation, 117
poisoning, 43, 81
Potterdale, 226-228

pregnancy, 131-132
    false, 138
progesterone testing, 131
pulse rate, 79, 138
puppies, 153-180
    birth of, 146-151
    evaluating, 161-163, 166-170
    illnesses of, 159-161
    newborn, 152-155
    weak, 157-158
    weaning, 165
pyometra, 140

rabies, 70
Raggmopp, 228
recessive genes, 100
Rescue Service, 33, 267
Rich-Lin, 237
road work, 65
routine care,
    anal glands, 58
    ears, 54-56
    eyes, 59
    feet, 57
    teeth, 57-58
    toenails, 56

Sammara, 226
selling, 171-180
    ads, 172
    contracts, 177-179
    follow-up, 180
    screening buyers, 174-175
service dogs, 95
Shaggylane, 232
sheath infection, 135
Sheiling, 233
shock, 79
shoulder, 11-13
shows,
    classes, 182-183
    entering, 187-188
    in England, 188-189
    judges, 192
    organization of, 182-184, 194
    superintendents of, 188
showing, 181-195
    gaiting patterns, 192
    handling, 189-192
Silverleaf, 235
singletrack, 22
size, 9, 15
    measuring, 12
skin disorders, 105
solar nasal dermatitis, 107
Southampton, 244-245

Standard,
    AKC, 8-13
    British, 14-15
sterility, 138-139
structure, 13, 17
stud dog, 111-112, 134-136, 173
Sunbree, 222
supplements, 64
swimmer syndrome, 157

tail, 13
Tambora, 218
Tamevalley, 225
tattooing, 43
teeth,
    bite, 8, 14-15, 162
    cleaning, 57-58
temperament, 2-3, 26, 199
    testing, 165
therapy dogs, 95
toenails (see nails)
tonsillitis, 77
tracking tests, 94-95
training, 38-39, 83-91
    basic, 87-89
    crate, 40
    early, 38
    herding, 201-206
    obedience, 88-89, 92
    psychology of, 83
    show, 90-91
    stud dog, 109
    table training, 49-50
trotting, 17-19
tube feeding, 157-158
tumors, 77

uterine infections, 140

vaccinations, 69, 70
vaginal smears, 130-131
vaginitis, 77
vomiting, 77

Walkoway, 245
weak puppies, 157
weaning, 165-166
whelping, 146-151
    box, 143-144
    chart, 142
    complications, 151-152
    prelabor, 146
Willowmead, 214-215
Windfiddler, 247-248
Wishanger, 216
Working Standard, the BCCA, 198